Black Cor

My Bipolar Marriage

A Memoir

By

Janey Robins

For Simon

and all the desperate souls who took their own lives,

and for their friends and families left mourning after their death.

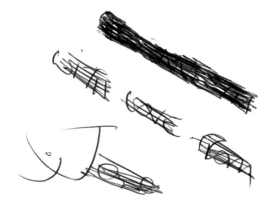

Acknowledgements

To my loved ones in this memoir who died before its completion:

Jane and Joe Lyons
My Dad, Edmund Robins

Wayne Milstead, my coach, editor and friend.

And to all my friends and family who encouraged and supported me on this challenging journey.

Contents

....Page

CHAPTER 1...3
CHAPTER 2...7
CHAPTER 3..13
CHAPTER 4..17
CHAPTER 5..24
CHAPTER 6..29
CHAPTER 7..34
CHAPTER 8..37
CHAPTER 9..44
CHAPTER 10...51
CHAPTER 11...54
CHAPTER 12...62
CHAPTER 13...67
CHAPTER 14...74
CHAPTER 15...78
CHAPTER 16...81
CHAPTER 17...83
CHAPTER 18...88
CHAPTER 19...93
CHAPTER 20...98
CHAPTER 21..103
CHAPTER 22..108
CHAPTER 23..112
CHAPTER 24..118
CHAPTER 25..122
CHAPTER 26..128
CHAPTER 27..137
CHAPTER 28..144

PART 2 147
CHAPTER 29...147
CHAPTER 30...156
CHAPTER 31...161
CHAPTER 32...169
CHAPTER 33...174
CHAPTER 34...183
CHAPTER 35...191
CHAPTER 36...200
CHAPTER 37...204
CHAPTER 38...208
CHAPTER 39...219
CHAPTER 40...231
CHAPTER 41...240
CHAPTER 42...246
CHAPTER 43...251
CHAPTER 44...263
CHAPTER 45...266
CHAPTER 46...274
CHAPTER 47...278
TWENTY-FIVE YEARS AFTER SIMON DIED 288

CHAPTER 1

One Saturday lunchtime after work, gripping his sun-kissed bald head and muttering, Simon landed like a bag of grey cement on our dusky-pink Habitat settee. Leaning close to hear him, I caught a whiff of apple cider on his breath as he rocked back and forth. Kneeling by his side on the dusty floorboards, I regretted pulling up the flea-infested, orange and brown swirled carpet, as it would have cushioned my knees.

'I can't do this anymore,' he said with a slight slur in his speech.

'Do what?' I asked.

'All this shit. I can't do it,' he mumbled.

'What do you mean, all this shit?' I demanded, pulling his wrists from his face to make him look at me.

'The business. This house. It's doing my head in,' he exclaimed.

'But we're halfway there. You've done so much,' I said, trying to assure him.

Rubbing his thigh, I picked at an oatmeal crust of dried cement on his ripped Levi's jeans.

'You don't get it, do you?' he insisted, pressing his fists into his eye sockets.

'What do you mean?' I said, prizing his hands away from his face as deep creases appeared in his brow like trowel lines in wet muck.

'I was on top of a building today where my toes curled over the edge and the black iron railings beckoned me down. I almost jumped,' he explained as he stared into space.

'For fuck's sake, Simon!' I screamed, spinning my wedding ring in my sweaty palm.

'Bob called me from the other side. Asked me to help him lift some blocks. He saved my life,' he relayed calmly. 'You're not serious, are you?' I asked, searching his watery eyes.

It was 1986. I was twenty-five and Simon had just turned twenty-six in the March. Looking back, we were so young. Simon was being harassed by the site agent to finish an office block in the middle of Slough's town centre. We were living on microwave dinners, and we had no kitchen or bathroom as we were renovating Number 34, our second Victorian house.

I was a district nurse and I knew nothing about mental health. I had learnt to cope with all things physical. Nothing like this. Only last week, I'd repeatedly tried to close Mavis's tissue paper eyelids as she took her final breaths, her three middle-aged sons weeping by her side. And the day before I'd dressed Philippa's fungating tumour. It had spread across her right breast, down her arm to her wrist; it resembled a baby elephant's trunk. She'd found an advanced breast lump the size of a grape the year before but did nothing about it. To stem the stench and halt my heaves, I surreptitiously sniffed Vicks Vaporub up my nose as I forced myself up the path towards her neat thatched cottage that sat on the village green by the pond.

With fine tweezers, I lifted the green infused gauze then peeled it off to avoid a haemorrhage, like steaming a stamp off an envelope. When it bled like a tsunami, it didn't stop. To distract Philippa from this torturous procedure, I made upbeat conversation about her eleven-year-old twins, Rachel and Rebecca, who were going up to high school in September. Josh, her handsome husband who looked a bit like George Michael, waited by the cloakroom with an embroidered hand towel. As I scrubbed my hands like a surgeon in their white goldfish bowl-sink, he gazed past me, as if she had already died. A final squirt of Lily of the Valley hand cream that Philippa insisted I used sent me on my way.

Like a toddler, I patted Simon in my arms as he rocked. I watched as particles of brick dust puffed across the triangular sun rays from his weathered, woolly jumper. I tried to imagine how he felt inside his troubled head. Did he face death in those moments when he said the railings beckoned him down? Or was it just talk? People often said things like that but didn't mean it. I hoped it was just a cry for help.

A shudder ran down my spine as I allowed myself for a split second to picture his beautiful body landing on the spiked railings like a battered teddy being tossed from a window by a child having a tantrum.

Stale air leaked from my lungs as I took a deep breath to calm myself. I recalled the copious clumps of cancerous cells that had multiplied like large chunks of cottage cheese across the gorge of Philippa's breast as she drowned in her decay. Nothing can be as bad as that, I thought. If I can cope with that, I can cope with anything. Can't I?

I honestly had no idea of the severity of the situation back then. Through my work as an occupational health nurse looking after mainly depressed and traumatised police officers, I know now that Simon was a high suicide risk and was having 'suicidal ideation', when he would have been thinking about, considering, or planning suicide. I thought he was a bit stressed, a bit overwhelmed. I'm not surprised he'd developed depression. Too many balls (pardon the pun) for any young man to juggle. He'd started a business on his own, we'd moved from an immaculate house into a wreck that needed complete renovation, and on top of all that, we were having sex by the clock and there was still no baby.

I also realise how naïve I was about depression and his suicide risk. Although I'd been horrified when he told me that he'd contemplated jumping off the building, I didn't think he was serious. And once we'd talked about it, I assumed that was it. He appeared to move on. But had he? I avoided the subject, tried to keep him upbeat. But with subsequently gained experience, I would come to know that if he talked about wanting to die or kill himself, feeling hopeless, having no purpose, and being a burden to others, he was feeling suicidal.

With hindsight, I realise that Simon suffered from mental health problems on and off for much of our marriage. I see it as two separate and different phases: this earlier breakdown, which I call his 'reactive depression', that came soon after we were married, and his manic depression/bipolar phases that came after his first Glastonbury festival thirteen years into our marriage.

CHAPTER 2

We first met one lunchtime, in a dingy working men's pub next to college in 1977, when I was seventeen. I'd just started my nursery nurse training and had gone with my new friend Helen who wanted to meet a bloke called Mario she'd shagged in the back of his van over the weekend.

'Bye bye baby,' bellowed from the jukebox as we fought our way towards the smoke-filled bar. Sticky, rickety tables, the ones that wobbled when you put your drink down, lined the edges of the room. A few old blokes threw feathered darts at the distressed dartboard in the corner, roll-ups stuck to the sides of their lips, waiting to be re-lit. Apart from them, a couple of one-toothed old men wearing grimy flat caps sat at either end of the bar. The Travellers Tavern, once filled with men from the railway, was now filled with tradesmen students. As Helen was assertive and tall, they parted for her as she wrestled her way to the bar. Feeling small and self-conscious, I got stuck behind broad-shouldered young blokes and gave up trying to get to the bar.

'What do you want to drink?' she shouted over the crowd.

'What are you having?' I shouted back.

'A pint of cider,' came back the reply.

'A pint?' I queried.

'Yeh,' she said.

I'd never had a pint in my life, but not wanting to appear weedy I agreed to have the same.

A pint isn't ladylike, is it, I thought, and I was worried it would make me too drunk at lunchtime to cope with the afternoon lectures. Plus, it was illegal to be drinking underage and I feared what my parents would say if I got caught. Looking around, I felt relieved to see other students my age drinking. And, this being the late '70s, most pub landlords turned a blind eye.

After being passed back through the crowd, my cider arrived in a slippery wet pint glass. Over a green Mohawk hairstyle sported by some bloke with his back to me, I peered on tiptoes in Helen's direction to give her a thumbs up, but her tongue was down the throat of a Mediterranean-looking lad with slicked, jet-black hair.

Jostling for my own space, I almost spilt my pint down the front of a handsome lad whose floppy black fringe hid one of his eyes. A line of cider dribble appeared on his smart, baby-blue polo shirt.

'Hey. Watch yourself, Ginge,' he said, smelling of Brut and beer.

'I'm so sorry but they pushed me,' I said as I steadied the glass with both hands.

Stepping back, he made room for me between him and his friend who stood sideways against the bar, trying to get served.

'She doesn't look like the kind of girl who drinks a pint, does she, Si?' he asked, looking down at the stain on his left breast. 'How rude of me. Let me introduce myself. I'm Mick. And this is my posh mate, Simon. We're at college together.'

I'd been so busy wiping the wet, sticky cider off my hands and onto my jeans that I hadn't noticed who he was with. I was startled by Simon's electric blue eyes and wide smile that teetered on the edge of a titter when he displayed his impeccable, uniformly white teeth. He reminded me of Paul Newman, the way his eyes followed me from a poster on my wall when I was fourteen. Amongst a bar full of loutish blokes, he appeared polite and sophisticated.

'And you are?' he asked, holding his hand out to shake mine.

I had trouble meeting his eyes without blushing. Squeezing his sturdy, warm hand, I was pleased when I realised it felt like Dad's.

'You can call me Ginger,' I said.

Frowning, he tilted his head, stroked his chin with his forefinger and thumb, then asked, 'Are you sure that's okay?'

'As long as you don't call me Ginge, I don't mind,' I said, frowning back at Mick.

'So, what is your real name?' Simon quizzed.

To hide my nerves, I gulped my pint, blotted my lips, and said, 'Have a guess.'

'Susan, Carol, Janet?'

'You're close,' I teased.

Mick joined in and between them, they reeled off a load more names.

'Come on, Ginger,' Simon pleaded. 'Tell us. And then Mick will buy you another pint.'

'Oh no. Simon will buy you another pint,' Mick joked in return.

'But I don't usually drink pints. I'd rather have a Babycham with a red sticky cherry on a stick,' I explained.

'Don't drink pints? What are you talking about?' Mick joked, pointing at the caterpillar-like mark walking down his top.

Babycham was the first alcoholic drink I'd tried. On Christmas Day, when the table was set with a crisp, white tablecloth and serviettes, Mum's ivy-edged, bone china dinner service, and tall stemmed wine glasses, each with different coloured stems, Mum would fill a cocktail glass with Babycham, then find me a cherry from her baking cupboard and stick it on the end of a wooden stick she usually saved for party sausages. It made me feel sophisticated, like an old-fashioned film star in the 1920s, particularly when the tiny bubbles went up my nose and then to my head.

9

'Okay. Mick will buy you a Babycham when you tell us your real name,' Simon said.

Giggling and looking from one to the other, I finally blurted out: 'It's Jane. Okay?'

'Oh no. That's my sister's name. Honest to god, she's Susan Jane, but we've always called her Jane,' Simon said, sniggering.

'Blimey, that's almost as bad as Jane Elizabeth. No disrespect to your sister, but I find Jane a bit plain,' I responded.

I caught a clean whiff of BLUE COMFORT fabric softener on Simon's sleeve when he tickled his nose and chuckled, and this somehow made him even more attractive.

'My little sister is called Elizabeth, but we call her Lizzy,' he whispered in my ear, leaning against me.

Throwing my head back, I giggled until Mick returned in a bit of a huff with my Babycham.

'I felt a bit of a big girl's blouse carrying Babycham amongst all these blokes,' he protested, shaking his head and pursing his lips.

'Thank you. That's lovely. You even got me a cherry,' I said, twiddling the cocktail stick, savouring the marzipan-flavoured cherry.

Flattered that they'd gone out of their way to buy me a drink, I felt tickled to have so much attention from two attractive blokes at the same time.

Leaning against the bar, sipping his pint with one leg crossed over the other and one hand slipped into his baggy painter-style jeans, I noticed how Simon's broad shoulders filled his soft, grey Lonsdale sweatshirt. Glancing down, I saw that his red Kicker boots were scuffed like a little boy's shoes and his laces double-knotted.

He had a strong jaw. A deep dimple appeared on his chin when he grinned. His eyes were evenly parted then curved into a natural extension of his fairly big nose. Very cool and trendy, I thought as I wedged myself even closer to him. Was he too handsome and stylish for me? I didn't stand a chance, especially once he knew about my hearing aids.

He giggled as I fired questions at him.

'So, what are you studying at college?' I asked.

'I'm training to be an artist in burnt clay,' he chuckled.

Mick doubled up, nearly spilling his lager down his trousers.

'We're bricklayers. Proper geezers. That's what Simon means,' Mick said, sniggering.

Helen joined us with Mario, who was also a bricklayer apprentice. We needed to head off as we'd be late getting back to class. Linking arms, we talked non-stop as we legged it back to college, making it just in time.

I didn't see Simon again until the end of term in June. He strolled past the woodwork department as I was rubbing down one of the legs of a table that I was making as part of my nursery nurse training. His eyes widened and he did a double-take when he saw me. I went all hot and felt the heat redden my neck. *Oh god, I hope I don't look shit in my buff-coloured, over-sized apron*, I thought as he leant through the open window. He cocked his head from side to side as I showed him the indent on the top of the table that was intended for tiles. He chuckled when I talked about struggling with the butt joints. I let him run his fingers over the bit I'd just rubbed down. He said he was impressed at girls doing woodwork. Not a comment that would go down well today, but back in the late '70s it was unusual for women to do things like woodwork.

Feeling a bit cocky, I leant further towards the window to get closer to him and said, 'So what are you doing in the summer holidays then Simon, going away with your girlfriend?'

'Oh no, not me. I'm going down to Cornwall with my family and cousins,' he explained. I caught a look in his eye that suggested maybe, just maybe, he liked me. A flush of embarrassment swept over me when the teacher called my name and told me to come away from the window. We barely said goodbye.

CHAPTER 3

The year after we met in the pub in 1977, Simon had already left college to start full-time work as a bricklayer, and I moved into the nurses' home to start my general nurse training. Bedding, books and pots and pans filled my kingfisher-blue Mini Clubman. Dad was already there to help me unload and walk everything up the fifty steps to the nurses' home that stood up the hill above the hospital. I was less than five miles from home, but when I locked the door to my room that first night, everyone felt a hundred miles away. The next morning, I ventured into the corridor and found it bustling with student nurses. After lectures, we bundled into each other's rooms, sat four astride on our single beds and got to know each other. It was such a buzz. I loved it.

A month later, on a cold Friday night in February, I drove Celeste, my old school friend, and three of my new nurse friends ten miles from High Wycombe to Slough to Blues nightclub that sat back on the busy Bath Road, not far from the Mars factory on the trading estate. Inhaling the sickly smell of chocolate, we bundled out of the car and hobbled on our pointy heels into the club.

Green, red and yellow lasers swirled and flashed to the beat of Abba, Michael Jackson and Blondie as I carried my Babycham onto the balcony that overlooked the dance floor. Settling to watch the talent below, my friends blew smoke in my face to entice me to try smoking. As I waved the smoke from my face, someone waved back at me from the bar below. And there he was, leaning against the bar surrounded by his mates.

'Oh my god. I don't believe it,' I said to Celeste. 'It's Simon. It's Simon!'

'Do you mean *the* Simon? Your dream boyfriend? The one you raved about from college?' she asked, nudging me.

'Quick. Take my glass so I can get to him. I can't let him go another time,' I squealed, thrusting my glass into her hand. 'Do I look okay? No lipstick on my teeth?' I said, rubbing them with my forefinger just in case. I'd worn a new mango lip gloss that rolled on like deodorant. Having a thin top lip, it tended to mark my top teeth. 'And how's my hair. Has it moved?' I said, pushing it in position.

In my tight black pencil skirt, which Mum would say looked like I'd had sprayed on, and black, patent stiletto boots that crushed my toes, I descended three steps at a time. Panting, I landed wide-eyed by his side.

'Wow. Steady there,' he said with his arms out to catch me.

He wore a racing green and white chequered shirt with a Persil white T-shirt underneath, his thinning fair hair standing out against his caramel tan. I noticed he was going a bit thin on top when we met at college, and with a neat short haircut, it hadn't distracted from his good looks.

'How come you've got a tan in February then?' I said, admiring the fair hair that stood out on the back of his hands like hair growing on a year-old baby's head, fine and soft.

'I've just come back from skiing in the French Alps with my mate,' he replied.

How swanky, I thought. He went up another notch in my mind. We talked all night, and I didn't move from the bar or dance with my new friends. When we said good night, Simon leant down to kiss me on the lips. Thinking it would be a snog I opened my mouth but he didn't. Then closing mine he opened his, and like a couple of goldfish searching for food, we did a weird kissing dance that ended abruptly.

Despite exchanging numbers, he didn't call. Two weeks later, and not being able to get him out of my head, I called him from the phone box in the nurses' home. It turned out that Angel, one of his friends, had been killed in a car crash the night we'd met. Simon said that he'd been too upset to call. Talking until my money ran out, we arranged to go out for a drink the following week.

I thought he was out of my league on our first date. I'd bought new clothes, hoping to appear as trendy as him. He wore denim dungarees and a navy Lacoste T-shirt that clung tight to his chest, and I watched as he climbed out of his silver-blue, 1600 E, mark 2 Cortina. In the wing-mirror he took one last look at his teeth and locked the car. 'You Send Me' by Roy Ayers span on my black-glassed stereo as I waited for the knock. As he kissed me awkwardly on the cheek, his Aramis aftershave acted like an aphrodisiac and filled my room as I got my coat and closed the door.

'What would you like to listen to, Ginger? George Benson or Marvin Gaye? You choose,' he said.

'I love George Benson,' I said, reading the back of the cassette box.

'Give Me the Night' bellowed from speakers perched on the back shelf as Simon drove one-handed with his elbow against the window ledge. I glanced at him from the corner of my eye and he threw me a wink that made me slump deep in his bucket seat as we motored to The Sheraton Skyline, a posh hotel near Heathrow Airport.

We could see our reflections on the marble floor as we pretended to skate towards the Caribbean cocktail bar where two large, floral cushioned bamboo chairs waited. I was captivated by the three middle-aged men wearing tuxedos. They tapped their sticks on steel drums and sang 'Fly Me to the Moon' as we settled next to the turquoise kidney-shaped pool. Their jingles rippled on the surface of the water and when Simon handed me a cocktail menu, I felt out of my depth. I'd never heard of a Nipple Twister, Task of Love, or Wicked Widow's Kiss before. Seeing me struggle, he suggested we had White Russians. The waitress delivered two large tumblers with green paper umbrellas, carried on a tray held high above her waist. The coffee-flavoured Kahlúa mixed with vodka and cream went quickly to my head, and after the third, I was ready to curl onto Simon's lap and swoon at him like a contented toy poodle who'd just won first place at Crufts.

He took me out again the following week, this time up to Baker Street to a jazz club. I'd never been to a London club before and I was impressed by its swankiness. Between my shifts, we saw each other twice a week and quickly our relationship took off. As we smooched on the spot in my room under the dimmed light to 'I Want You to Want Me' by Marvin Gaye, Simon cupped my face in his burly hands and I lost myself in his large, tender lips. I could have stayed there forever and thought of nothing else but him, and vice versa. That was our first meaningful kiss, the one I'll never forget.

He appeared vulnerable and talked openly about the devastation of losing his hair. He'd examined the top, back and sides of his head with three mirrors. When he saw a shine from his scalp through what was left of his baby-fine hair, he was gutted. His fine blond hair covered the top of his head, so you couldn't see his scalp. He kept it short and I liked how it curled slightly behind his ears. And I loved the smell of the top of his head; it was as pleasing as a baby's smell.

CHAPTER 4

A few weeks later, Simon invited me as his special guest to his bricklayer award ceremony, where he was going to be awarded a prize for being one of the best apprentices.

'We'll go for a Chinese afterwards. You can meet my whole family,' he said, rubbing his hands together.

Anxious about meeting his family, I had my hair permed; the first of many of my ridiculous hairdos, and highly fashionable in the 1980s. I bought a new black and white polka dot dress with massive shoulder pads and a thin red patent belt and matched it with red patent stilettos and clutch bag. I wore it with the collar up which took a bit of confidence, but the girl in the shop said that's how it had to be worn. I didn't wear dresses as a rule, but I was keen to impress the family.

'Wow. You look amazing,' Simon said as he came into my room. 'Love the curls. It suits you.'

Like a chauffeur, he opened the car door for me.

'By the way. My mum and dad will be at the ceremony, so you'll meet them there first. Okay?'

'Sounds good,' I said, smoothing my dress over my knees.

Secretly I was nervous. It was a big thing, meeting The Parents when you're nineteen and in a public place. Plus, Simon told me how close he was to his mum. He talked about her more like a friend than a mum. Told me that she was a great listener and how everyone would confide in her about their problems. He also said that it drove his dad a bit mad having to listen to everyone's troubles.

In the college foyer ahead of us, they waited. Michael wasn't as rotund as Brenda, but you could see he liked his food. Brenda beamed, greeting Simon with outstretched arms and hugging like they'd been parted for weeks, not three hours.

'Love the pink roses, Mum,' he said, eyeing her dress up and down. Floaty and mid-calf, her dress was pale green with a pattern of massive peony-like pink flowers, and long-sleeved with a high-frilled neck. In his chocolate-brown suit and diamond-patterned tie, Michael nodded hello and lightly shook my hand.

'Hello, my darling,' Brenda said in a surprisingly posh voice. 'You must be Ginger. We've heard all about you. Now, come here and let me say hello properly.'

I was knocked out by her spicy cinnamon smell and clutched into her bounteous, J-cup bosoms, and she squeezed the air from my lungs as she gave me a bear hug.

'Simon tells me you're training to be a nurse, just like my Jane. And I hear that you're a Jane Elizabeth. Just like my girls. What a coincidence, isn't it?'

I don't think I'd ever met such a jolly and dynamic mum in my life. I dropped my shoulders and within minutes we linked arms and walked towards the stage like she had known me for years. She fired questions at me like I was on a quiz show and I instantly saw why others confided in her. She made you feel like you were special. Her aristocratic voice, however, didn't quite marry with her appearance. I later learnt at Michael's funeral that she and her brother had had elocution lessons to increase their opportunities later in life.

The lights dimmed in the sports hall full of bricklayers, carpenters, plumbers and electricians, plus their chattering girlfriends and parents, as the ceremony began. Brenda's eyes widened. Crinkles appeared around her nose and I saw where Simon got his smile from. She beamed at him with pride whilst he rubbed his hands together and fidgeted nervously. Putting his hand into mine, it felt moist with sweat, then he rubbed them on his trousers and gave them back to me, widening his eyes and shrugging his shoulders.

Trying to control his grin, he looked down at his feet as he walked up the steps onto the stage. The mayor's gold chain of office glistened under the stage lights as he shook Simon's hand several times. Coming down the other side, Simon raised the antique silver trowel like a football cup to the whoops and cheers of his classmates. *Blimey*, I thought, *he must be popular – no one else got a cheer.* In turn, Brenda and I hugged and kissed him. Michael shook his hand and said, 'Well done, son. Well done.'

'Thanks, Dad. That means a lot,' Simon said, patting Michael's shoulder.

In the first year of secondary school, Simon was almost expelled for playing the fool and disrupting the class. He'd sit at the back of the class with his friends and talk for much of the lesson, be cheeky to the teacher and make the other kids laugh. As a result, Michael sent him to a private school in London as he was of high intelligence and expected to do well. But he played up. Failed all but a few of his exams. He'd dreamt of being a quantity surveyor and begged his dad for another chance to re-sit, but Michael said he'd spent enough on his education and that Simon needed to go out and get a job, earn some money. Reluctantly, he enrolled for the closest thing – an apprenticeship in bricklaying. However, Simon never came to terms with that lost opportunity. Hence, when Michael challenged some of Simon's behaviours, like me, Michael got the worst of him. Simon appeared to hold a grudge against his dad for the rest of his life.

In the car on the way to the Happy House, a Chinese restaurant, Simon squeezed my knees and rubbed my thigh in excitement.

'I think Mum likes you,' he said. And I liked her. She put me at ease. Brenda was reassuring and comforting; the kind of person who would drop everything to help you in a crisis.

'Just your sisters now then,' I joked as I turned Anita Baker up, topped up my mango lip gloss and let her words soothe my nerves.

Straightening my dress and clutching my bag tight under my arm, I shrugged my shoulders and gave Simon a cheeky wink as he opened the door for me to go in first. The lip-smacking smell of sweet and sour pork balls, chow mein and chop suey tantalised my taste buds as Brenda leapt up from a large circular table in the middle of the restaurant and greeted us again like we'd not seen each other for months.

'Come, Ginger. Come and sit next to Jane,' Brenda said, pulling me by the hand like a child between the tables.

Wearing a shocking pink, black and white striped, power-shouldered dress, Jane pulled up her collar with both hands and embraced me with a warm squeezy hug. Her pink bubble gum lips shimmered as we chatted about our nurse training and the wards we'd been on. Sharing Simon's Colgate-white smile, she exchanged a puppy dog look when he handed her the menu across the table. Fluttering her long black eyelashes in response, their eyes shot sparks at each other spontaneously, like twins connected by an invisible language.

Jane was dating Joe, a fellow ginger whose edginess made him striking. He was also one of Simon's best friends. Ahead of his time, he kissed me on both cheeks. Smelling of Paco Rabanne, he gave me a reassuring smile and nod, and said, 'All right, love?'

A well-built, confident and stylish bloke, Joe towered over Lizzy, Simon's younger sister by nine years. She was sat between him and Michael. A few beguiling freckles that dotted her nose and cheeks made her look pretty. She appeared shy and small amongst the rowdy adults.

I felt intimidated sitting around the huge circular table, as I had never eaten with chopsticks before. They all appeared at ease with each other and familiar with the menu, as plate after plate appeared until there was no more room left on the table. I felt a flush in my cheeks when spareribs appeared as part of the set meal. Simon had to show me how to eat them. I didn't want to coat my fingers or get cherry-pink goo around my mouth. In our house, we never used fingers to eat food. Not even a chicken leg. Only recently, I'd watched Dad dissect a chicken wing with his knife and fork!

I loved the freedom of speech and banter between them. In his deep cockney accent, Joe told a blowjob joke between courses. He described the origin of a blowjob. It meant 'below job', meaning – get down below a man's waist. Lizzy shuffled in her chair and hid her face with her long fair hair as we all rolled about in raucous laughter.

Hot flannels cleaned our fingers and faces, followed by After Eight mints. I was overwhelmed, not only with the food but also with the family. They embraced me like one of their own. Brenda and Jane asked me about my own family. I felt a bit disloyal talking about my parents and I was worried I was making them sound dull! In comparison to Simon's family, any family would appear dull. There were no limitations as to how much anyone could eat, which would explain why Simon had had a weight problem in his teens which I later found out about.

Training to be a social worker and working full-time, Brenda was absent when the kids came home from school, so they ate what they liked and lived on taramasalata and pepperoni sticks. Not long before I met Simon, he'd been on a diet of Bovril and Lift, a powdered energy drink. He'd lost two stone in weight and had the appearance of a rugby player.

Mealtimes were formal in my house. Nothing of importance was discussed. For example, Mum would comment on how nice the beef was even though it was usually as tough as old leather. Or she would say the potatoes were cooked well when they were like bullets.

Things of any seriousness were kept away from us. I only heard that my granddad had died when I was drying up after dinner one day. They threw it casually into the conversation as if someone had died on TV. I don't remember reacting. I don't remember being upset much as a child. Only when I was smacked for being naughty at the dinner table for playing with my food and not eating it. I was frequently sent to my room to sulk for three hours after lunch. Situations were never discussed. Everything went under the carpet or over my head.

Simon's family would discuss anything; there were few boundaries. Brenda was trained in counselling and, working with clients suffering from serious mental health problems, she thought nothing of delving deep into someone's emotional history, even at a party or a wedding. It was just Brenda's way.

She jumped to help others in any way she could, whether it be sorting out their problems, rehousing a dog they didn't want, or making their dinner; she'd put everyone before herself.

Our families were different in many ways. Mine were slim for a start, mainly as a result of Dad being a controller. We were never allowed more than two biscuits at a time and when Mum opened a box of Black Magic chocolates, we were only allowed to take one. It was forbidden to peek under the next layer for something you preferred; the top layer had to be eaten first. I hated Turkish delight and orange and strawberry creams; they were always left until last.

In Simon's house, the biscuit barrel had a huge selection of assorted chocolate and cream-filled biscuits that were left out on the lounge coffee table. You could take as many as you liked – whenever you liked; it was encouraged. And when a box of Milk Tray came out during a film, you could delve down into the next layer. The empty box would be in the bin within an hour or two. I was in food heaven when I joined their family, but I gained half a stone in the first few weeks.

CHAPTER 5

I fell in love with an insightful, selfless, comical and compassionate nineteen-year-old Simon. He brought me tea in bed at the weekends and made scrambled eggs and bacon just how I liked them. Regularly he bought me my favourite orange gerbera flowers. He surprised me on my birthdays with several unique gifts that he'd wrapped himself. He listened to me and reassured me when something troubled me. And when I was ill, he couldn't do enough for me.

A few months into our relationship in 1980, I became ill with a pelvic infection that I assumed was caused by the buckled coil (intrauterine device – IUD) I'd had fitted at a private family planning clinic. I'd been advised by a neurologist to stop the combined pill as it was causing me to have focal migraines. The symptoms mirrored having a stroke: flashing arcs around one eye, slurred speech and slight weakness down one side of my body. He said that if I carried on, my risk of a stroke would have increased.

Picking me up from the GP in High Wycombe, Simon drove me back to his mum's and, like a princess, he nursed me on the sofa. He brought the quilt and pillows down off his bed. Placed a silver satin covered hot water bottle on my tummy. Iced water with lemon, magazines and the television remote control sat on a small table by the settee. Trained by his mum, a nurse, he made sure I took my antibiotics and pain relief on time.

I would usually have confided in my mum, but as she wasn't impressed with me dumping my old boyfriend of three years, who she'd hoped I'd marry one day, to go out with Simon, I thought discussing my method of contraception would tip her over the edge. Instead, Celeste, my oldest friend from school, and I went to a private family planning clinic that was happy to fit me with the coil.

24

Within six weeks, I'd developed a fever and had excruciating pelvic pain. It was then that I had climbed the stairs to Mum's office on the third floor of an old Victorian house where she was a health visitor at our GP's.

Jumping out of her chair, she peered in the corridor hoping no one had seen me, then pushed the door shut.

'Oh my goodness. Whatever's the matter?' Mum said in a hushed voice.

Rage flashed over her pale cheeks as I spilt my tale.

'They put a coil in a young girl like you who hasn't had a baby? Why on earth didn't you tell me? I would have told you not to do it.'

'Exactly, Mum. That's just why I didn't tell you,' I said, crouching forward and clutching my tummy.

'Right. I'll get Dr Hunt to see you after surgery,' she said.

I realise now it probably hurt Mum's feelings because I wanted to go to Simon's house and not home to her after seeing the GP. She never mentioned it. She wasn't one to confront things head-on.

Whilst I was ill, and for several weeks afterwards, Simon tended to me tenderly and respectfully. Being less experienced than me and practically a virgin, he didn't push me for sex until I was fully recovered. Once things settled and I was established on the mini pill, he suggested we go to Bath for a weekend. He booked us into a posh hotel. The same one we would visit on our honeymoon three and a half years later.

In his usual cool style, he drove with one elbow on the window ledge and his hand on my thigh. Parking in front of what looked like a stately home, Simon produced a gold curtain ring from his Levi pocket.

'Don't panic. I'm not asking you to marry me. Not yet, anyway,' he said, rolling the ring between his thumb and forefinger.

I wouldn't have minded if he was, I thought as I tilted my head and pushed my hair away from my fringe and said, 'What's it for then?'

'Mum said that we couldn't book a room unless we were married.'

Like azurite gemstones, the blues of his eyes sparkled when he leant in closer to me and slipped the ring on my finger. It was a perfect fit. Our lips coupled and lingered. I can still feel the warmth from his hand as he caressed the side of my face.

'What if they don't believe we are married? What then? Will they call your mum?' I teased him all the way up the stairs and into the reception.

Giggling and hiding behind Simon in a teenage fashion in the hotel foyer, I listened as he talked with authority to the receptionist who looked a bit like Mum. She referred to us as Mr and Mrs Pillsbury. Simon had thought Smith or Jones would be too cliché. We must have looked like children. And at twenty, we *were* children playing at being grown-up. Yet we believed we'd got away with it. I now realise that no one would have given a damn what or who we were, but at that age you still fear grown-ups and getting into trouble.

A restored Georgian townhouse with a bar and restaurant, The Blueberry Hotel was a bit like Downton Abbey but on a smaller scale. Heavy gold drapes, thick flock wallpaper, low lights and oak wooden floorboards covered with deep red rugs scattered here and there. Feeling like naughty children, we walked up the two flights of stairs. Carrying my bag all the way, Simon unlocked the door. The high bed looked big enough for three people. We jumped on it and met in the middle, laying side by side like pencils on a desk, so close that we went cross-eyed as we went to kiss.

'Wait a minute, I haven't cleaned my teeth,' Simon said, jumping off the bed, searching for his toothbrush and a large bottle of Listerine.

'Oh, me neither,' I said, rooting for my toothbrush.

Settled back on the bed, we lost ourselves in each other's eyes and mouths. Over our winter clothes, we explored each other's bodies and became highly aroused. And again, Simon jumped off the bed and said, 'Right, let's unpack and explore the city. I've always wanted to see Bath. We'll start with the Royal Crescent and finish with the Roman Baths. How's that sound?' I didn't care that much about sightseeing, and I would rather have got into our hotel room bath with him than explore the Roman Baths in the city. Simon loved exploring new places. He researched before we went anywhere, and always bought an OS map of the area to take us off the beaten track. It was only 11 a.m., and we'd come all this way. *He doesn't want to waste time*, I thought as I zipped my boots back up and checked I had my scarf.

We scouted the trendy shops searching for a new pair of jeans for Simon. With large, muscly thighs, he struggled to get the right fit. Trying on a couple of pairs, he wouldn't let me peep behind the curtain until he was dressed. He quickly gave up as they wouldn't go up to his thighs. I fell in love with him a little bit more in the next shop, as he tried on a leather bomber jacket with a thick collar and cuffs. It made him appear stockier and even more handsome.

'Right, it's your turn now,' he said, rummaging through the lady's leather jackets. Shoulder pads, leather jackets and trousers were high fashion following the release of the film *Grease*. He found me a short-cropped jacket with two zippered breast pockets. I felt cool when I looked in the mirror. It wasn't what I would have chosen for myself, and without sounding bumptious, it suited me. Standing behind me in the full-length mirror, Simon pulled the collar up, placed a kiss on my ear lobe and made my hearing aid whistle.

'You look fit, babe,' he said, gripping his hands around my waist. Swaddled in his bulk, I felt petite. Simon insisted on buying it for me. He produced two crisp £50 notes and handed them over to the cashier as easily as I would have two tenners. Bricklayers earned good money. Plus, Simon was exceptionally generous. He didn't bat an eyelid at the price. Skipping out of the shop, we sang the lyrics to 'You're The One That I Want'.

CHAPTER 6

The following year, Simon and Joe bought an old white Ford Escort with a wide racing red stripe that ran from bumper to bumper across the top of the roof. It had plump Pirelli tyres beneath its bulging wheel arches. The steering wheel was chunky and small, and the low black bucket seats were fit for racing at a Grand Prix. It was a bit of a scrapper, but they were determined to become rally drivers and didn't care.

After Michael had dieselled off to towards Heathrow in his black cab to pick up his first fare, they prepared to fit a new carburettor. They dragged the faded red wooden doors open and flicked on the fluorescent tube that swung on chains overhead. Metallic silver metal toolboxes opened to display new gleaming spanners, ratchets and sockets. Grinning and playing at mechanics, they finally adorned a pair of navy overalls each.

Michael's garage sat at the back of the house and was small and long, only a car's width wide, so there was no room for me to watch, not that I was bothered anyway if the truth be known, so I slunk off to study the anatomy and physiology of the brain as I had an exam the next day.

Brenda popped home in her lunch break with fish and chips at lunchtime and we sat on the grass whilst the boys took a brief break.

'You will be finished by eight, won't you, darling?' Brenda asked Simon. 'You know Daddy will go mad if he even knows you've been in the garage, let alone if he can't get the cab back in,' quizzed Brenda, licking her vinegary fingers.

'Yes, Mum. I know. Don't worry, we'll be out, I promise,' huffed Simon.

As it got dark, I heard Brenda's car door slam, followed closely by her navy court shoes trotting at speed down the drive as she returned from work. She came through the back door with a line etched between her brow and confided in me that she didn't think Michael would let them leave the cab in the garage overnight.

'None of his cabs have ever been left out. Not in twenty-eight years,' she exclaimed, leaning against the Formica worktop. 'I always try to patch things up between Simon and Michael, you know. Simon's a vulnerable boy. I can't have Michael knock his confidence any further. Do you know what I mean?' Brenda ranted.

Being a social worker, I assumed she knew what she was talking about, so I listened and nodded appropriately, until she abruptly stopped in her tracks. Together, we watched as Michael's bulky black cab creeped up the road like a fat black beetle searching for its prey.

Barging past me and almost knocking my tea out of my hands, she intercepted Michael, and blurted, 'Hello, darling, how was your day? Your dinner's ready. Shall I dish it up?'

'Why haven't you moved your car, love? It's about to rain,' Michael quizzed, peering over her shoulder towards the garage.

Standing across his path, putting her hands on his chest, Brenda replied, 'Well, we have a little problem, darling. And I want you to deal with it with sensitively. I know it will be difficult for you, but please try, and do your best not to be cross.'

'What do you mean, don't be cross? And why is the garage light on? And why were Simon and Joe's cars parked up the road? What the hell's going on?' he barked, forcing himself past her and into the garage. 'What on earth do you think you're doing?' he shouted at Simon. 'Get this heap of shit out of my garage right now.'

'But Dad, the engine's in bits,' Simon pleaded.

'I don't care if it has no fucking wheels. It's not staying in my garage and that's it,' Michael responded firmly.

'Michael, darling. Can't the boys leave it in here just for tonight? They can't get the part they need until the morning. One night won't hurt, surely?' Brenda pleaded.

'Yeah, Dad. It's only for one night. It will be gone tomorrow, I promise,' Simon added to his pleas.

Embarrassed, Joe busied under the bonnet as Simon pointed and jabbed his finger close to Michael's nose as their voices revved up.

'Only one night? My cab can't stay out for one night! Or even one hour. Get it out, now!' Michael shouted.

'But it's only a stupid fucking taxi, for god's sake. What do you think is going to happen to it? Is the paint gonna fall off, eh?' Simon ranted, baring his teeth and almost spitting at his dad.

'How dare you speak to me like that, son? I'm your father, now show me some respect or I'll show you what for.' Michael firmly held his ground.

'Oh yeah, so what you gonna do about it, big fella? Hit me, eh? Come on then, I dare you,' Simon incited.

Michael puffed himself up like a cockerel about to fight, replying, 'Don't you dare me.'

Wrestling her way between them like a referee in a boxing ring, Brenda looked up at Michael and said, 'Now don't be so ridiculous, darling. Come on. Give Simon a break.'

'But *he's* being ridiculous. Not me. Anyway, you should be on my side, not his.'

Joe stepped in and said, 'Simon, calm down, mate. Just calm down. We'll get it out of the garage. We can wheel it out. Come on.'

'See, at least Joe shows me some respect,' Michael said, scratching his forearms.

When Brenda finally came in to the house, I pretended to be looking for some papers on her piano in the dining room so she didn't catch me spying.

'Oh my god, Ginger. Can you see how unreasonable Michael is now? He's always been difficult. Every time he comes in from work we all have to drop what we're doing to accommodate his needs – honestly.'

Taking another cup of tea out to the boys, I found Simon fuming and ranting to Joe about what a bastard his dad was. Stroking his back, I handed him the tea.

'Do you see what I mean now, Ginger – about my dad?'

'Kind of, but I also get that he needs to look after his cab for work – doesn't he?' I delicately replied.

'No, he doesn't. Don't you get it? Cos it's not just about his cab, is it? It's about the way he treats me. He's never given a shit about me, he only thinks about himself,' Simon ranted.

And that became Simon's mantra. All our married life he slagged off his dad. Harped back to how badly he was treated by him.

Half an hour later I heard raised voices and looked out of the lounge window to see Simon and Joe pushing the car back up the drive, Brenda sat in the driver's seat steering the car backwards out on to the main road, whilst Michael sat in the dining room slipping spaghetti down his throat, his white cotton serviette tucked at his Adam's apple to catch the drips. Closing the sliding doors between the lounge and dining room, I settled to watch *Some Mothers Do 'Ave 'Em*, a sitcom on the TV, until I became aware of a silence in the house. I peered up the road and saw the rally car on the verge, the garage light off and the doors closed. Brenda's Fiesta was back on the drive. There was no sound apart from Michael washing up in the kitchen. Puzzled, I crept up the stairs where all the doors were open as normal apart from Simon's bedroom door which was closed. I stood for a while. Listened at the door. Couldn't hear anything. Gently, I pushed it in. Through the gap I saw Simon on his bed with his head pillowed in Brenda's bosom. Stroking and kissing his head, she rocked him like a toddler, to and fro. Pulling the door open from behind, Joe ushered me into Lizzy's bedroom next door.

'Blimey. Is everything okay?' I asked.

'Yeah, don't worry, Ginger. He'll be fine. He's just upset,' said Joe, patting my shoulder.

'But isn't he overreacting?' I said.

'I suppose so. But that's Si. Don't worry. You'll get used to it.'

That kind of reaction became normal to anything that was out of Simon's control. I reflect back to that evening and think how curious it was. But it wasn't for them. Brenda was the most nurturing mother I have ever met. She would do absolutely anything to take her children's suffering away. Brenda nursing him like a child was a bit over the top. But as no one else seemed to think it unusual, even Joe, I assumed it must be the norm. But with what I now know, I wonder if Simon was born with a sensitive predisposition, and that's why he was unable to cope with stressful situations.

Simon suffered severe headaches after that episode and was referred to his GP for an electroencephalogram EEG to check everything was okay with his brain. Nothing abnormal was detected, so we put it down to the stress of him needing to leave home. We'd saved enough for a deposit on our first Victorian house in Slough, a few miles away from Brenda and Michael; we moved out a year later.

CHAPTER 7

It was around Christmas 1982, three years after we met, and we'd barely settled into our new home when my mum phoned and asked, 'Isn't it about time you two got married, dear? October's a nice month. Lots of orange and bronze leaves on the ground.'

Afterwards, I discussed it with Simon.

'Yeah. October's nice enough,' he said. 'How about we go and get you a ring then?' There was no proposal. No going down on one knee as I'd hoped there might be.

In fairness however, Simon made up for it with what followed. In an antique market in Windsor, we chose a vintage gold set ring with three small diamonds. Keen to make it official, Simon insisted on asking my dad if it was okay to marry me. After a couple of glasses of wine with Sunday lunch, Simon followed Dad into the lounge whilst I stayed in the kitchen to dry up with Mum. Being business-like and rather formal at times, Dad could appear intimidating. Fortunately, however, they came out smirking and Simon put the ring on my finger. And that was it. We were engaged to be married.

Jane and Lizzy were my bridesmaids, and Joe was Simon's best man. I remember praying for a hint of sunshine as I peered up at the featureless sky, and the rain and wind made my hair frizz. As we pulled up to the church gates, Michael tried to take a photo as I stepped out of the car holding a red, blue and yellow umbrella in one hand and the camera in the other. I shrieked as he stumbled on a gravestone, slipped backwards and landed on his side. He jumped back up, but his grey suit tails and backside were sodden. Once I saw that Michael was okay and he was laughing, I laughed too, but I didn't think the state of his suit would go down well with Brenda. The vicar had told me that few wedding ceremonies went off without something going wrong, so I shouldn't be nervous. But I was nervous as most brides are, and my hands trembled so much that my flowers quivered.

Gripping onto Dad's arm with one hand as he hoisted the brolly over our heads with the other, I lifted the huge hoop of my dress above my knees to stop the rain from soaking it black.

Sheltering under the cream-coloured stone porch, smelling of Brylcreem and Old Spice, Dad pressed his crooked nose to mine. Matching like a reflection in the mirror, our crow's feet laughter lines crinkled and his thin upper lip arched up like mine.

'Ready?' he asked.

I was unable to answer, and Dad pulled out his white pressed hankie with *E* for Edmond embroidered in maroon; one of a pack of three bought by my Nanny Davis every Christmas. Catching a tear about to spill from the outside of my eye, he dabbed it and said, 'Come on, Tozzy. You'll be fine. Grip my arm tight. Stride slow and tall like a queen. Look into the eyes of those who love you.'

Tozzy was my pet name; only he called me it.

As I strolled down the aisle, Simon's cheeks were rose and his mouth parted as he ran his tongue over his perfectly even and striking white teeth. I could tell he was struggling to remain serious. Like me, Simon saw the funny side of things. It was his sense of humour and the way he threw his head back and bent forward when he laughed that had attracted me to him. Appearing smart, but a bit stiff in his grey striped cravat and crisp white shirt, he winked and nodded as we shuffled like penguins towards the vicar.

We had been to our wedding rehearsal a few days before, just the two of us. It was then that we both felt we got married. There were no distractions and I heard every word that Simon said to me. Tilting his head to one side, he'd nodded a reassuring look as if to say *You ready?* then he'd emphasised the words, 'To love and to cherish. Until death do us part.'

No children were crying behind us. No choir boys looking bored. And the vicar was in his casual clothes, not dressed up like an archbishop. We hadn't taken our eyes off each other. I can remember wanting to hear and savour the words 'I do', but the vicar told us not to say them, to save them for the day. So when we got to that bit, we mouthed them like blowing a kiss at each other. And on the day, they were the only words I heard. *I do* love you was what it meant to me, and *I do* want to spend the rest of my days with you.

At the reception, in the cottages next door to the church, our friends and family laughed out loud at Simon's speech. He'd rehearsed night after night as he was determined to read it by heart, and he did. With the guests raising their glasses to us, Simon held a long kiss on my lips. The crowd cheered. We had borrowed Phil's new Mark 3 red Escort to go on honeymoon to Bath. They'd dressed the car in multicoloured balloons, old tin cans, streamers, and sprayed the back window with *Just Married.*

CHAPTER 8

A year later we moved to Number 34, our second Victorian semi-detached house. We bought it in 1984. It sat upon a hill on a corner plot in a nice area of Maidenhead, opposite a primary school. It was a wreck and needed complete renovation, yet it had planning permission for a double-storey extension. The foundations had already been dug when we moved in. With Simon being a builder and me being creative, we thought we could smash it. We'd talked about having four children and chose this house as it had huge potential as a family home.

Grey curly mushrooms seeped through cracks between mouldy tiles in the downstairs bathroom. Orange imitation-brick wallpaper covered the chimney breast in the lounge. Laminated pine panels boxed in the stairs. Worst of all was the shit-brown and orange swirled carpet on the floors downstairs. The rubber underlay was crumbling and bugs tumbled out when we ripped it up.

At the same time, after much haggling with a large building contractor, Simon got his first deal to build twenty houses. Inspired, he managed well at the start, but as he took on more contracts to build an office complex and warehouses, he struggled.

Admittedly, Simon didn't manage his emotions well. If an event didn't turn out as planned, he could lose his temper easily. Sometimes simple things, like if I didn't hold the dustpan under the drill and the dust spilt, he would kick off. I chalked this up to his perfectionism. I understood that he wanted things to be just so. I acclimatised to his frequent temper tantrums. My passions ran high as well, so I figured this explained why we were driven to work well during those years.

Plus, I wasn't getting pregnant. I wrote a large capital *P* in my diary for the first day of my period each month. I worked out when I was ovulating and made sure we had sex around that time. 'Don't forget to buy a sprinkler for your hose, and don't forget tonight's the night, darling,' I shouted after him with a saucy pout on my glossed lips as he drove off to the DIY shop one Saturday morning.

Simon was particularly stressed as we prepared for both sets of parents to inspect our progress. I'd planned an afternoon tea for Simon's twenty-sixth birthday. As the day approached, Simon worked hard on the house. We had finished the kitchen and were now focused on the small back bedroom that we'd converted into a bathroom.

I was weeding around the yellow and blue pansies at the bottom of the garden when I heard a couple of thuds followed by a yowl from the bathroom window. It sounded like the lion in Simon had escaped. Unlike all the times I'd heard him holler in temper, this sound was different, like the roar of a desperate soul. Dropping my fork, I hurled myself through the patio doors, sprinted up the stairs three steps at a time and found him in a foetal position on the landing. Dropping by his side, I stretched my arm over his bare sweaty shoulder and took the weight of his head on my knees. Like a motherless child in a foreign orphanage, he rocked.

I can remember feeling shocked and thinking that this was serious shit. We'd stopped socialising and were in what we called our 'love bubble'. Simon had encouraged our togetherness and when I challenged him about his hermit-like behaviour, he'd

reassure me by saying, 'Let's just be you and me, babe. We don't need anyone else when we've got each other, do we?'

He made me feel special, like he only wanted me. I liked that, so I went along with it. Hence I didn't share my true concerns about his mental health with other people as I didn't want anyone to think anything was wrong in our relationship. I was very good at putting on a smiley face and saying everything was wonderful. I never let on that life was pretty shit living on a building site, having no money and not getting pregnant. Away from the home situation, when I was at work in the community with my patients, I was distracted and felt uplifted. Simon being my world back then influenced my thinking more than anyone. Under the blind umbrella of love, either he'd convinced me – or I'd convinced myself – that his outbursts were normal.

With only the splashback behind the sink to go, we were close to the end. Peering into the bathroom, I saw tiny tile spacers spewed from their boxes like rejected kisses amongst the debris on the bare floorboards. The tile cutter lay buckled and bent in the corner. It looked like a fight had broken out between a half dozen tradesmen. But it was the work of just one young bloke attempting to tile a bathroom. The remaining turquoise tile sat cracked in the sink. The space where it should have gone, against the splashback, was empty like the missing part of a puzzle.

Modest weeps of blood leached through his scuffed and raw knuckles as he clutched his sun-kissed bald head. Lifting his hand to my face, I tasted the coppery beads of blood on my lips as I kissed his knuckle clean. *Fuck me*, I thought. I'd seen him punch holes in things before, but usually he'd walk away from the situation, not curl up and cry. Hole punching was commonplace – I was used to it, but I didn't like it. I now realise this was unusual behaviour.

'I've got to move, darling,' I said as the fumes from the Evo-Stik adhesive made my eyes burn.

'Okay. I'll stand up,' he mumbled under his breath.

As we stretched ourselves into a standing position, Simon leant against the shower door, pulled me by my belt loops to him and dropped his head on my shoulder. My lips brushed the hairs on the back of his neck as he rested his hands in the small of my back, a position we adopted after an argument when we were equally sorry for the unkind words we'd spat at each other.

'Shall we go and sit on the bed and talk about this?' I said.

Avoiding my direct eye contact, he stared at the worm-like white wiggles of sealant swarming over the bathroom floor.

'I'll go down and make us a cup of tea. Do you want a couple of Hobnobs?' I called from halfway down the stairs.

Leaning over the landing banister, he shook his head no.

Catching sight of my brows snapped together in the reflection of our silver kettle as it boiled, I shrugged my shoulders at myself and wondered how I could comfort Simon.

We were so much more united back then. Often when Simon was feeling low, he'd let me cuddle and reassure him. I didn't know what I was talking about much of the time, but he appeared to listen to me. And I had little idea of what we were dealing with. Ignorance was bliss. If it were today I would access Google, probably do my own diagnosis in a flash and find where to get help.

Stirring two large caramel cups of builder's tea and adding two sugars for me, I dunked three chocolate Hobnobs for energy before going back upstairs.

Walking along the landing towards our bedroom, concentrating on not spilling the tea, I felt rubble under my feet and gasped as I saw two punch holes in the landing wall. I'd never seen the inside of a wall before. Sandy wisps of straw-like horsehair, broken lolly sticks of splintered wood and powdered pink nuggets of plaster poked out of the fist-shaped, lath and plaster hole. He must have done this earlier when I'd heard the thuds from the garden. Blimey, he must have punched them hard, harder than the punches in his van roof and our bedroom door.

It wasn't unusual for him to punch holes in things here and there. It scared me when he did it, not that I was afraid of him as such, but the way he lost control frightened me for him more than anything. But this was another level, and he'd gone a bit too far this time.

I propelled myself through the bedroom door. Treacle strands of tea dribbled down the newly painted vanilla walls as I banged the mugs on the windowsill. Turning around, I saw Simon's mound curled under our patchwork quilt that Mia, one of my nurse friends, had made us as a wedding present. He'd pulled the fabric taut over his face like a child hiding from an angry parent.

We loved that quilt and appreciated the hours of work that went into making it. For a moment, I flashed back to Mia at the nurse's station swimming in an ocean of Air Force blue and white floral patchwork squares, her head bowed, as she sewed like an old lady with black cat eyeglasses perched on the tip of her nose. Her pointy fingers poked the white threaded needle down, then up in the air, conducting a symphony orchestra of fabric. Amidst the beeps of the cardiac monitors and puffs of the life support machines, she sat on a plastic hospital chair, sewing as she listened for the patients.

I loved the fact that Simon was into interior design. Like me, he appreciated colours and liked things to coordinate. A few years into the renovation and as the house started to take shape, we spent a weekend in Sussex and visited Charleston House, the home of Vanessa Bell and Duncan Grant. We'd been so inspired by the bohemian nature of their décor that Simon encouraged me to source similar material for our lounge curtains. Bizarrely, I found the very same material, yet in a pinkie colour that hung in one of the bedrooms in Charleston House; it had been repeated by Laura Ashley that year.

Inspired, Simon went on a course to learn more about modern artists like Matisse, Picasso and Klimt. Klimt became one of our favourites as the image reminded us of ourselves entwined in a mosaic twinkly blanket, just like the famous *Kiss* print. Whenever I see that image I think about us at our best, in love, smooching at each other as we once did. Not like living on a building site for four or five years. I too had had enough of sitting on our bed in the evening watching a tiny portable TV because the lounge had become a makeshift kitchen and we were eating microwave dinners whilst the kitchen was being refitted not to mention the fact that our clothes were covered in thick builder's dust, and we only had cold water to shower with in the winter. The house was a shithole and bad enough without Simon adding holes in the wall.

Jabbing a finger at him under the covers, I screeched. 'For fuck's sake, Simon. You've got to get a grip. You can't punch holes in the walls when you feel like it. And you can't bury your fucking head hoping it will all be okay, cos it won't.'

I was scared. I'd never seen a grown man in such a broken state before. I felt that I had to be the strong one. But I wasn't. And it wasn't what I'd expected in my marriage, bearing in mind we were both only twenty-six. That seems so young to me today. And I can't believe as I look back that we kept it all a secret. Our parents would have been mortified if they'd known what we were experiencing on our own. I also wondered if he was having what used to be called a 'nervous breakdown', not that I knew what that looked like.

He didn't respond. Laid as still as a corpse. Jumping up on our antique wooden bed, I straddled him like a sumo wrestler. Grabbing the quilt with both hands, I tried to force him to look at me. But he wouldn't let go. We battled. Backwards and forwards. Harder and rougher, like a tug of war, until the quilt ripped along five of the handsewn bluebell and white patchwork squares. A high-pitched screech escaped from my throat. Pummelling his chest with my fists until he wrenched both my wrists apart, I dropped with a thump on his trunk. My cheeks scorched red against his unshaven bristles.

He held me tight until my whimpers ceased. Leaning up on one elbow, he gazed down at me with shameful eyes. It was then that I noticed two mouth-sized curves of broken skin and a crescent-shaped bruise just below his left shoulder. I tried to imagine what kind of injury or implement would leave that shape. Turning his head to see what I was looking at, he saw what I'd seen. His unsullied white teeth had made the marks. Frowning back at me, he shrugged his shoulders. Raised his eyebrows and grinned with what appeared to be embarrassment.

An uncontrolled shudder swept through my body as I imagined Simon's teeth biting into his flesh. The thought of piercing his skin made me cringe in horror. I pulled my knees into my chest. Rolled into a tight ball and turned away so that I didn't have to face him.

CHAPTER 9

What the hell can I do to cover the holes? I thought, knowing that our parents were bound to want a tour of the house to see our progress. I could put the print of Picasso's, *The Dream*, over them (the one where the nose looks like a penis), but that wouldn't be big enough, I thought, giggling to myself, trying to find humour in the awkward situation.

I searched in the cupboards above the wardrobes and spread out all my sarongs, but they were too thin. I even considered a large navy Ralph Lauren polo towel, but I couldn't pin a towel to the wall, could I? The punch holes were a few feet apart so it had to be something large enough to cover both holes and not look ridiculous.

The next morning, I climbed into the loft searching for anything I could find to cover the holes. Balancing on the top rung of our rickety aluminium ladder, I pointed my torch into the gables and heaved myself up inside. Sitting with my legs dangling out of the loft hatch, I had a terrible thought. What if I don't find anything? We'd spent last month's spare cash on the tiles and were up to our limits on both Barclaycards, so we couldn't afford to buy anything new. And if we stuffed the holes with Polyfiller, they would stand out like two snowballs against the timeworn, tattered wallpaper, left by the previous owners. I imagined the feeling of nakedness as I explained to our parents that Simon 'had gone a bit berserk'.

Bending, stretching and swaying like a ballerina in *Swan Lake* along the splintered wooden beams, I imagined Dad on my shoulder saying, 'Never, tread between the rafters or you will go straight through the ceiling and break your leg, or even worse, your neck.'

Concentrating hard, I shined my torch over boxes of photos, piles of records, an old sideboard and bag of old curtains and bedding waiting for Oxfam. Pulling out the curtains, I sat with yards of green, floral lined material across my lap, wracking my brain with how I could cut them up and spread them across the wall. *For god's sake, don't be so stupid*, I said to myself, stuffing them back in the black bin liners and tearing the bags as I went.

About to give, up I shone my torch deep in the eaves right at the back of the roof. And there I saw the answer. I released the tension from my chest as I fondly stroked the rug's coarse faded fibres, like finding a long-lost childhood blanket. Mum and Dad had bought it for my new room in the nurses' home. When you qualified as a nurse you automatically upgraded to a double-sized room. For years I had waited to walk from one end to the other and not be cooped up like in the student rooms where there was only space for a single bed. Its deep Eden-green, pepper-red and tangerine twist had drawn me towards it, and I'd liked the way each stripe was sewn in tiny individual squares and triangles that resembled beach huts and ice-cream cones. It was perfect.

It weighed over a stone and stank of musty old hessian sacks, but I heaved the rug onto my hip and lugged it back across the beams. Relieved not to have broken my neck, I forced it down through the loft hatch. It landed with a heavy thud.

Simon said that I was being absurd when I plucked up the courage and asked him to help me put it up the next day.

'What do you want to do that for? Just leave it. It doesn't matter as that wall's got to be plastered anyway,' he said, waiting for his toast to pop out of the toaster.

'But what will people say if they see the holes?' I said, spreading Marmite on my toast.

'I don't give a shit what people say. It's none of their business,' he said, sitting opposite me, stirring his tea, making it spill over the edges of his mug.

By that stage in the house renovation, he'd punched quite a few holes, mainly in the doors that were made of veneer. They were shit doors anyway, he'd say afterwards. And they were all going to be replaced as we decorated each room anyway. The holes usually appeared after an argument about something. I'd put art posters we'd collected from galleries over them, one by one. But I couldn't put a poster in the middle of a wall, as that would draw too much attention and require further explanation.

After discussing other options, he could see that this was the only solution and that I wasn't giving up. Grudgingly, he agreed to my plan and went to search for a hammer and nails. Fortunately, it was quite hip to hang a rug on the wall back in the '80s, so I hoped it wouldn't appear too preposterous, although I knew it would be placed against the russet and beige '70s anaglyptic-like tattered pattern.

With his heavy, chipped, metallic toolbox and drill, Simon met me on the landing.

'How do you want this to go then?' he said with a face like a bulldog chewing a wasp.

'I think it should go at an angle, don't you?' I said, demonstrating with widespread arms like I was flag signalling to an opposing ship during the war.

'I don't give a shit what angle it goes. Let's just get on with it. I've got to clean up the bathroom in a minute.'

I don't remember him being worried about our parents seeing the holes like I was or showing much remorse, unlike the first time I'd seen him punch something a year or so after we met. It had been snowing heavily and we'd borrowed Brenda's old silver Fiesta to get back to the nurses' home as Simon's car was off the road. The snow was thick and falling fast. By the time we arrived, the roads were covered. The car slid out of control as Simon tried to turn around at the end of the road, and he desperately yanked on the handbrake. With a crunch, it slipped towards some concrete bollards. A crunching noise stopped it in its tracks. *Oh fuck*, I thought. What would Michael say? Jumping out of the car, Simon gripped his head in his hands and let out a primal scream. Reared up like a frightened horse. Thrashed his arms up and down. Thumped the bonnet with his fist and almost burst out of his clothes like the Incredible Hulk. I had never seen anyone lose their temper quite like that before, except on the TV.

With outstretched arms, I pinned the rug in place as Simon shrouded me and hammered the first nail into the friable lath and plaster. But it buckled under the force. Each time he swapped for a stronger nail, he revved up a notch. And after ten minutes, I could hold it no longer and the rug slunk from my grip and crumpled in a mound over our feet.

'What the fuck are we doing this for anyway?' he snarled through clenched teeth.

'Look. Our parents are coming tomorrow and we can't let them see the holes in the wall, can we?' I said, lifting the carpet, the fibres itching my hands.

'You're worried about your mum and dad, aren't you?' he sneered.

'Of course I am. They'll think we can't cope.'

'Actually,' he shouted, pointing his finger at my nose, 'let's call it all off.'

'What do you mean, call it all off?'

'My birthday.'

'But your mum's made your favourite lemon drizzle cake. Please, Si, let's try again. Come back,' I pleaded, pulling at his elbow.

Turning around, he said, 'I'm sorry, darling. I'm just so sick of this house. The work's never-ending.'

'But we've broken the back on it now. We have a real kitchen, and a bathroom upstairs. It's only the painting and decorating left. Come on, let's do this, and I'll make us a nice roast dinner,' I said with as much encouragement as I could muster.

He rummaged for rawl plugs in his toolbox and fixed a screw to the drill head. Dust and rubble flew into my eyes and mouth until it held enough for me to let go. The other five screws went in easily by comparison. When he had finished, I ran my hand over the coarse fibres to check that the bumps couldn't be felt.

The next morning, I placed red tulips, daffodils and a handful of blue hyacinths I found in a cluster beneath the apple tree into a vase. The sun was kind and made it warm enough for us to sit on the patio. After a slice of cake and a cuppa tea, the dads drifted into the garage to look at Simon's new workbench, leaving Mum, Brenda and I washing up.

'Are you going to show us what you've been up to, Ginger?' Brenda asked, brushing the crumbs off her tartan pleated skirt.

'Come on, Joan. You want to see, don't you?' she said, nudging Mum's elbow.

'What do you mean? What we've done?' I asked.

'Si said the bathroom's almost finished.'

'Oh, of course,' I said, steadying myself against the wall as I led them up the stairs and ushered them into the bathroom so they didn't have a chance to look back at the landing wall and see the rug.

'Wow. This is amazing. Did my Simon do all the tiling himself?' said Brenda, holding both of her cheeks.

'Of course. And he put the bath and shower in. I helped with the painting,' I said, running my hand along the top of our new bath which was big enough for two.

'He's so clever, isn't he, Joan, don't you think?' Brenda said, beaming at Mum.

'But there's a tile missing. Why is that?' Brenda observed.

Taking a deep breath, I replied with my rehearsed white lie.

'I broke it. Dropped it when I got it out of the box. I'm collecting another one next week. The man in the tile shop is very kindly giving us the display one.'

'Well, that's very lucky for you, Ginger. Isn't it, Joan?' Brenda said, stoking the empty space and making eyes at Mum whilst I kept them in the bathroom for as long as I could.

'What on earth is that on the wall?' Mum gasped, entering the hallway, pointing to the rug.

'Oh, it's all the rage, Mum. It's a bit ethnic and trendy.'

'All the rage? Well, it wasn't in our day, was it, dear?' she sighed, sticking her nose up in the air and raising her eyes at Brenda, who was tilting her head from side to side and frowning.

'Ethnic and trendy? I think you've been going to too many of those art galleries in London,' Mum muttered.

'Don't you remember, Mum? You and Dad bought the rug for my room in the nurses' home as a celebration when I qualified.'

'No, I don't. I'm sure your father and I wouldn't have bought you something as odd as that as a present. Isn't it meant for the floor?' she said, shrugging her shoulders and folding her arms tight over her cream polo neck.

'Well, at least you could have put it up straight. I think that's what your mother's trying to say,' Brenda said in support of Mum.

'Si and I like it. We think it brightens up the hall,' I said, shimmying them along the landing. 'So that's it. The show's over now. There's nothing else to see. Shall we go and see what the boys are doing downstairs?' I clapped them down the stairs like shooing a cat out of the house.

Once I could see they were downstairs and in the kitchen, I sagged against the wall and covered my hands with my face, shaking my head. My body felt heavy and my heart felt like it had shrunk. I tapped the bumpy faded carpet fibres like playing the piano as I drifted back to being in my nurse's room surrounded by friends who'd encouraged me to sparkle. I can recall the pride I had felt when the rug was the centrepiece on my floor; my parents were proud.

Simon distracted my thoughts as he shouted upstairs.

'Are you staying up there all day, Ginger?'

'No. I'm just coming. I'll be there in a minute.' I jumped up in response and skipped down the stairs, as though nothing had happened.

Lighting a green candle in the shape of a 2, then a red one in the shape of a 6, we sang 'Happy Birthday' to Simon. Brenda cut him a super large chunk of cake as we sat around the table and made small talk about the house and what a talented young man Simon had turned out to be. *If only they all knew*, I thought, slurping my last drop of tea.

As we said goodbye, I was relieved to think that despite feeling wounded, I'd gotten away with hiding the holes in the wall, and in my marriage!

I'd been brought up not to tell the truth. Not to lie exactly, but to protect people from what was going on in case they became upset. Like as kids, we were sworn to secrecy by my mum not to tell Dad if we'd been in trouble in any way. He had no idea what we got up to. So I suppose that white lies came easily to me.

CHAPTER 10

It was a few weeks after this that Simon talked about jumping off the building at work.

We talked about him getting help, but he refused. I made an appointment for him with the GP anyway. When I told him, he said I'd overreacted, yet on the day of the appointment he came with me. But when it came to going in and after a big argument, he got out of the car and walked home, said there was nothing wrong with him. Reluctantly, I went in on my own, told the female GP everything. Walking out of the surgery and back to the car, I felt relieved, not only because I'd unburdened myself, but because the GP didn't think I was overreacting by asking for help. I was impressed that she referred him directly for psychotherapy without seeing him. I don't remember her saying he was depressed, and she didn't prescribe any medication as most GPs would today, but she must have been worried about him and trusted my explanation. There was no follow up that I can remember, and Simon never saw a GP at all during that time.

Psychotherapy is also known as 'talk therapy'. It can be any method used to help people living with emotional, psychological or behavioural challenges.

The prefix 'psycho' comes from the Greek language, and means 'soul' or 'mind,' and its part of many words related to mental health, including psychotherapy.

I dreaded telling Simon the outcome, and he still had the hump with me when I got home. Initially, he wouldn't even talk about it. He continued to say that I'd overreacted. Later that evening in bed, I told him that his GP had been concerned that he was struggling to juggle everything. Reluctantly, he agreed go to see the psychotherapist.

'I'm only going to one session, mind you,' he said, reaching out to turn the light off in bed. 'If I don't like it, I won't go again. And I'm only going for you. Remember that. Okay?'

Snuggling in his arms, I felt relieved. It was a step in the right direction, and I prayed it would help; not only him, but me.

It wasn't until I was working as a school nurse that I realised that when Simon bit himself and occasionally punched himself in the face, he was self-harming. I associated self-harm with young people cutting themselves, not punching or biting themselves. I now understand that self-injury or self-harm is something you do to damage your body as a way of managing or expressing intensely difficult feelings, without intending to kill yourself. It's mainly used to keep feelings under control, rather than to get a response from other people. Many people have difficult times in their lives and feelings can be hard to put into words, and sometimes the only way to manage the intensity of what you feel is maybe to hurt yourself. When hurting yourself becomes a way of managing these pressures, it means there are other things wrong in your life that need sorting out. Self-injury can become compulsive – a way of coping because the underlying issues haven't been sorted out.

Punching holes in something occurs when uncontrollable anger washes over you. This can fuel physical discomfort and internal distress. Your thoughts race, your heart pounds and your chest tightens. You might go numb or even see red as anger takes hold and you battle the urge to lash out in response. It can be a sign of underlying anger issues caused by things like chronic stress, conflict with loved ones, life challenges and untreated mental health conditions such as depression. Simon was suffering from all of the above, so it wasn't surprising he was punching holes in the walls and harming himself out of sheer frustration.

To this day I don't know what he talked about during his sessions, or if he even talked at all. He appeared embarrassed and humiliated. I made him have Sundays off. We stayed with Jane and Joe and met close friends for lunch. He went to galleries and art exhibitions with his friend Mark and slowly things improved. He declined new contracts and went back to being a self-employed bricklayer. Eventually, the house became home.

CHAPTER 11

By 1989, six years into our marriage and despite never using contraception, I failed to conceive. After several investigations, I was referred to Hammersmith Hospital in London, where I was diagnosed with blocked fallopian tubes.

The pain seared through my pelvis like I'd been branded with an iron as they rolled me off the theatre trolley onto the crisp, cold sheets. I'd been sliced from hip to hip in an operation to unblock my tubes. Peering over his silver-rimmed glasses the following day, Professor Robert Winston, the pioneer of in-vitro fertilisation (IVF), told us that the operation had been tough. Appearing as he did when I'd seen him on the TV, his bushy black moustache moved up and down as he spoke. He said the infection I'd had when I'd had the coil fitted had scarred my fallopian tubes and knotted the ends together like mittens and that he'd done his best to fix them. It was 1989, and I was twenty-nine years old.

His expression softened as his eyebrows drew together and he delivered the final blow. 'I'm so sorry. You only have a 20 per cent chance of pregnancy.'

Throwing my head back on the pillow like I'd been sniped with a tranquilliser dart, numbness infused my body as my brain made sense of what 20 per cent meant.

Like a tile falling off a roof, Simon's face fell as he dropped my hand. Staring at the recently disinfected floor tiles between his Timberland boots, he said, 'What does that mean, exactly?'

'It means that if you don't get pregnant after another year of trying, you should consider IVF,' Professor Winston said.

Bowing his head, Professor Winston shook both our hands and left us to absorb the news. *All this fucking pain for 20 per cent*, I tried to say as my mouth opened and shut, but no sound came out. As visiting time drew to a close, I gripped Simon's arm as he kissed me goodbye, pinned him with my eyes and said, 'You do still love me, don't you, Si?'

His eyelids drooped as he pressed his forehead against mine.

'Of course I do. I'll always love you,' he said, wiping my tears with his thumbs.

'I need to go now, darling, as the car park ticket will run out. I'll come tomorrow. Same time,' he said, popping a kiss under my fringe.

Sorrow shredded my insides when he didn't do his usual wave as he went out the door. All night as the pain stopped me from sleeping, I repeated *only 20 per cent, only 20 per cent* in my head like a mantra.

Desperate to offload to Mum the next day, I clutched my urine bag on its plastic frame like a yellow handbag and trudged my way to the payphone. As I pushed through the heavy swing doors, the sight of pregnant women and new babies smacked me like an airbag going off in my face. I'd landed in the maternity ward. Squeezing my eyes shut, I nibbled on my bottom lip and waited for the nausea to pass. *How cruel*, I thought as I tried not to look at the new-borns. Like a snail with the weight of the world on its back, I set off to hike to the end of the long Nightingale Ward. Wafting past the new mothers cradling their new-borns, like a barren ghost amongst a flock of fertile females, I hungered to snatch their babies. Put them in my cot, in my nursery, and I'd swathe them in my arms.

Eighteen months later, when I still wasn't pregnant, as the crisp, bronze leaves fell from the trees and the afternoons drew in, the time came for our first attempt at IVF.

Over a four-week cycle, I sniffed drugs like crack cocaine every six hours, and my skin became a dartboard for injections and blood tests to stimulate my ovaries to produce eggs.

Lounging in bed one Sunday morning as Simon stroked my bloated belly, he said, 'One of the nurses said fifteen is the golden number of eggs. You can have success with three to six, but it's safer to have more.'

'Maybe that's why people have twins and triplets. Wouldn't it be amazing if we had twins? But I wouldn't want triplets, would you?' I said, nestling in the crook of Simon's arm.

We talked like that every day. Like a pouch of a seahorse full of progenies, I imagined how many babies could be brewing in my belly. Having high hopes for several, we talked about freezing the spare ones for the future or giving them to other women. We'd already worked out what day they would transfer the eggs to the dish and join them with Simon's sperm to produce what we jokingly referred to as 'a balding ginger baby'.

One nippy November morning when I was finally ripe, the Royal Masonic Hospital summoned us into a dim ultrasound room. Mounting the bulky black, vinyl examination chair, I felt the warmth from the previous hopeful woman. As I spread my legs and loaded my ankles into the stirrups, Simon took my hand and we settled to scrutinise the screen like watching a film on TV.

Miss Bleak, whose name badge had more social skills than her, squeezed KY jelly from its white and blue tube onto a dildo-like probe. She thrust it deep into my vagina. Her sidekick, Mr Ming, a meek young houseman whose greasy black fringe flopped over his silver-rimmed glasses, fingered letters on the keyboard like he was learning to play the piano. Together they scanned the monochrome screen for eggs.

Squinting at the screen, Simon squeezed my hand and said, 'Wow, is that all the eggs? All those black dots?'

They didn't respond. And after only a few minutes of probing and pressing on my belly, Miss Bleak looked heavenward and came to a halt. Mr Ming looked at her and said, 'Shall I try?'

Manipulating the probe like a gearstick in a sports car with his childlike hand between my thighs, they frowned and peered even closer at the screen. They halted, like doing an emergency stop in a car, and plucked out the probe.

Warm jelly ran down my legs as Miss Bleak announced, 'Sorry. No eggs.'

'You have no eggs,' Mr Ming echoed.

'What do you mean, no eggs?' Simon said in a higher voice than usual.

'There were only three eggs. And they're no good,' Miss Bleak said, looking towards the door.

'But can't you use them anyway?' I asked, wiping the jelly off my belly and from between my legs.

'Afraid not. We'll call you later and talk if you like,' Miss Bleak said as she twanged her luminous green gloves into a yellow hospital sack and slunk from the room, Mr Ming on her tail.

'No fucking eggs. Poor fucking quality,' I screeched.

'Calm down. Calm down,' Simon said, trying to soothe me.

Dropping my head to my chest, I slumped in the bucket of the bulky black chair. It felt like I was being sucked down a dark tunnel into the basement where every door was locked. Like a rag doll, Simon manoeuvred me. Slipping off the chair, my knees buckled and together we crumpled like a pile of soiled washing on the cold steel tiles. We were scooped up by a middle-aged nurse and she led us like children into a small room next door. She brought us tea and custard creams, like in a counselling scene from *Casualty*.

I dwelled on the couch all day that day. Simon had become a master at looking after me. He brought the quilt and pillow down from my bed. He moved the little table I made at college when he peeped through the window at me that day, next to the sofa. On it, he placed a glass of iced water with a floating slice of lemon, a hot chocolate in my favourite spotted pink polka dot mug, a plate of custard cream biscuits and the remote control. He closed the lounge curtains. Left me, as he went off to phone everyone to tell them the gloomy news. I couldn't bear to speak to a soul, not even Mum.

In the afternoon he phoned the hospital who confirmed that I'd only produced three eggs and that they were of poor quality. I'd failed. We were advised to go on holiday. Let my body rest. Try again in six months.

That was such a sad time for me. Probably the closest I'd come to being depressed. I was grieving, but I hadn't realised. Grieving the loss of a baby I might have had. Another six months were lost. Another year to add to the seven childless ones.

Jane too was trying for a baby and we expected the news every time we saw her. Simon and I had conversations about how we would feel. I knew as soon as we walked into her kitchen on Valentine's Day 1991 that she'd conceived. With her arms stretched out towards me, ready for a hug, we patted, squeezed and swayed like we hadn't seen each other for years. She stood back, her lips curled up, and she held my gaze, nodded and stroked her heart.

My eyes and mouth widened as I let out a squeak: 'Oh my god. Are you? Are you pregnant?'

Nodding her head and rubbing her forearms, she nodded.

I took a sharp breath in as Simon engulfed us both with a hug that crushed my head between theirs. I couldn't breathe. I wanted to be pleased. I did. And I was for her. But deep inside, my heart split.

Joe ushered the three of us onto the sofa next door. Tears tumbled as I collapsed like someone bereaved in Joe's arms. Jane was the worst. And the best. My best friend. My 'sister-in- love' as we referred to each other. She'd shared my pain like no one else. But she'd now moved into the pregnant club and was no longer in the trying-to-conceive club.

Once we'd regrouped, we talked about her dates and our expectations. After lunch, on my way to the bathroom upstairs, I saw her and Simon deep in conversation on her bed. She patted his back as he stared into his lap, a tissue in his hand. I pretended I hadn't seen.

As Jane approached six months, we prepared for the next round of IVF. Weeks of sniffing. Daily injections. Blood tests to see if I was ripe. But I wasn't. This time there were no eggs at all. The door slammed shut. It was over. I'd lost my potential baby.

Mum and Dad were on the doorstep when we arrived home. I cried so hard that day, it felt like my brain was being stabbed inside my skull.

I thought my grief was greater than Simon's. I realise now that his was equal to mine. In my experience the focus tends to be on the woman, as more times than not it's women who carry the burden of infertility. Men's feelings can be neglected in this scenario. Only recently I heard two men talking about their loss of being dads and granddads on Radio Four. It bought home to me how Simon must have suffered as the attention had been on me, as I was the patient. It must have been draining for him, having to look after me during that time.

I felt responsible and guilty for not giving Simon a child. And there were times in our marriage when I'd suggested he go and find someone who could give him children. I wondered if he saw our inability to procreate as a failure. I didn't, and still don't see it as a failure, more a misfortune. A cruel affliction of nature.

Jane's baby, Jess, compensated for our loss as we spent every weekend with her. Through caring for her, she met some of my mummy needs. We would fight to change her nappy and carry her in her sling. Simon often snuggled her inside his leather jacket, and only her fair wispy hair could be seen peeping out.

Almost thirty years on, Jess has qualified as a midwife and has delivered many babies herself. She still loves to hear the story of us all fighting to look after her.

Simon and I had previously agreed that we would only have two attempts at IVF; apart from the cost, I'd seen too many women have failure after failure. I believed in fate to a certain degree. 'What's meant to be will be' was another one of Mum's mantras that I'd adopted back then.

As a distraction from my grief, the following year I undertook more training and became a practice nurse. I absorbed myself in learning new skills and setting up clinics. I felt proud when my name was placed on the door and patients asked to be booked in with me. Simon went with his friend Mark and my dad to practical philosophy classes where they discussed the meaning of life. Simon learned to meditate, appeared more accepting of things and practised being in the present.

A few years later, Jane became pregnant with their second child, Theo. I had given up hope of ever having one of our own. We were on our way home from Jane's one Sunday evening when I asked Simon about adoption. Oasis sang 'Don't Look Back in Anger' on the radio. Simon said he wasn't keen, so I didn't press him.

Then a few weeks later out of the blue, he said, 'A social worker called Alison is coming tomorrow at seven to talk about adoption.'

I almost dropped a plate as I bent to put it away after dinner.

'What? Don't wind me up,' I said, standing up to face him. Pulling me close, he linked his arms in the small of my back and smiled like sunshine coming out from behind the clouds.

'Do you think I would joke about something like that? Anyway, it's only a chat. We don't have to make a decision.'

'Oh my god. I can't believe it. Are you sure?'

Pressing my head against his chest, I squeezed him until he squeaked, 'I'm sure. I'm sure.'

His words felt like swollen kisses on my face. We talked non-stop that night. We made love like we hadn't in months. It was tender and slow. Afterwards, I nestled in his arms. Stroked his soft, furred chest. I counted his breaths as he drifted off to sleep. It was like someone had opened the Venetian blinds. Through the slats, I saw hope.

Infertility is the cruellest thing to endure. The thought of having a baby never left me. Not even for a day.

CHAPTER 12

As Alison was arriving at seven, there was little time to prepare. Simon bought fish and chips on his way home so the house didn't smell of cooking. We stuffed it down our throats, and I placed red gladiolas on the sideboard and cleaned the sink in the bathroom. It wasn't dirty, but as we were going to be scrutinised within an inch of our lives, everything needed to shine. I even swept the leaves off the front doorstep as the winter wind whipped them onto the step. We panicked over what to wear. Shirts tucked in or out? Slippers or shoes? Perfume? Aftershave?

At seven on the dot, Alison appeared. Formal, middle class. She wore a mint scoop-neck jumper, pearl beads, black skirt and patent shoes. It turned out that she wasn't much older than us and had a good sense of humour. Her husband was a lawyer in the city.

'There's no guarantee of a baby, I'm afraid. A good chance of a child under five,' she admitted at the end of the evening.

Simon leant forward, covered his face with his hands and broke eye contact with Alison. Picking up on his disappointment, she said, 'You're a young couple in your early thirties. You may be lucky.'

A hope of a baby had long gone for me. I was grateful for the chance of any child.

The process was intense: our relationship scrutinised, childhoods analysed, values and beliefs challenged. Attending a six-week course with other couples, we were assessed and prepared by three different social workers who painted horrific stories of physical and sexual abuse. I sensed they meant to put us off.

A few months later when I was halfway through my morning smear clinic, there was an urgent knock on my door. I was in the middle of searching for a lady's cervix. Releasing the speculum, I closed her legs and left her to get dressed. Rosie, one of the receptionists, said that Alison was on the phone. That could only mean one thing. Yes. She'd found us a child!

Alison arrived with Chris, the child's social worker from the placement team, a quiet lady in her fifties with a motherly smile. Like well-behaved children, Simon and I had sat close on the sofa. We made small talk and drank tea until we all settled. They'd found a match. An eight-month-old baby girl called Bee. A baby girl. Fuck me. I couldn't believe it. I was fit to burst. But having just met Chris, I thought it inappropriate to jump up with joy. Instead, I nudged Simon's elbow with mine. He pushed back with his knee as though we were like kids messing about in assembly at school.

Chris sat back, closed the buff folder on her lap and frowned at Alison. I gripped Simon's hand in his lap, curved my shoulders forward and clenched my jaw as I waited for the punch line. It all sounded too good to be true: no abuse. No learning difficulties. No health concerns. Nothing. Chris shuffled to the edge of her seat and looked like she was going to say that Bee's father was a mass murderer, or that he'd been in and out of prison for something nasty. Alison brushed a hair off her collar and tried to contain a grin, then said, 'Do you want to tell them or shall I?'

Chris nodded yes as she cleared her throat. My heart raced. My mouth was dry. I gripped Simon's hand and waited.

'Baby Bee is ginger. Just like you,' Chris said, smiling.

I smacked my mouth with my hand. 'Oh my god. No way!'

Tears burst from my eyes like a dam breaking free. I jumped up, rushed over to Alison whose tears had already

63

spilt over her powdered cheeks, and hugged her. I then hugged Chris. Simon let out a 'Whoop'.

'Do you want to see a photo?' asked Chris.

I couldn't believe it. Here I was in my lounge about to see my baby. My baby. Our baby. A real fucking baby. I blotted my tears so I could see the picture. And there she was. With uncertain eyes, she looked straight at me, her bottom lip sucked in. Dainty like a doll, her fine orange hair framed her pincushion flushed cheeks. She wore a red and white Minnie Mouse dress that didn't suit her pale skin.

I felt Simon's breath on my neck as we gawped at her in awe.

'She can be here in a month,' whispered Chris.

'A month! Blimey. We'd better get moving then, ladies. Chop chop,' urged Simon as he ushered them out of the lounge.

The month before she arrived was frenzied. With both sets of parents, we went to Bare Necessities, the baby shop in town that, for several years, I'd walked past hoping for the day when I would go in and buy something for my baby. We bought everything: a buggy, bibs, bottles, baby-grows; highchair, nappies, wipes and more. Both mums kept asking if we liked this and that, and when we said yes, it went into the trolley. Dad chose a soft, fleecy white rabbit with velvet floppy ears and a pale green, candy-striped suit, who later became known as Rabbi-Rabs, and Brenda bought a shocking pink monkey with yellow paws and long arms and legs.

On the floor in Bee's room, we ate smoked salmon and cream cheese bagels swished down with Bucks Fizz as Dad assembled my old cot in the corner. He'd restored it to new. It smelt of Cloud Nine fresh white paint. Inside the cot, Mum placed the Babar Elephant quilt set she'd handmade. We were transfixed by the rabbit and monkey laying inside where I imagined Bee tucked up. Content and asleep.

Bee was ready and waiting for us in Sharon's lounge on the day we bought her home. Propped up against a cushion on the sofa like a Paddington bear waiting at the station, Sharon went through her routine with me as Simon gave her a bottle. She clutched his finger as if to say, *I trust you now.*

'Everything's in here,' Sharon said, lifting a bulging black bin liner and carrying it out to the car like she was on her way to the dustbin. She took a final photo of us standing by the car. Bee is in Simon's arms; his other arm is around me. As I look at it now, Simon and I had a honey glow and our eyes gleamed like new pound coins.

Bee was like a glass statue that could break at any time. Simon smooched with her on his hip into the house. Showed her everything: the kitchen, the lounge, balloons, toys and cards. Like a limpet, she clung to his neck as fear shadowed her. For a long time, we sat on the floor in her bedroom until, at a tortoise pace, she left his grip and crawled around the room. I saw a hint of bravery as she poked the toys. Stroked the furry animals and pulled a few books from the shelf. Every few seconds she peered back over her shoulder to check we were still there.

We fell in love with her that first week. She ticked all our boxes. Her tangerine fringe framed her little pearl face like glass beads on a lampshade. Her eyes were blue like ours. She even had a hazel fleck in her left eye like Simon's. I could cradle her in my arms and feed her as I'd always imagined. I couldn't breastfeed of course, but it was close enough for me. I watched in awe as she wiggled her toes, sucked hard on the teat, made bubbles in her bottle. I sat her up, supported her chin with my new muslin cloth, rubbed her back and waited for the sound of her burp.

Each day she ventured a bit further away, always looking over her shoulder to check we were still there. Eventually, she took herself off to her toy box in the lounge next door. I didn't leave her for more than thirty seconds just in case something happened. We'd mastered the car seat, the highchair, the buggy. Walked proudly to town to show her off. Frequently strangers would stop and say to me, 'Well, there's no doubt who she belongs to is there?'

Slowly, and not without tears, we settled into family life. Bee gave us daily joy and soon called us Mummy and Daddy. Simon couldn't wait to get home after work. I would watch as he jumped out of his van and run across the road to where we waited at the front door. He used to say it was like coming home for Christmas every day.

CHAPTER 13

I first noticed a significant, almost manic change in Simon's behaviour in June 1996 after his first trip to Glastonbury. I had spent the weekend with Jane, at her house just outside Swindon. The weather was scorching. We'd lounged in our peach and cerise sarongs, sipping strawberry Pimm's and splashing with the kids in the paddling pool, wondering how Simon and Joe were getting on at the festival as they'd talked of nothing else for months.

When they returned on Sunday evening, we did a second take. Wearing wooden beads, white cheesecloth shirts open to their belly buttons and multi-coloured harem pants with crutches that hung around their knees, they appeared like a pair of balding hippies. Moving in slow motion and looking like they hadn't slept for a week, they recalled stories about fairies and dragons in The Green Fields, raving all night in the dance tent and playing their air guitars to 'I Wanna Be Adored' by The Stone Roses.

Having bought a handheld cigarette-making machine at the festival, Simon revelled in demonstrating how to roll a spliff. Spreading peach tobacco and breaking musky weed on a small red plastic sheet, he fed a Rizla between metal rollers. Out popped a perfectly made joint that resembled the white sugar candy cigarettes we'd pretended to smoke as kids.

And this is how it went. For three to six months Simon was frantic, then for three months he was flat. We'd pretend nothing had happened and I'd pray we were over it. However, when the clocks went forward in the spring, he would unfold like a poppy stretching open its red crepe petals to show its deep purple hearts inside. And off we'd go again.

For the first couple of years I was baffled by the change in him, and had no name for his affliction. And despite being a nurse I knew little about mental health.

His moods seemed to rotate around Glastonbury Festival. I now think of them as 'the Glastonbury cycles'.

Leading up to Glastonbury, he was like a child counting the days down to Christmas morning. He couldn't stand still, talked at speed and was so enlivened that he couldn't get his words out quick enough, and became irritable and agitated if I told him to calm down. In retrospect, Simon always turned a bit melancholy and would tend to hibernate a little through the winter; perhaps it was a small touch of seasonal affective disorder. But it wasn't until his first Glastonbury that he experienced mania; he'd been reasonably balanced before then.

Simon found joy and escapism whilst at Glastonbury, I thought. He loved everything about it: the live music, performing arts, comedy, the dance tent and food from around the world. He was in heaven for twenty-four hours a day for four days in a row. It was a place where he could play like a child, revel in music and entertainment, as well as entertain others. It gave him energy and something to look forward to after spending much of the winter glum. Of course, it was purely a chronological coincidence that the mania coincided with the festival, a yearly landmark for me to keep track of his moods. Had it not been that, it would have been something else.

Whilst he had his ups and downs and an episode of 'reactive depression' during our first ten years of marriage, there was no discernible pattern. I had chalked it up to the stress of renovating our house, running a business, not getting pregnant and the gruelling nature of the adoption process. Normal things faced by many young couples.

Maybe after thirteen years of marriage and all the things we'd been through, the romance was simply cooling.

Perhaps we had entered that mid-relationship slump that happens to many couples when they lose themselves to parenthood, work and other demands. But this felt different. Like something was changing beyond our control. There still had to be love. *I* had it. I did wonder sometimes if he still had love for me, especially when he slagged me off and accused me of not being fun anymore. He said that I controlled all our money and said I was a crap wife and mother. But even in these moments, it did not feel like I was dealing with Simon at all, but rather some alter ego. It was like someone else has taken control of my Simon.

We were halfway through the process to adopt our second child. With Alison, our social worker, due to see Simon for his interview, I became seriously concerned that she would notice his hyper behaviour and that it could jeopardise our chance of having another child. I was worried that something had changed, but I didn't know what it was. I put it down to him smoking too much weed.

The first adoption process had been exhausting and Alison reassured us that the next would just be an update as we'd now proved ourselves to be capable parents.

I heard Simon shouting in the lounge. Peeping through our glass door, I saw Alison wedged into the corner of the settee clutching our file across her chest as he strutted up and down.

'So that's it, Al. Bee loves me. I'm a great dad. You can tick that box and get us the next kid?' he said, pointing his finger at her nose.

During our first interview three years ago for Bee, we sat side by side on the sofa. Only spoke when we were questioned. Listened intently to the copious amounts of information Alison gave us. For eight weeks we did this and by the end, Alison knew everything there was to know about us. Not a stone was unturned. Each week we relaxed and opened up in her company, but we were always aware that all our behaviours were being judged.

69

Speechless and flushed, Alison left without saying goodbye. She phoned a few days later to say she had grave concerns about Simon's mental health.

'What's happened to Simon, Ginger? I don't understand.'

Defending him, I said, 'I just think he believes he's proved himself as a father and is keen to get our next child. You know how much he loves Bee.'

'I had to go back to the office and have a debrief with my colleague as Simon had intimidated me. Something's changed. I know he can be a bit over-enthusiastic and animated, but this was on a different level. Just keep an eye on him, will you?'

Deep down, I agreed with her, but I couldn't tell her that as it would jeopardise our chance for another child. This idea terrified me, but I also felt a strange sense of relief that someone else noticed what I had over the previous months. It wasn't all in my head.

We had to get a letter from Simon's psychotherapist during the first adoption saying that the episode of depression he'd had in his early twenties was due to normal stressors and not a chronic condition. He was depressed then. He barely spoke. Didn't look forward to the usual things he enjoyed. Stopped answering the phone.

But this was different. He spoke and moved twice as fast as usual and was easily distracted by trivial things. I had never seen this exaggerated side of his personality. Admittedly, he could be bouncy, wave his hands about like a caricature of an Italian, and twist and warp his face to make us laugh when he was buoyant, and amuse us with a story. But this was on a different level. And now Alison had validated my suspicions.

A couple of weeks after that, early one Sunday morning, Simon woke me and said, 'Shut your eyes. I have a surprise for you.'

Stirring from a deep sleep, I covered my eyes and sat up.

'I've bought you flowers, my princess,' he bellowed.

Balancing on my bedside cabinet sat a muddy, yellow builder's bucket brimming with floppy, pink carnations. Their necks were still tied with blue nylon string. He'd nicked them from a roadside stall. Smelling of nutmeg and cinnamon, Bee toddled in carrying a plate laden with chunky squares of bread pudding. Simon had been up all night baking.

'Thank you, my darling,' I said, springing out of bed to catch it before she dropped it.

Being a toddler, Bee absorbed everything. She thought bringing me cake and flowers in bed was exciting. She had no idea that flowers normally lived in vases, and baking was usually done during the day. She mirrored Simon's mood of heightened eagerness, but it was only seven on a Sunday morning. Usually, we laid in on a Sunday until 8.30, and yes, Simon would bring me a cup of tea and bring Bee into me if she was awake, but baking in the early hours and having already been out just to get me flowers was bizarre.

'Si, don't you think you're being a bit hyper, darling?' I said whilst loading the dishwasher a few hours later. Bee had fallen asleep on the sofa. 'Even Alison said you were full of beans when she interviewed you.'

'Who the fuck does she think she is? Nosey bitch,' he spat.

I curled my toes in fear.

'Well, maybe it's just that the weed has gone to your head a bit. You're having a bit of a reaction,' I offered, trying to diffuse the situation.

'I'm just fine,' he said. 'This is the new me. And babe, if you don't like it, well, that's bad luck. I ain't changing for no one.' He opened the patio door and went outside to roll another joint.

I phoned Jane to see if Joe's behaviour was altered, but it wasn't. She did tell me, however, that they were smoking super strong skunk that was twenty times stronger than normal marijuana in Glastonbury. And they'd both tried magic mushrooms. Simon hadn't told me as he thought I'd go mad. And despite Joe still smoking the skunk, it had the opposite effect on him; he appeared more chilled than usual, which Jane was grateful for as Joe could be argumentative at times.

We thought it was funny at first, some of the wacky things Simon did. But as his behaviour worsened over the next few weeks and this became his new normal, where he barely came to bed, talked loud and fast and found fault in everything I did, I became more concerned.

He became obsessive about hygiene and went to a sauna most days after work and scrubbed his skin until he had no scent.

'Smell me, babe. Do I smell?' he asked as he stepped out of the shower each evening after work.

Steadying myself with my hand on his hairy chest, all I could smell was Pears soap.

'You smell clean, darling,' I said.

'Are you sure?'

'Sure.'

'What about my armpits?' he said, sniffing them both.

'You smell soapy. Nice,' I said, taking his towel and hanging it on the radiator, noticing that his thighs were red raw from where he'd scrubbed them with a nail brush.

Midweek, he returned early from work with two bulging green plastic bags full of body massagers and essential oils from The Body Shop. As he tipped the contents of one bag onto the kitchen table, out fell a smooth wooden handheld massager resembling male genitalia with two balls attached to a handle. He said it was designed to alleviate buttock tension. Another, like a knuckle duster with numerous small balls, relieved deep tissue tension, and there was a body back roller that resembled a belt full of bullets. From the other bag he pulled a beautifully handmade, walnut Tisserand aromatherapy box containing twelve essential oils, a bag of tea-light candles, three bottles of massage oil and a Buddha's head oil burner. It filled the house with floral and musky smells, but when he poured too much oil into the bath, his skin became blotchy and red.

Each evening he got in the bath, dripped geranium, patchouli and lang lang oil in the steamy water and lined the edge of the bath with tea lights. He took our CD stereo in with him and soaked with Jeff Buckley's version of 'Hallelujah' at full volume. On the fourth night, I became worried when he locked himself in and talked about wanting to drown. I didn't think he was serious, but his behaviour had been so out of the ordinary that I called Jane who sent Joe up to help me get Simon out of the bathroom. Shouting back and forth through the stripped pine door whilst I let Bee watch any video she liked on TV to distract her, Joe got nowhere. Simon told him to fuck off and stop interfering. Joe phoned Jane who had already sent Simon's mum, Brenda, to come and talk to him. We believed she was the only person who could persuade him to calm down and talk about his behaviour change.

I left her in the hallway as Joe settled me and Bee in his car and then drove us an hour back to their house. I don't know what happened after we left. Brenda played it down. She told Jane the next morning that Joe and I had overreacted, that Simon was just being a little playful. Again, I questioned myself. Thought it was possible I had overreacted, taken his eccentricity too seriously. But still, I thought of what Alison, a professional who knew us inside and out, had said. I felt torn, unsure of what to think or do. I knew something larger than us was at work, but I did not have a name for it or know what to do.

CHAPTER 14

Although Simon appeared to be calming down after that first Glastonbury, he remained a little twitchy through to September 1996. With Jane and Joe, and their younger sister Lizzy, we had planned a surprise sixtieth birthday picnic for Brenda. We'd hired two small motorboats to cruise up the Thames and managed to keep it a secret right up until we arrived at the river.

I felt optimistic. Simon was coming to bed at a reasonable hour and was less obsessive about his hygiene. He was still irritable, especially with me, but overall seemed to be his old self in most ways. He did wheel spins at each set of traffic lights like he did when he was young and swerved the car from side to side. He found this hilarious and flared up when I asked him to calm down.

'Shut up, Ginger. I'm going to be with my family now. I can do what I like,' he said as we got out of the car.

The tension between us must have shown, as after the initial surprise and excitement of the picnic, Brenda took me to one side and said, 'Darling. Don't fight with him. He's just a little florid. Just go with it. You'll find it much easier that way.'

So I listened to his mother and shut up. I went in the boat with Joe, his father Michael and the kids. Simon took Jane, Brenda and Lizzy. Revving up the throttle, he sped up the river so fast that he quickly went out of view. I offloaded to Joe and Michael about the recent events. They both agreed that he appeared a bit volatile, but not as bad as he had been following Glastonbury.

Simon could be hot-headed at times; that was part of his normal personality. He was the fun one in the family group, the one who took the lead and was full of ideas. He would examine *Time Out* magazine each week and find us new places to explore. He made us walk miles to find the best spot on a beach, and he'd get us tickets for fringe shows and art exhibitions in London.

Under a tumbled down old bridge we found a pretty grassy area that was flat enough for us all to sit down. Unfolding our chequered blankets, we emptied the hampers of all Brenda's favourite foods: corned beef and tongue sandwiches, pork pies, Liquorice Allsorts and a Miss Piggy cake. Miss Piggy always made Brenda laugh out loud as she was such a diva.

'Oh my goodness. I can't believe you kept this a secret,' she said, holding her face and shaking her head as we handed out Van Gogh party plates and napkins as Michael popped the champagne. After a few large slurps, I felt the rush of bubbles as they lightly sprayed the top of my lip. Finally, I breathed out and relaxed. Waving a champagne bottle and cocktail sausages in his hands, Simon chased the kids up and down the riverbank.

'Right, come and sit down now for food,' Jane ordered the kids as I filled plates with Hoola Hoops and snack bites for them.

It took me a while to notice that Simon had disappeared.

'Where do you think he's gone?' I discreetly mouthed to Joe.

He grinned and raised his eyebrows. Mimicked rolling a joint with his hands. Ten minutes later, Simon jumped out like a clown appearing on stage, climbed up onto the bridge and wedged his feet between the wrought iron railings above us. The sky had an unreal brightness like a bulb that was about to blow, making it hard to see him.

I held my breath until he balanced himself, using one finger on the roof of the bridge.

'Oh yay, oh yay. Thank you all for coming today. Mum, you are an amazing woman. You don't look a day over sixty. Ha-ha. We all love you so much. Three cheers for 'The Forces' sweetheart'. Hip, hip, hooray! Hip, hip, hooray!' he sang like a town crier. His pet name for her was 'The Forces sweetheart, after Vera Lynn, whose songs helped raised morale in World War Two.

We raised our glasses towards Brenda, whose smile was like an umbrella whooshed inside out. In her eyes, Simon could do no wrong. There were many times over the years when Simon had been upset and she would comfort him in her huge J-cup bosom.

Simon offered his smiles like canapés. Gesticulating and entertaining us with his humour and wit, as he always did. Glowing with self-contentment like he was in a one-man show and we were his number one fans, he bowed as we cheered and clapped. As he crouched to jump down the six-foot distance, his foot got stuck. He toppled and impaled his thigh on the rusty railings. He yelped like a dog being trodden on as Joe and Michael grabbed his arms to steady him still as they prised him off the spike. Freed, he collapsed in a ball, right on top of Miss Piggy's pink face. Blood seeped through his ripped jeans. Jane and I flew into nurse mode and applied pressure to the wound. We agreed it was a hospital job.

Brenda distracted and reassured the children, who were all in tears. Scooping up the picnic in the blankets, we bundled everything into the bin bags. Joe dragged Simon into one of the boats with Jane and me. Michael took Brenda, Lizzy and the kids. We were somewhere up the Thames in Oxford, but none of us knew where.

As we cruised close to the riverbank to find help, Simon's face drained white as he drifted into shock.

'Go faster, Joe,' screeched Jane. 'This is fucking serious.'

'I'm going as fast as I can,' replied Joe.

As he pulled the throttle, the boat jolted and made a throaty chug noise. The engine cut out. We'd run out of fuel.

'Look out for anyone in their gardens and ask for help,' Joe bellowed, steering us towards the bank. 'Ask anyone where the nearest hospital is.'

As Simon lay with his head on Brenda's pink cotton jumper, drifting into shock, I felt love and compassion for him.

We stopped at the first family in their garden we saw. As they tossed steaks on their barbecue and soaked up the last of the autumn rays, Jane explained what had happened. They jumped up to drive us to the nearest accident and emergency department. We hauled Simon, who was shivering and grey, out of the boat and covered the back seat of their red BMW with black bin liners. As we arrived at the hospital, he was taken straight into the emergency room. The wound was as deep as it was wide. It needed internal stitches. He was given a pethidine injection for the pain and wrapped in a foil blanket. The others arrived an hour or so later, just as the hospital discharged him.

A frail ET-like smile appeared on Simon's lips when Brenda rushed in, in her usual blue-light fashion.

'I'm so sorry, Mum. I've ruined your birthday,' he said in a quiet voice, gazing at the floor like a naughty five-year-old.

'Don't worry, darling, it's fine. As long as you are okay, that's all that matters,' she said, pulling him into her bosom, hugging and kissing his head, holding him there like a babe in her arms.

CHAPTER 15

Once we'd returned from A&E after the riverboat trip, Simon went straight to bed. He didn't appear until half past one the next day. We reflected on what had happened whilst Bee played with the kids next door. He agreed to stop smoking weed and confessed that he hadn't been feeling right since the festival. I still had no idea why Simon's behaviour was so changed.

By the following weekend, he'd withdrawn from everything and was full of remorse for ruining Brenda's birthday. He talked about feeling worthless and helpless. He stayed in bed beyond lunchtime and hid under the duvet when Bee peeped in to see if he was awake.

Distracting Bee at breakfast one morning, I asked her what sort of birthday party she would like. Usually there was a theme. That year it was horses. She was going to be four on 5 October 1996. I'd enquired at the local Shire Horse Centre if they did parties, and they did. My neighbour made her a chocolate cake that resembled a stable yard with plastic horses, jumps and green icing for grass.

When Simon disengaged, I don't remember calling it depression, not as I would today. I just thought he was a bit moody, pissed off with himself. Yet the symptoms had been glaring at me in the face. Even with Bee's excitement, which always motivated him, he had no interest in her birthday at all. I wasn't sure if he would even join us.

Her birthdays were always a bittersweet time for me. I loved the thrill of buying and wrapping her presents, getting ready for her party where both families would celebrate with us. But each year, just before her birthday, a buff brown envelope from social services landed on the mat. Inside were two opened cards, and a letter from 'The Letter Box' administrator. When we adopted Bee, we agreed to an annual exchange of cards and letters from Gemma (Bee's birth mother).

The first time, on Bee's second birthday, I placed the envelope on the kitchen table like it was tainted. I didn't want it in my home. I know it sounds selfish and ungrateful, but we'd only had Bee for a short time and it hadn't been easy. Plus, Gemma was refusing to sign the adoption papers. I was now Bee's mum. Her only mum. She called me Mummy. I'd earned that name. I had waited ten years for it and wasn't prepared to share it.

This year, I put Bee down for her afternoon nap, made myself a cup of tea and sat at the kitchen table. I looked at Gemma's card. Dreaded it saying something like, *To my daughter, from Mummy*. That would have killed me. The card was large with a huge teddy waving on the front. Inside it read, *To someone special*. She wrote in childlike print, *Love from Gemma and Beth xxx*. Beth was her second baby who was now a year old. The court decided that it was best for her to be placed with her father (not the same father as Bee). Gemma was sixteen and under the care of social services when she fell pregnant with Bee. I rested my forehead in my hands. Felt all mixed up. Like one minute I'd been flying in a glider, the next the wind dropped and I had crashed onto the black tarmac.

Sharing the card with Simon when he returned from work, he showed little emotion. I felt mournful and solo. We'd been deemed suitable parents, able to give a child shelter and stability, and Bee had been placed with us after much scrutiny. I now felt guilty as Simon showed Bee little attention as he lay in bed at the weekends, or got distracted with his latest obsessions during the high times. I felt more and more like a single parent.

What made it worse was that each year I had to write back to Gemma by Christmas and tell her how Bee was getting on. I didn't want to tell her how my daughter was. It stung. But in the back of my mind, I felt desperately sorry for her. So I painted the perfect picture that year. Reassured her that Bee was absolutely fine. Which, outwardly, she appeared to be. I stuck to the facts and wrote something like this: *She loves playing outside in the garden and likes digging with her toy spade. She collects all the apples in her blue bucket. She loves books and going to the library, and is very patient and gentle.* Each time I enclosed one close-up photo of Bee's smiling face, plus a full-length shot.

As the years passed and I grew in confidence, these birthday letters mattered less. Today I feel proud that I did that. Any feelings of insecurity I had then were replaced with empathy for Gemma who went on to have five more babies.

CHAPTER 16

After Simon had his interview with Alison for our second child, I eventually had mine. I'd rehearsed my answers to any questions she may ask about Simon's elevated mood. My toes curled in my sheepskin slippers as I lied and said everything was okay. Simon was still restless and had started going for a daily sauna and steam again to cleanse himself. Alison appeared to go away reasonably content to find us our next child. But as Simon's mood dropped following Brenda's riverboat incident, and his depression lingered over the winter, I feared he couldn't cope with another child.

The following Easter weekend as I flicked through photos of Princess Diana at a royal function wearing an elegant black dress in an old copy of *Hello Magazine*, I decided to sound him out. He'd just placed his favourite mulligatawny soup in the microwave for three minutes when I said, 'Si. Feeling as you have these last few months where you've found things a bit of a struggle, would it be less stressful if we stopped the second adoption? What would you say?'

Attempting to appear casual, I stroked Diana's wedding ring on the centre page. I didn't give him eye contact, and I held my breath.

Leaning against the white worktop, he appeared to search on the black and white tiled floor for answers. He still hadn't said anything when the microwave pinged, so I pressed him.

'Would you prefer to stay just the three of us as Bee is a known quantity or take on another child who may not be as easy and potentially change the dynamic of our little trio? And possibly add to your anxiety?'

Watching the cheese spread as it melted in his soup, and after what felt like an age, he replied, 'Life hasn't been easy lately, has it?'

'So that's a no then, is it, darling?' I said, searching his face to be sure.

'I think so. I'm sorry,' he said, sitting down opposite me.

I put it to him in other ways to test his decision and the answer was the same.

Sadness clouded his features as he stared at the melting cheese circles as he stirred his soup.

My body felt heavy, like I was coming down with the flu, as I crept around to his side of the table. I hugged him from behind, felt his warmth as I nestled my head in his neck and whispered, 'It's okay, darling. Don't worry. We'll be okay.'

I left him at the table still stirring his soup. Crept upstairs. Curled into a ball on our bed and quietly wept.

I was gutted. Had never wanted only one child. Of course, I was grateful for Bee, but I didn't want her to be an only child. It didn't feel like a complete family to me. Plus, we'd always fantasied about four children. I felt resentful and angry. But I knew the decision was right. Another child may have compounded things. What made it worse, however, was when Alison called a year later to say that Gemma was pregnant again with child number three, and we could have a baby from birth. Despite Simon having had two manic phases by then, I still asked him. Hoped he'd say yes. Thought I would cope with anything to have another baby. But he still he said no.

And that was the right decision. Another baby would have added huge stress. Neither of us would have coped.

CHAPTER 17

When the second Glastonbury rolled around in June 1997, Jane and I decided to join Simon and Joe. We had learned from last year and thought maybe if we went together we could help keep an eye on the boys. I'd packed and unpacked twenty or more times; it was tight stuffing everything into my new rucksack. Simon and Joe had gone ahead on the Thursday and found a top spot for our giant, grungy old army tent. It was larger than most, slept eight people and overlooked the whole of Glastonbury village. Simon's younger sister, Lizzy, now in her twenties, came as well with her new boyfriend, Foz. They trooped us up to the Green Fields, to a fairy-lit marquee where we downed vodka jellies, scoffed hash brownies and simmered in a solar-powered Jacuzzi. On Saturday night, I clung to the loops of Simon's jungle greens as he dragged me through a crowd of 70,000 to the front of the main stage, just in time to hear Bjork sing 'Venus as a Boy'.

Jane and I weren't impressed the next day when Simon and Joe shared a tab of acid (LSD). Simon was quick to react and, like when a curtain goes up on a stage, he walked out and performed. Every five minutes he stopped like a toddler at a fairground in awe of something. He bought a long blonde wig from a black guy with dreads called Red who wove green and orange braids into the wig. For the rest of the day, he wore it like a trophy on his sun-kissed baldhead. People looked at him twice and cracked up with laughter, especially when he said, 'You're not taking the piss out of my hair, are you?' as if it was real.

He described everything with exaggerated detail and behaved like a child with ADHD. He kept saying: 'You're either a party maker or a party taker.'

We chilled out the next day in the acoustic tent and listened to unplugged sounds from a host of top names. Simon still appeared altered, yet mellow. Drifting back to the car on Sunday, we stopped by a camper van painted with yellow and white daisies and bought a dream catcher for Bee. It was made from small willow branches tied together with garden string, decorated with dangling beads and shaped like a fish with a mother-of-pearl button for an eye.

Bee had spent the weekend with my mum and dad and was asleep when we got home. Desperate to see her, we ran up the stairs and crept into her room. Simon carefully pinned the dream catcher over her bed. We watched in awe as her tummy rose and fell with each contended breath; we still couldn't believe she was ours despite it having been over four years.

In a similar way to the first Glastonbury, Simon's behaviour changed again once we were home. He became irritable, edgy and hyperactive. Spent money like water. Stayed up late. Rose before dawn. Became friends with our neighbours who he'd only waved at before. When I reached across the bed one morning around 6 a.m., he was gone. *He's been up all night baking again*, I thought. *Or maybe he's gone to work early*, I prayed as I slipped out of bed. Pulling on my dressing gown, and peeping into Bee's room, I was relieved to see that she was still fast asleep.

Orange and yellow Post-it Notes clung to all the doors along the hallway, giving me instructions on what needed to be got rid of in each room. For example, on our office door, it read in capitals, *Get rid of all Ginger's old nursing books*, and on the bathroom door it read, *Clear out the crap from under the sink and throw away old bath toys*. Before I even got to the loo, Simon beckoned me downstairs.

'Quick. Quick. Come down. Close your eyes, my princess. I've got something to show you.'

Creeping down the stairs, afraid of what I might find, Simon met me in the hall.

'You always said I was a bit arty. Well, art I have produced. Now close your eyes.'

Leading me by the chord of my dressing gown, he counted down: 'Three, two, one... Da da. Open your eyes.'

And as a magician pulls the black cloth off the rabbit, he whisked off a tea towel and with a booming laugh said, 'What do you think. Eh? Fucking amazing. Bet you couldn't create that, could you, babe?'

And there on the table was what he called a sculpture. It was a pair of his Timberland work boots lying on their sides with our pink and white spotty dustpan and brush balanced next to it with a roll of green garden string in the dustpan!

With my hands on my hips, I said, 'Are you fucking serious?'

'What do you mean? Of course I am. Don't you like it?'

'It's ridiculous. Please tell me this is a joke?'

Simon did have a creative flair, and when he was depressed early in our marriage he'd taken up pottery, hand-coiled an earthenware vase that weighed a ton and glazed a fruit bowl yellow and black like a bumble bee. I'd been so impressed with his handy-work. But this was not what I would call a sculpture.

'What the fuck is wrong with you? What bit don't you get? I did this for you, babe. I thought you'd like it. But nothing's ever good enough, is it?' he said, moving closer with each word. 'Why do you keep challenging everything I do?'

'I challenge you because I don't like your behaviour. You're spending too much money on shit. You're not doing a full day's work. And you're nasty to me. I wonder if you love me anymore, Simon. Do you?' I shouted until I shook and my knees nearly gave way.

And then with spit flying from his mouth like a dog shaking as it comes out of a river, he said, 'Love you? Of course I fucking love you. What do I have to do to prove it?'

His shouting savaged the air. He didn't just raise his tone; his muscles tensed and the veins in his neck bulged with blood like a thrombosis swelling into a clot. His face was so close to mine that his spittle landed on my lips.

'Just be gentle for once. Don't be so angry. Please, Si. Please.'

I wiped my eyes and nose with my sleeve, pushed past him and sobbed as I walked up the stairs. I heard the front door bang behind me and prayed he'd gone to work.

Relieved that Bee hadn't appeared when we were shouting at each other, I crept along the landing, knelt by her bed and watched as her tummy moved Rabby Rab's floppy white ears gently up and down in time with her breath.

What has she done to deserve this chaos? I thought as guilt laid heavy, like an iron pressed on my chest. I consoled myself that she thought that all Simon's lively behaviour was fun and normal. Kneeling by her by bed, I kissed her forehead as she turned and opened her eyes.

'Mummy, what are you doing?' she asked, pushing me away, clutching Rabby Rab to her chest.

'I'm just loving you, my gorgeous, scrumptious girl. Now, come on, sleepyhead. We've got to get you to the nursery to get that collage finished, haven't we?' I said, choosing an outfit from her chest of drawers.

I could barely walk down the hall for boxes and packing when I returned from the nursery. I could see that Simon had bought a large pair of expensive headphones. When I swung through the kitchen door, he announced with his arms outstretched like an opera singer reaching a high note, 'Da da. There you are, princess. I thought cos you're a deaf old bird and you can't appreciate music quite as I can, or even hear the words properly, I'd buy these for you. The bloke in the shop said they were the best you could buy.

They sound wicked. I got a deal on them. Instead of £995, I got them for £895. What a bargain. I thought you'd think so.' He said this without drawing a breath.

Tension built in my neck and shoulders as I pictured our bank balance further in the red. Then, like showing me to a table in a restaurant, he said, 'Right. Sit your pretty self down, and I'll set you up. Okay?'

Like a robot being programmed, I did what he said. Sat at our bare kitchen table with my hands placed in my lap like I'd been handcuffed. Watched as he unravelled cables and plugged things in around me.

'I've bought you this album by John Martyn. Music for your soul. I want you to listen to the words. Really listen to it. Like you've never heard music before. Well, you haven't, have you, babe?' He sniggered to himself inappropriately as he busied himself around me like he was about to operate on me.

Before the words even shaped in my mouth, or my feet had the chance to take me to him where he might hear my words, I battled with my wits. I wanted to stand up to him and tell him to stop. But every time I went to speak, he shushed my lips with a charming 'Joker' kind of smile. Like a puppet, he pulled my strings.

Taking the cardboard sleeve out of a plastic CD case, he underlined a track several times with a red biro then, thrusting it in my hands he said, 'Read that.'

'Couldn't love you more. I just couldn't love you more,' I read, as John Martyn's voice tried to sooth my mind.

CHAPTER 18

I'd been struggling to live with Simon's agitated pace since the second Glastonbury. Hence, in the winter of 1997, I developed a chest infection that left me fatigued. I went with Bee to Mum and Dad's to recover. During that week, Simon convinced his family and friends I was a useless wife and mother and said that I never cooked, cleaned or looked after Bee. Brenda phoned one day with the same message; she said I needed to listen to him a bit more, otherwise things wouldn't work out for us. Jane came on the phone after Brenda and said the same. I came off the phone feeling confused. I vacillated between thinking they must be right and then thinking I wasn't that bad. Or was I? I usually believed what Jane told me. She was my friend. I trusted her. Admittedly, I had no energy of late, but I was ill. Wasn't I?

Making a surprise visit to my parents' house a few days later, Simon barged past me. 'Where's your mum?' he asked.

She was cleaning the bathroom in her pink rubber gloves, and he pinned her against the avocado sink and said I was useless. It was all her fault, he said. Dad tried to reason with him as he ranted like the Joker in *Batman*. After throwing Bee in the air and spinning her around a few times, as quick as he came, he was gone.

Dazed, Mum perched by the fire on the edge of her chair. Her pink nails trembled as she sipped a double Harvey's Bristol Cream sherry. Once Bee was settled for her afternoon nap, we discussed Simon's behaviour and Dad decided to visit him a few days later to see if he could make sense of the situation.

Dad had great respect for Simon, especially after he built them a fancy wall around their patio. He found Simon intelligent and enjoyed discussing politics and modern art with him. The first time Simon came to dinner, they served lunch in the dining room with a white starched tablecloth, best china and tall-stemmed wine glasses. Dad shook his hand. Mum asked him lots of questions about his family. Nanny, who'd lived with us all my life, smiled and nodded at him but didn't say a word. Mum had made a cherry pie for the occasion. She smiled and rubbed her hands together as Simon finished off the last slice with custard. It was unusual for anyone to have seconds, as the pie was normally saved for the next day when Dad came home from work.

A few days after Simon had stormed in on my mother, Dad visited him and found him wearing yellow leather Indian slippers and his multicoloured harem pants. His chest was bare and he had wooden beads around his neck. Simon paced in and out of the garden clutching our orange paisley biscuit barrel. He ranted as he fed custard creams to the birds.

'See, Edmund? This is what I mean about your daughter. She's fucking useless. She lives on biscuits all day. Doesn't cook. Doesn't clean. What's a man meant to do?'

Several times Dad tried to defend me. But Simon wouldn't let him. He reported back that Simon had lost his mind, and our marriage was over.

Fucking hell. That's a bit harsh, I thought. I knew Simon wasn't quite right. But I thought we could work it out, surely. But Dad's mind was made up.

Shortly after that, I told Dad that I felt better and needed to go home. Simon arrived to collect Bee and me. He paced up and down Mum and Dad's entrance hall, rushing his words like a walking power surge. I barely had time to say goodbye. He scooped Bee up in one arm and our bags in the other. He then sped down the dual carriageway at 85 mph.

'Please slow down, Simon. Bee's in the back,' I begged.

'What? Don't you like the way I drive?'

'It's too fast. I don't feel safe,' I said, gripping the overhead rail.

'Well, you'd better get out then if you don't like it,' he said, doing an emergency stop on the hard shoulder. 'Go on, then. Get out.'

'No. No. I don't want to,' I begged as he shoved my shoulder until I got out.

The pit of my stomach fell and my chest tightened as he sped away. I had no coat, cash or phone. A flock of birds rose and flew off as I stood not knowing if he would return. It seemed the mist itself had screamed and covered me in a wet cloak as I felt drizzle in the air. The next exit was three miles away and it would take him twenty minutes even if he did come back. I walked quickly between cars, jumping onto the grass verge as they honked their horns.

Quickening my pace, I strode towards the orange street lights in the distance. Where shall I go? How will I get home? I know, I'll knock on a nice house. Call Phil, my brother, not Mum or Dad.

Beep. Beep. Beep. Beep. I leapt out of my skin. It was him. He swung open the door. As I tried to get in, he pulled away. My hands trembled. Eyes watered. Eventually, I climbed in.

'Where have you been, Mummy?' Bee asked.

Simon answered.

'Mummy's been for a little stroll on the bypass, darling. What a silly Mummy!'

I reached back to hold her hand, and our fingertips touched for a moment until Simon hit the throttle and ranted all the way home about us having too much junk in the house. He kept going on about getting rid of my things.

My jaw dropped as we pulled up outside the house. The curtains had gone. The contents of the entire dining room were piled high on our eight-seater, waxed pine table. It resembled an auction room with my dinner service, knickknacks, table lamp and all my books piled high as if they were about to be sold to the highest bidder.

Simon repeated, 'We've got too much junk. I want you to go through everything and decide what you want to keep. I'll take the rest to the dump tomorrow.'

Nodding, I knew not to respond. I wandered in a trance around the table trying to make sense of what was going on, and one voice in my head said, *Brenda and Jane were right; I should listen to him more. Make him less angry and frustrated with me*. Yet my instinct said that this wasn't normal behaviour.

Working my way through the psychiatric section in my *Black's Medical Dictionary* desperate to find some explanation for Simon's erratic and increasingly unpredictable behaviour, I discovered a few lines about 'Manic depression', as it was called in the 1990s:

'An exaggeration of feelings that we all experience from time to time. It is the opposite of depression – a feeling of well-being, euphoria, energy and optimism… Feelings can be so intense that one can lose contact with reality… Believing strange things about yourself… Behaving in embarrassing, harmful – even dangerous ways. You may feel very happy and excited, and show anger or aggression toward others who don't share your outlook. Depression usually follows a high.'

Feeling delighted, relieved and frightened all at once, this definition described Simon to a T. At last, I had an answer to his uncharacteristic and erratic behaviour. All I needed to do was get help for him. But I feared that Jane, Brenda and those who could reason with him wouldn't think there was a problem.

I too felt like I was living life on the edge, like being in a bumper car on your own at the fair. One moment I had a smooth space free of other cars to regain my tracks, and the next the sparks would fly from the metal mesh embedded in the ceiling above and I'd be bashed in the back.

Things reached a peak one morning after the second Glastonbury, when Simon was found in a frantic state by our neighbour Joyce at the entrance of the multistorey car park. She was on her way to the dentist, where she worked as a receptionist. Appearing lost and bereft, he appeared to have lost our Volvo estate. She told me how she followed him up and down every floor of the car park, rubbed his back as he sobbed on the concrete stairwell when he couldn't find it. As Joyce offered him a lift home and he got in her car, he remembered he was in the wrong car park.

Making an emergency appointment with our GP the next day, from what I described over the phone, they said Simon sounded seriously mentally unwell, but not ill enough to be sectioned. They suggested he could be assessed as an 'informal' patient on a voluntary basis. But there was the problem. How could I get him to agree to go to hospital?

Being sectioned means that you are kept in hospital under the Mental Health Act 1983 – a piece of legislation that covers the treatment, assessment and rights of those with mental disorders. It states that:

You can be sectioned if your own health or safety are at risk, or to protect other people.

Sectioning is a legal process which allows people to be detained in hospital where they're not prepared to go in as a voluntary patient or informally.

It's a process that allows you to be detained without consent.

CHAPTER 19

The next day I called Jane, hoping she'd agree with my findings, but she defended Simon and said that I was being melodramatic. She agreed that he was a bit more hyper than usual, but to say he was a manic depressive, in her view, was going too far. I felt alone and doubted myself. I wasn't a psychiatrist. I didn't have any mental health training. But what I knew for sure was that Simon's behaviour was unbalanced. And Dad, who I'd always believed to be right, said the same. By now, both families had experienced Simon's mania. They had seen his hyperactivity, agitation, elevation in mood and impulsive behaviour. This was when our loyalties became divided and I hated not being united with Jane. I felt a sick feeling when she said she thought I was overreacting.

I confronted Simon that night, told him I thought he might be a manic depressive. He went mad, repeated that I was the one who needed help, not him. I called the surgery again in the morning who advised me to coerce him to take himself to hospital. They said to call them as soon as he arrived back home and they'd send an on-call GP to assess him. He'd gone out for the day with his bricklayer friend Gary who'd noticed a significant change in Simon, particularly at work, where he spent much of his time on his phone and not laying bricks. Gary had shared his concerns with me and agreed to persuade Simon to consider seeing a doctor.

Dad had never been involved in our business until then. I'd gravitated towards Simon's family for years. I had a more superficial relationship with Dad. I'd always painted a picture of normality to him. Never told him details. But things had reached beyond a tipping point and Dad had seen the truth with his own eyes. I knew Dad thought I needed out of the relationship, but I had no alternative but to ask him to help me save it.

He arrived after I'd put Bee to bed as she wouldn't have gone if she'd seen Grandpa. We sat opposite each other at the kitchen table, Dad in Simon's usual chair against the radiator, me with my back to the patio doors. We shared a bottle of Cabernet Sauvignon that he'd brought, his favourite wine, and he loosened up. We talked honestly for the first time, adult to adult.

Every time we heard a noise, we both jumped a little. As the wine lubricated our thoughts and tongues, we reassured each other it would be fine. Simon would be compliant. Go willingly. We had the GP on call and waiting at the surgery up the road. He said he would come as soon as he got the signal. I can't remember how he arrived in the evening or who called him, but he was there just after Simon came back with Gary, who knew what was going on.

Surprised to see Dad sitting in his place, Simon was initially playful. Not angry. But when the GP arrived, he became suspicious and flared up.

'What's all this then? Who's this little bloke?' he ranted, pointing at the middle-aged smiling Sri Lankan doctor.

'Now, come on, Simon, your wife tells me that you've not been feeling yourself lately,' the doctor said.

Standing on our black and white kitchen tiles, he was surrounded by us , like in a game of chess. He turned from the GP, to Gary, to Dad, to me, and said, 'I've been set up, haven't I? You've done this, haven't you?' His finger was inches from my nose. 'It's her who's got the fucking problem. Not me.'

His rage boiled over like hot lava. White skittles of froth formed in the corners of his mouth as he showered me with spit. Stomping like a racehorse trapped at the start of a race, he flailed his arms and pointed his fingers and fists at the doctor as we tried to calm him down.

Reluctantly, he finally agreed to let Gary to take him to the psychiatric unit. Backing out of the front door, he bawled, 'This is your fault. You've set me up. It's you who needs fucking help. There's nothing wrong with me.'

He was sedated and admitted for three weeks, and they diagnosed him with bipolar disorder (BPD). I visited and took him out for a drive. Still fuming with me, he blamed me for putting him in what he called a hellhole for nutters, where there was a cage on the roof and you couldn't get out. He was prescribed lithium (a mood stabiliser). He hated taking it and said he felt like he was hearing his life through a radio channel, or having an out-of-body experience.

I still feel guilty for making him go in that day, especially as he had a reaction to the sedatives; his tongue swelled for three days. Dad reassured me that I'd done the right thing, and I knew he was right. But I felt so disloyal to Simon and hated the disapproval, especially when his family and friends visited him in hospital and appeared to agree that he shouldn't have been admitted. It felt like being back at school, when you've been sent to Coventry by your friendship group for saying the wrong thing. For the first time in my life, I'd stood up for what I believed was right: to get help for my ill husband.

Many years later, reading *This Fragile Life* by Charlotte Pierce Baker, who writes about her son's struggle and acceptance of BD, reinforced to me how much Simon needed medical intervention for his own well-being and safety. She too talks about how her husband and her son's girlfriend did not believe that he was ill and the fact that they'd blamed his drug-taking for his nonsensical behaviour. Fortunately, with psychiatric help, family support and medication monitoring, her son manages his life. However, fear of a relapse is never far away.

Simon wouldn't accept his diagnosis and nor would Brenda, Jane or a couple of Simon's close friends. Joe and Michael agreed he was unwell. Lizzie had mixed feelings.

I talked to one of the psychiatric nurses on the ward one day. I told her about his elevated moods and agitation.

'Don't worry, love. He's just another manic depressive kicking off. I see it every day in here,' she replied.

As the summer of 1997 progressed and his behaviour worsened, he would bark, spit and tear me to shreds with his acid tongue. He was experiencing euphoric highs, followed by lows that were like diabetic hypos where his blood sugars dropped, and he would collapse in a chair and rant for food. Years later, I learnt that he was experiencing rapid cycling, one of the more severe forms of bipolar disorder characterised by frequent mood swings. It is diagnosed when a person with bipolar disorder experiences four or more mood episodes within a twelve-month period. An episode may consist of depression, mania or hypomania.

Hypomania is an abnormally revved-up state of mind that affects your mood, thoughts, and behaviour. It commonly manifests with unusual gaiety, excitement, flamboyance, or irritability along with potential secondary characteristics like restlessness, extreme talkativeness, increased distractibility, reduced need for sleep, and intense focus on a single activity.

Rapid cycling is considered one of the more severe forms of bipolar disorder. The condition can seriously impair ability to function as well as quality of life and not only places individuals at greater risk of alcohol and substance abuse, but it also increases the likelihood of suicide and self-harm.

Within weeks of being discharged, he stopped the lithium. He said it took his personality away. He appeared subdued; shocked by his hospital experience. Said he could no longer trust me.

I was gutted. It was at this point my relationship with Jane became tenuous. She was torn between Simon and me, and naturally she chose Simon, her brother. I'd looked to her for guidance, but Simon had absolutely convinced his camp that I was the cause of his problems. I couldn't do anything about it.

Mental health wasn't a word you heard when I was growing up. My only experience was of a supply teacher that the boys in secondary school threw rubbers at and nicknamed 'Mrs Shaky', as she shook when she couldn't get control of the class. She didn't return after Easter. They said she'd had a nervous breakdown.

Simon's nana had spent months on and off in St Bernard's, a psychiatric hospital. She sat in her chair in the corner, staring out of the window, looking skeletal, and mumbled, 'Bloody Bob, bloody Bob,' repeatedly under her breath as she picked at the quicks on her nails each time we visited. We didn't even think about what was wrong with her. She was just Simon's nutty nana.

People back then who suffered from mental health issues were referred to as being 'nutters', 'living on their nerves', or worse still, 'lunatics'. They were housed in what used to be referred to as 'lunatic asylums', where they were mainly sedated with drugs, and often spent weeks, months or even years in these institutions.

The Mental Health Act in 1959 set out to deinstitutionalise mental health patients and look after them in the community. With the passing of the care in the community act in the 1980s, many of these institutions have since closed; only a few of them remain open and in the use for mental health services.

CHAPTER 20

As Guy Fawkes Day, 5 November 1997, approached, the crazed glaze I'd started to recognise returned to Simon's eyes. And I knew it was time to say goodbye to my Simon and hello to Sid. He stopped coming to bed, wasn't there when I woke, talked at speed and didn't stand still. Appearing edgy and impulsive, he insisted we had a firework party. On Sunday afternoon Simon rounded up the kids in the street and together they made a few Guy Fawkes. They built the bonfire and balanced each guy on top amongst the twigs, leaves and old copies of *Time Out* like dead bodies in a funeral pyre.

The next day Simon returned early from work, with not just one, but several boxes of fireworks. Bile rose in my throat when he placed box after box on the kitchen table to show the kids. All I could think of was our bank balance draining away. How would we pay the mortgage and bills if he kept on spending?

Early the next morning, our neighbour Joyce knocked at the front door. Pursing her rebel plumb lips and frowning, she crossed her arms tightly across her maroon, scoop-necked jumper. Leaning in towards me, she said, 'I'm sorry to be a spoilsport. But it's your bonfire. Well, Ian says it's just too close to our shed, Ginger. Do you think you could take it down, or at least move it further away?'

Stepping outside, I pulled the door closed behind me and whispered, 'I'm so sorry, Joyce. I totally agree, but I can't get through to Simon. He's dead set on doing this. It would help if you had a word with him. He won't listen to me.'

Her face contorted as she walked backwards out of my gate into hers, like a film rewinding.

'No, don't worry. It's okay. I don't think that's necessary. You just have a word with him and tell him that we're not happy. Okay?'

'But Joyce. Please. I don't think you realise. He won't listen to me and I'm as worried as you are about it. He might actually listen to you. Really. Please try.'

With her arms still folded, she followed me down the hallway like a marching soldier during a remembrance service.

'Stay there. I think he's in the garden,' I said.

Closing the patio door behind me, I crept down the steps towards the shed.

'Si. Joyce's here, darling,' I said, casually walking into the shed to find him rummaging around. 'She and Ian are a bit worried that the bonfire's too close their shed. She wants you to move it a bit. Make it safer?'

'Tell her to fuck off. It's my garden and I can do what I like.'

Waving my hands in his face and pointing towards the kitchen to show him that Joyce was only yards away, I said, 'But please. Just come and reassure her it will be okay.'

Baring his teeth like a horse whinnying, he snarled and pushed past me to meet Joyce head-on in the kitchen.

'Right, Joyce. What's the problem exactly?'

A red stress mark appeared on the side of her neck as she shared her concerns. Simon towered over her, his hands on his hips. She was visibly shaking.

'Right. Come with me and have a look. You'll see it's miles from your fence.'

Joyce stood aghast as it was clear that the bonfire was only a few inches away, and some of the leaves even stroked the shed roof.

'But Simon. Surely you can see when that's alight it will set the shed and all your trees on fire within minutes.'

Screwing his eyes closed as if to shut her out, and in a patronising tone, he replied:

'Okay, Mrs Joyce. Just cos I respect you and Mr Ian, and we don't want to fall out with our lovely neighbours, do we, I'll drag it away from your fence. Okay? Will that be okay, madam?'

The red patch on her neck had spread across her throat like a scarf strangling her.

'Yes. Well. It had better be, Simon. Else you'll have Ian to deal with.'

Folding her arms even tighter across her pert chest, she marched off down the hallway shouting over her shoulder at me, 'Don't worry, I'll let myself out.' She slammed the door in my face.

'Who the fuck does she think she is? Little busy body, telling me what to do. And yeah, I'm so scared of Ian, aren't I? Not!' Simon ranted behind me.

Usually, Simon was respectful and courteous to our neighbours. He had got on with Ian and Joyce for years. We'd become friendly, particularly when Simon built a six-foot brick wall between us and them. Ian knocked-up the cement as Simon laid the bricks. Joyce gave them endless tea and custard creams. They were delighted, as their wooden fence had started to fail. Another time, I'd taken Megs, their eldest daughter, away with me on a riding holiday. They watered our plants, and us theirs, when either of us were away. Simon had believed it important to 'keep the neighbours sweet', as he put it.

Plus, he would have usually listened to me and seen reason. When we were building the extension on Number 34 and Mr Careless – our neighbour in the bungalow on the other side – came to look at the boundary between us, Simon was pissed off as he thought he might jeopardise the building of the extension. But once we sat him down with a cup of tea and he'd looked at the drawings, he was satisfied that we were not encroaching on his land. Simon moaned about him afterwards, but continued to involve him as the extension's walls went up.

I left to get Bee from school and when I returned Simon had moved the bonfire. But only by about three feet. I was still worried.

On the day, he sent me off to buy thirty sausages, burgers, frankfurters, plus baps. It seemed excessive but it wasn't worth arguing about. We'd asked our neighbour, Bax, and his wife to supervise the barbecue to free me up to do drinks. It was two degrees that night. We could see our breath. We all wrapped up in gloves, scarves and hats and I asked our neighbours and their children to come round the back of the house.

At speed, Simon set off the fireworks one after the other: rockets, roman candles and fountains. In the middle of the lawn, they whistled and banged with sparks of gold, green and red. The beer and wine flowed. Kids drew their names with sparklers as the whoops and cheers grew louder.

'Hey, Bax. You take over the fireworks. It's time to set these guys on the bonfire off,' Simon said, swinging a small can of paraffin in one hand and clutching a box of extra-long matches in the other.

Dread owned me. Like a coward running away from a battle, I kicked off my wellies, skulked up to the bathroom and hid. I didn't turn on the light as I didn't want anyone to see me from outside. As I sat on the loo, I saw Joyce, Ian and their teenage daughters, Megs and Emma, standing on white garden chairs, huddled around their shed with buckets and a hose pointed towards our bonfire.

Orange flames licked at the skirt of the bonfire, flicking and playful at first. Showers of sparks crawled up the Guy Fawkes' legs like ants. Within seconds it was an inferno, licking their deformed faces as they melted like waxworks.

'Fuck. Fuck. Fuck,' I cried.

Three at a time, I lurched down the stairs. Bolted out the door. The whizz from the rockets and whoops from the kids were so loud that no one heard me shout. The fire rumbled and rampaged like Simon's temper. Sparks caught the feathery foliage of our conifer trees alight. *Whoosh*. They went up.

'Stop. Stop,' I screeched in Simon's direction.

But my yells were lost amongst the crackles and roars of the fire. A spray of water came over the wall from Ian's hose. Megs waved her arms and shouted, 'You fucking wanker, Simon. You fucking wanker.' She was only fourteen.

I ran towards the fire, as if it could burn up my inner rage and frustration, and the heat stung my face as I grabbed at Simon's sleeve. Pointed at the bucket. Like a trickle from a teapot, it did nothing to stem the inferno. I looked back towards the patio where the onlookers stood with their mouths wide open, clutching their children, whose squeals of excitement were now replaced with screams.

'Shall I call the fire brigade?' I shouted at the crowd as I ran past them towards the phone.

'There's no need. You watch. It'll be out in a flash,' Bax shouted.

He'd dropped his barbecue tongs and spun the tap on to full. Like a professional firefighter, he aimed the hose to the middle of the twenty-foot conifers.

As the devil's blaze waned, a huge gap appeared where there had been three trees. I saw the houses behind for the first time in years. Garden lights came on. Neighbours gathered to watch in the street. The stars were swallowed by swirls of grey smoke. I tasted ash on my tongue. Like a wedding party, our guests were showered in black confetti. When the fire died down, so too did the mood. We gathered in the kitchen. The men thought it was a great laugh. Like me, the women were concerned about Simon's cavalier attitude. Hostile and angry after everyone had left, he said I'd embarrassed him by overreacting and had become a bore.

CHAPTER 21

After the trees caught fire on Bonfire Night, Simon crashed into a deep depression that lasted through to his thirty-eighth birthday in March 1998, and I feared a pattern emerging. It was like he was hibernating again as he had in previous winters. He laid low, didn't want to see anyone, moped about and took little interest in everything apart from Bee. Thankfully he still managed to go to work. But having reacted so badly to his hospital admission the previous year, he wanted nothing more to do with clinicians, so there was no chance of any treatment.

It's not until now that I realise how odd it was that there was no follow up from anyone at all, the GP or the psychiatrist. Patients are usually followed up after hospital admissions. My gut feeling is that Simon may have been offered an appointment, but either he didn't tell me or he just didn't go. It was such a sore subject that I didn't dare ask him. If it were today, however, Simon would be under the NHS mental health teams (MHTs).

Mental health teams are part of the NHS. They support people and their carers living in the community who have complex or serious mental health problems. I too would have been able to access help from several mental health charities like MIND or MDF.org for example. And with that joint help, we could have weathered the ups and downs, and I for sure wouldn't have felt so isolated and undermined.

As the evenings lightened and we could get out in the garden, he slowly picked up. Walking to town with Bee on his shoulders one Saturday morning, he bounced her up and down as she jabbered with excitement about having pancakes with syrup and lots of butter in McDonald's for a breakfast treat. I saw his smile coming back; plus, we'd started to socialise a bit more and went down to see Jane, Joe and the kids whenever we could.

Beaming through the lounge window one Saturday morning a few weeks later, the May sun made a diamond shape on our royal blue carpet, lifting our spirits as we talked about Jane and me joining the boys for Glastonbury again that year. Wrapping my arms around Simon and Bee, I could feel the warmth from the sun on my shoulder as we smooched in what Simon called our 'love triangle'. As we pulled our heads together, sandwiching Bee tight between us and pushing her fringe up so she could feel her bare skin against ours, Simon sang 'We're Almost There' by Andy Williams.

Things are going to be all right, I thought. Maybe I had over-dramatized it all, and perhaps the previous year's hospital admission had been a mistake just like others said it was. Anyone looking through our lounge window at that time would have said what a perfectly happy family we were.

Simon first played 'We're Almost There' one morning in June 1995 (a year before the first Glastonbury), the day we went to court to officially adopt Bee. I heard it playing, crept down the stairs and peeped through the glass to see him twisting and turning with Bee giggling in his arms.

Despite Bee having been with us for two years by that point, it took that long to get to court for the official adoption where she would legally become ours. For several months leading up to going to court, Alison visited to make sure things were going okay. Not all adoptions are a success, with some infants being taken back into care. I lived with that fear. Visiting one day, Alison informed us that Gemma wouldn't sign the papers to allow Bee to be adopted. She explained that Gemma had felt guilty, like she was giving Bee away without a fight. I tried to put myself in her shoes and still to this day I can't imagine what it must be like to give your baby to strangers.

I felt terrible for her not being able to keep her first baby; and also by then, the father of her second daughter was fighting for custody. Despite months of assessments, social services concluded that Gemma's parenting skills were not good enough for her to keep her babies, meaning that she wasn't able to meet their basic physical or emotional needs or keep them safe from harm. We had fallen in love with Bee. She felt like ours. I couldn't bear the thought of giving her back. Feeling anger and frustration towards social services, Simon believed he had proved himself to be a good dad and resented the level of supervision we had to have. He wanted them out of our hair so that we could crack on and be a normal family. Natural families are able to get on with their lives without their parenting abilities being assessed, judged or criticised. They have no one else to consider; only themselves and their children.

As a thank you to both social workers, Alison and Chris, we planned a picnic in a park, a short drive from the county court. We gathered everything the day before: smoked salmon, Parma ham, olives, vine tomatoes, picnic blanket, bubbly and plastic glasses etc, fresh French bread was all we needed to get the next day.

We were due to court at midday, but we were late setting off as Simon couldn't decide which tie to wear. Wanting to look smart and impress the judge made him agitated and nervous. Even when he'd decided on his Paul Smith silk floral patterned tie, he gave up putting it on after three attempts to get it the right length. I had to calm him down and do it. Tightening it around his neck, I pulled his head towards me, kissed the end of his nose and said, 'Don't worry, babe. She'll be ours this time tomorrow. Really.'

I'd planned mine and Bee's outfits the week before as I hated being unprepared. I'd bought Bee a blue and white striped cotton dress from Next and pink sandals. She'd insisted on wearing a pink bead necklace from her dressing-up box to match her new shoes. I wore a deep-purple silk top over a short cream skirt. I'd ironed Simon's white shirt and navy trousers and brushed the shoulders of his jacket the night before.

The court was in the centre of the next town to ours. We hadn't been there before. We couldn't find a parking space in the multi-storey. And worse still, we couldn't find a bakery. We still needed to get some French bread. As I tottered after Simon in my new cream, bowed suede shoes, he stormed up and down the high street until we arrived outside Marks and Spencer.

'Let's try in here,' I shouted after him, my heels beginning to rub.

Clinging to the sides of her buggy as people jumped out of Simon's way, he whizzed Bee around the aisles like he was doing handbrake turns in his rally car whilst searching for French bread.

'How about these?' I said, holding up a variety pack of mini rolls.

He ignored me so I left him to find the French bread. Sensing his agitation, I knew that whatever I said would be wrong. So I hid amongst the tall orchids in the flower section of the food hall and watched as he scooted straight towards a shop assistant who took him off towards the bakery section. At the till, I wanted to break the two French sticks over his head as we were running late and had to race to find the court.

Leaving the buggy outside, Simon carried Bee on his hip as we tiptoed into the windowless, hushed courtroom and waited with Alison and Chris, plus a handful of other parents and infants, to hear our fate.

'All stand,' said the court clerk, as a sombre looking judge dressed in black robes and a bobbed cream wig started proceedings.

I stilled every synapse in my body, gripping Bee's leg which was tucked around Simon's waist, and he reeled off the list of children's names to be adopted.

'Bee Emily Burdall, I announce that from this day forward, you are now officially the daughter of Mr and Mrs Simon and Jane Burdall.'

Biting my lips between my teeth as heat flushed in my cheeks, I clasped my cheekbones with my fingers and thumbs, trying so hard not to burst. Alison sat me down and slipped a tissue from a new plastic packet into my hand. Elated, Simon jiggled Bee up and down. And when the judge had finished, clapping and cheers sang around the room.

Simon shook the judge's hand as he received Bee's additional birth certificate with our surname on it. Alison called us for a photo and the judge positioned himself between Simon and me. Just as Alison had clicked the shutter, Simon seized the judge's wig off his head and slapped it on his bald pate. Doubling over, Simon laughed so hard that he went beet-red in the face. The court fell silent. Alison and Chris's jaws dropped; I held my breath. I couldn't believe he'd done that. Fortunately, a slow smile crept across the judge's face, steadily turning to an ear-to-ear grin. Fucking hell. It could have gone either way, I thought as I joined in the fake laughter.

I can see that that wasn't exactly normal behaviour, but it was normal for Simon. That's why it took me and others such a long time to notice that Simon was ill, as this kind of behaviour was normal for him. It's what made him unique and entertaining, and at times unpredictable.

CHAPTER 22

Chasing Bee up the stairs for her bath on May Day 1998, six weeks before the third Glastonbury, I caught a glint in Simon's eye that concerned me. Fearing he was on the turn, I cuddled up to him on the settee and said, 'Si, you don't think you're going up, do you?'

'What do you mean, "going up"?' he replied, astounded.

'You know. Going up. Becoming a bit altered again?' I said in a jokey way, followed by a nervous laugh.

He nudged me so hard that I rolled off the settee.

Then, pointing his finger at my nose, he said, 'Call me manic depressive and you sentence me to death.'

'What? Are you serious?' I gasped, taken aback by his sudden shift in mood.

'What bit don't you get, eh?' he said, shooting sparks at me and bearing his Sid teeth.

I was frozen to my royal-blue carpet, and fear filled my blood vessels like icy water. My pulse slammed in my neck. Fuck me. How could he turn so quickly? One minute we were cuddled up and the next we were standing in the middle of the room facing each other like we were about to spar.

'But I thought we were back in love. I thought all that shit was behind us,' I said, fighting back the tears.

'Don't you ever call me a manic depressive again? Do you fucking hear me?'

he said, thumping up the stairs, slamming the office door shut and turning up Manic Street Preachers' 'You Stole the Sun From my Heart' at full blast.

I was stunned. Shocked. Scared. Like it was all going smoothly and somehow I'd ruined things. It was my fault.

His expression and words are as clear to me today as they were when he threw them in my face on that May Day evening. It's only now I believe he feared that he did have bipolar disorder. And, if he admitted it to himself, he knew he would be facing an erratic and unpredictable future, something he couldn't cope with. Having tried lithium, the treatment for bipolar disorder, he couldn't face his personality being suppressed and annulled. Latterly, he admitted that he enjoyed the highs, but couldn't tolerate the lows.

His reaction confirmed my fears, and he was gone when I woke up in the morning. And within days he was frantic. He cleaned himself up. Lost a few pounds. Smelt of patchouli oil and was never without a spliff. Never a skinny one, but a big fat one made with three Rizlas.

Drinking excess alcohol or taking drugs often goes hand in hand with bipolar disorder. It's used as self-medication, a way of coping with the shifts in mood and energy levels. These substances provide temporary relief of the mood swings and allow you to feel normal whilst your mind is altered.

One weekend at Jane and Joe's, Simon raced around their cul-de-sac, amusing us and worrying us at the same time. Their neighbours were having a barbecue. Having met them several times when we were visiting, Simon invited himself! Bare chested, wearing his beige India prayer hat and playing his child's plastic blow-up guitar, he sang, 'I Wanna Be Adored' as he raced between the houses. He took a banana from their fruit bowl to make a super-sized joint. Several times he tried to sit down in Jane's lounge to make it, then he insisted that Jane and I learnt how to make it too. We didn't know how to behave around him as he was highly capricious. He became angry and shouted at us if we didn't do what he asked. At one point, Jane and I had a fit of giggles and hid in her downstairs toilet in case he caught us laughing at him, which was out of nervousness.

Kneeling on Jane's bedroom floor the following morning having been up most of the night, we watched aghast as he shaved his head, decked himself in a green army vest and camouflage combat trousers, strapped a water bottle and a Swiss army knife to his belt and took on the appearance of Marlon Brando in *Apocalypse Now*. He talked about becoming a Druid, and he wore a Vadra around his neck like a voodoo charm to give him power and energy. And off he went in his van, wheel spinning away from Jane's house.

Sitting around Jane's kitchen table in a daze, nervously laughing, we discussed Simon's behaviour and agreed that I should phone someone for advice. Jane phoned Brenda to update her and warn her that Simon may be coming her way. After several calls, I finally got through to the ward where he'd been a patient the year before. The on-call registrar insisted I get him to stop smoking the skunk as he believed it could be making him worse. But I had more chance of stopping a juggernaut in its tracks than stopping Simon when he was on a high.

Naively, I believed that Brenda could influence him, but approaching her about his drug-taking was a no-no as at the time I didn't think she knew he was smoking the weed or had taken any other drugs like LSD or magic mushrooms. I found out later that she had tried to get him to stop smoking the weed, but Simon reassured her it was only a bit of harmless herbal-like grass. Little did she, or any of us, know that smoking skunk triples the risk of suffering a serious psychotic episode.

A study found that people who smoke skunk every day have five times the normal risk of experiencing extended episodes during which people heard voices, suffered delusions or demonstrated erratic behaviour.

At this stage, my communication with Brenda was mainly through Jane as she was completely in Simon's camp. Like during the previous year when Simon had told Brenda that I was a crap wife, that impression and belief about me remained. It didn't help that Brenda was a bit of a domestic goddess. She fed and watered anyone as soon as they set foot in her door. She would often have a shepherd's pie, spaghetti bolognese or chicken curry on the stove, ready to feed you up. I could never come up to her standards and meet Simon's needs quite like she did, no matter how I tried. Naturally, I felt inadequate, like I believe any daughter-in-law would.

Brenda told me many years later that she did know about Simon smoking and had tried to persuade him to stop. She said that he often called her in the early hours of the morning to rant and offload to her. He would sometimes arrive at her house early in the morning on his way to work for comfort and reassurance. She also told me how worried she'd been about Simon, especially when he would break down and cry to her for no obvious reason. For years, I believed that she didn't think he was ill. However, years later she said that she wasn't able to think of his erratic behaviour as an illness, and that she couldn't bear to think that he was suffering and she couldn't make it okay. She blamed his dope smoking rather than an underlying mental health issue.

CHAPTER 23

As the third Glastonbury approached, our relationship deteriorated to the point of not being able to have a normal conversation. We agreed to go to the third Glastonbury separately: Simon with Mark and his girlfriend, and me with Jane and a couple of other friends. It was the wettest Glastonbury on record. We waded through brown sludge and it was difficult to stop it seeping over the top of our wellie boots. We were caped in shapeless cagoules with no cover between constant rain showers; it wasn't much fun. We didn't see any bands, swapped midsummer for a monsoon and bailed out early and left Simon there like a pig in shit.

He called me from a call box on Tuesday morning as he'd lost the three mobile phones he'd acquired, and told me how disturbed he was at people leaving their things behind: tents, sleeping bags, rucksacks and all sorts. Cars and vans got stuck in the mud and were pulled out by breakdown trucks. He couldn't understand why people would abandon such 'good gear'. Scooping sleeping bags and blankets, he piled them in a wheelbarrow and carted them to his van in relays. He was furious because the police wouldn't let him back in to collect more, and he was complaining that his feet and hands were blistered and sore. Abruptly ending the call, he said he didn't know when he'd be home.

Trembling and troubled, he finally appeared a few days later stepping out of his clothes on the front door mat, as they were sodden with mud. Dripping ylang ylang and geranium oil into a hot bath to soothe him, I settled next to him on the loo and listened as he raged about how he'd lost his tent and had to make a *Basha* (temporary shelter) from remnants of other people's tents. He'd worried about his

112

stuff being nicked and said he had no money for food or drink. He shouted each time I stood up to leave or interrupted him.

Lust glistened in his eyes as he went on to describe finding himself in a tipi full of swinging hippies.

'They were all naked,' he said, grinning.

'Naked?' I screeched.

'Yep. Everyone. Absolutely everyone. And they were all having sex around me,' he said, nodding and looking pleased with himself for telling me.

'What the fuck! What did you do?'

'I'm not sure.'

'What do you mean, "not sure"?' I snapped, standing up and pinning him with my eyes.

'A couple of middle-aged women were massaging me with musky oils. Their breasts dangled on my face.'

'You what?' I shouted, waving with my arms in air.

'Don't worry, babe. Calm down,' he whispered. 'It was lovely. Soothing. They made me feel safe. Like a baby.'

I thought I would have a fucking baby if he carried on.

'I think I was involved in a Bacchanalian orgy,' he said, nodding and smirking.

'A what kind of orgy?' I fumed, not knowing what he was on about or even if any of it was true. Every time I tried to ask more questions, he said, 'Shut up. Sit down. Let me finish. Just let me finish.'

But he never did. For two and a half hours I stayed there. Strangely, he appeared traumatised. With tears in his eyes, he said that nobody could imagine where he'd been and how bad it was there. He compared it to being in battle. He said none of our friends had ever experienced anything as awful. Feeling sorry for him, I gently washed between his split toes and soaped the blisters on his heels. I'd heard on the news that several people had got trench foot. He was one of them.

When I think back to that story, I now believe he was experiencing a psychosis.

Sometimes, a person with bipolar disorder may experience symptoms of psychosis that occurs during a severe episode of mania or depression where they may have delusions and distorted thinking that cause them to believe that certain things are true when they are not.

It didn't take him long however to get back on track and start planning for his own festival. The following week he persuaded our bank manager to give him a loan of £30,000 to fund it. He was leaving the building site on and off through the day, and Gary told me that he was threatened with the sack if he carried on spending most of his time on the phone finding sponsors, bands, caterers and a venue in Bath. I feared he was losing touch with reality and updated Jane most days, and vice-versa. Unlike me, she'd become involved in helping organise his festival and continued to believe in him. He was her brother whom she adored and wouldn't let down.

Plus, she got the fun bits as she wasn't obstructing him like me, hence she didn't get the aggression. I believe he could have been a cult leader. He had the charisma, enthusiasm and power to convince people to follow him, and they did, without question.

Things came to a head one morning during an argument about money. He barricaded me in our bedroom, pushing our pine chest of drawers against the door. He wanted me to sign a declaration he'd written on an orange Post-it Note. It said that if we separated he could have full custody of Bee. Of course, I refused. After a tussle, he hung me upside down out of the bedroom window. I saw my jeans standing the right way up on the washing line. As I struggled to pull myself back in, I knew with certainty that it wasn't safe for Bee and me to stay any longer.

At this point, my relationship with Jane and Brenda broke down as their loyalty lay with Simon. There were two camps of thought: me, my family, Michael and Joe, who, like me, were in the firing line. In the other camp with Brenda and Jane were Simon's other friends, Mark in particular, plus new hangers-on. Lizzy was in between, because although her loyalties were with Simon, his unpredictable behaviour troubled her and instinctively she knew it wasn't right.

Once Simon had left the house, I threw a few things into a bag. This time I was scared and needed to protect Bee. He was raging like a bull. I believed he'd lost the plot and become psychotic. He displayed all the symptoms: delusions, incoherent or irrational thoughts and speech, decreased performance at work, unwarranted suspicion of others and lack of awareness.

It was at this point I moved out into my brother Phil and his wife Michelle's house. They too had experienced Simon's frenetic behaviour during a family party for Michelle's mother the previous year. It wasn't until recently that they told me Michelle's brother-in-law, who was a doctor, had said that he thought Simon was suffering from bipolar disorder. I don't remember them telling me that as Phil hadn't got involved in my marital issues at all, yet he was always there to pick up the pieces when I needed him most.

It was Bee's first school sports day. Feeling the hot July sun burn down on my neck, I watched as she picked herself up after she fell out of her sack in the sack race at the finishing line. Twisted orange rope marking the track prevented me from running over to her to pick her up. She didn't appear bothered that she'd come last, and she came over to me to ask if I was okay! As we skipped and swung hands back to the car, I noticed the teddy on Bee's navy drawstring PE bag had faded and was peeling off. A bit like me, I thought – worn out and hanging on by a thread.

Bee was delighted that we were going to stay with Uncle Philip and her cousins Charlotte and Monty in their big old

115

Victorian house that stood on the hill in High Wycombe. When we arrived, however, their new au pair had moved into the spare room. I was given sanctuary in their tiny attic amongst old rolls of wallpaper, dusty magazines, antique books and a frilly, floral lampshade. Paying particular attention not to brush my face against the fibreglass when I turned over during the night, I slept under the eaves. Bee shared a bedroom with Charlotte and Monty.

After dropping Bee at school a few days later, I popped back home to collect my post. Feeling like a trespasser, I turned my key in the lock. On first inspection, things appeared tidy. But as I ventured into the lounge and looked out of the back window, I gasped. I counted ten sludgy, muddy sleeping bags and six soiled, shit-coloured blankets spread over the fences and slung over the washing line. A frayed Union Jack flag waved from my window box amongst the yellow and purple pansies. A large plastic gorilla climbed the ivy in my wicker hanging basket. Brenda had helped Simon wash and hang them to dry.

Shaken, I went down the hall into the kitchen. In the middle of the black and white chequered floor flapped Fanny the goldfish. She must have done a backflip to escape from her tank. I hated fish. Couldn't bear them. Seeing her flap on the floor was the final straw. I flew back to my car and wheel spun away from my home, distraught. Jane phoned me later that night and told me that Simon had been livid that I'd left Fanny to die. He'd resuscitated her somehow and returned her to her luxury tank. He'd been obsessed with her before I left. She went from living in a plain round goldfish bowl to a tropical, oxygenated, glowing tank with a fairground ride of her own inside it.

Bee and I lived at Phil's for three months whilst I decided what to do. I loved Simon so much but didn't want Bee growing up thinking his behaviour was normal. If only he would admit that he was ill, I thought, then I knew we could cope. With the right treatment, I could look after him. Without it, I didn't hold out much hope.

It was a strange time, because I'd moved back to my hometown and become much more involved with Phil and Michelle, got to know them a bit more. They were compassionate, diplomatic and non-judgemental.

Behind the scenes, Dad phoned Phil most days to see how he thought I was doing. Together they talked about my prospects like project managing a sales negotiation. Discussed the best way forward for me. Phil was good at seeing everyone's viewpoint. And never took sides.

Phil hinted that Dad was hoping I would see sense and not go back to Simon. But neither of them knew Simon and I found myself defending him when they pointed out some of the things he'd done. It's a funny one, isn't it? Somehow it's okay for us to criticise a loved one, but we don't like it when someone else does.

CHAPTER 24

Jane phoned at the beginning of September 1998, just as Bee started in year 2, to say that Simon's granddad Bert had died and asked me if I wanted to go to the funeral. I was fond of Bert, who we'd spent many Sundays playing rummy with around the table after one of Bren's notorious roast dinners where we couldn't breathe afterwards. Jane also said that Simon was on his way down and appeared a bit more level. A couple of days later I phoned him. Appearing jovial and cheeky despite the sad circumstances, we agreed to go to the funeral together. By the third Glastonbury cycle, I'd noticed a small window of relative normality when Simon came down from his mania before he slipped into a depression, where briefly I saw my old Simon.

His tanned skin glowed as smooth as honey spilt on a table against his crisp black shirt. The scent of Issey Miyake aftershave oozed from his pores as he opened the front door. Feeling coy, I dropped my head as he kissed me on the cheek, and I fiddled with my silver moonstone earrings. It reminded me of our first date when he picked me up to take me out. There was still a strange look in his eyes, and he was a bit jumpy. I sensed if I wound him up, he would ignite like his embers were still burning. Gripping the steering wheel at ten to two like I did in my driving lessons, I imagined Mum offering advice in my head: *Don't provoke him. Keep the conversation light*, she said.

Standing side by side during the funeral service, getting closer the more emotional it became, our little fingers entwined as I cried. He put his arm around my shoulder and I nuzzled into Simon's chest and wept. I wasn't only crying for Bert; I was crying for us. All we'd lost. All the hurt. The backbiting. The love we'd buried. We barely spoke at the wake. Much of the time he was animated, went from cousin to auntie to uncle, sharing stories about his grandma and granddad. I took a photo of him and Brenda together. Bren put it in a frame high on a shelf in the lounge amongst the photos of the grandchildren. In it, he's staring hard, like boring holes into the camera lens. Intense. A bit harricd. Preoccupied. Jane agrees with me; we say the same each time we look at that photo, even many years later.

On the journey home, he was edgy as we talked about me moving back home or separating if I didn't. I'd had the house valued when he was at work one day. He'd gone mad. Hadn't agreed. Refused to sign the papers to let it go on the market. I couldn't see our future together. Jane told me that he'd said he couldn't believe that *I* was considering leaving *him*. He must have realised that I was serious because his family went around one Sunday, tidied the garden, made it presentable for potential buyers.

Granddad's funeral was a Thursday, which was when I usually worked with a female GP at the local family planning clinic from 4 to 9 p.m. Simon had continued to look after Bee whilst I was at work like he always had. He'd picked Bee up from the child-minder at five and Dad collected her and brought her back to Phil's after Simon had given her tea and bathed her ready for bed. I promised to give him a decision when I picked Bee up that night. June, the receptionist at the clinic, had followed my story every week as it unfolded. I spilt out my dilemma as we set up clinic, and she said something that made me make up my mind.

'Why don't you give him one more chance? What do you have to lose? Then if it doesn't work out at least you know you have tried your best.'

That was the answer, I thought to myself on my five-minute route home. Deep down I knew I didn't want to separate. It seemed too drastic. But equally, I didn't think I could face another distressing year. At least if I gave him one more chance I would know for sure if he became manic then depressed again that without treatment, it would likely be repeated for the rest of our lives. And I was adamant that I didn't want Bee to be exposed to any more distress and uncertainty; she'd had too much already, and she hadn't yet turned six.

I didn't know it at the time, but I wondered if finally, he'd realised the seriousness of his illness and needed me to help him through it.

Creeping up the stairs towards the bathroom, I heard Bee giggling and water splashing in the bath. Peeping through the gap in the door, I watched them playing. Bee had come a long way from that first photo we'd seen of her taken at Sharon's, the foster mother's house. Sat in the stainless-steel kitchen sink surrounded by unwashed pots and pans and a deep fat fryer, she'd looked pasty and bewildered. *Not treasured and adored like she is now*, I thought as I watched Simon's sturdy builder's hands support her waist as he swooshed her up and down the bath to 'Row, Row, Row Your Boat', the water spilling over the sides. As they laughed out loud in unison, I melted with love for them both.

Making them both jump, I announced myself and said, 'Shall we move back in with Daddy at the weekend then, darling?'

'Yes please, Mummy,' she squealed with delight.

Simon nodded and puffed out his lips, and his head bowed with relief as Bee splashed so hard the water wetted my face.

Sitting in Phil's kitchen that evening, I told him and Michelle my decision. There was a long pause before either of them spoke. Michelle gave Phil a nod as if to say, *You tell her*. They'd been there to mop my tears and listen to my woes, sometimes in the early hours. But they'd never judged me or told me what to do. They let me make my own decisions.

'Have you thought it through?' Phil asked.

'I've thought of nothing else since I've left,' I said, then went on for half an hour about the pros and cons etc.

'That's fine,' Michelle said. 'But be prepared for a frosty reaction from your father. That's what Phil is trying to warn you of. Okay?'

Hugging them both good night and thanking them for all their support, I made my way up to bed. Stopping by Bee's bunk, I watched her cheeks puff in and out in a contented sleep. I felt guilty for the stress we'd put her through as I inhaled a hint of blue Comfort fabric conditioner from her Harry Potter pjs. Tucking her arm inside the quilt, I popped a kiss under her fringe before ascending into the loft.

I'll go to tell Mum and Dad at teatime tomorrow. I won't tell Dad I'm coming; he'll be more relaxed then, I thought, rehearsing my speech, tossing and turning, trying to get to sleep.

CHAPTER 25

I was still wearing white linen trousers and turquoise Birkenstocks despite it being the end of September 1998. On the radio they spoke of an Indian summer. Some of the leaves had already turned from khaki to copper and crunched under my feet as I waved goodbye to Phil. He gave me the thumbs up symbol through his lounge window, clutching Bee on his hip. During the three-mile drive to my parents' house, the air blew thick and warm.

My parents had journeyed with me these last three years, Dad in particular as Simon had become increasingly difficult to live with. He'd been a part of the intervention when we tried to get him help. He had been supporting me, but his patience had worn thin lately. He loved Simon, respected him, enjoyed his humour and intelligence and admired his skills as a craftsman. But Dad dealt with facts, not emotions; his training as an accountant had taught him that. However, I wasn't sure he'd think the facts were in my favour today. I'm not sure I knew for certain they were either.

Driving along the valley road to my childhood home, I saw, high on the hill, the church where Simon and I had married fifteen years earlier. I made an instant decision to stop, and like on automatic pilot, I turned my green racing VW Polo left up the hill and over the cattle grid to where a handful of caramel cows mooed as I parked. The water sparkled from the stream where I'd spent countless childhood summers with friends rolling up our trousers and daring each other to walk across the wall, over the waterfall in the middle, to the other side. We always lost our nerve halfway across.

Standing there fifteen years later at the kissing gate next to the graveyard, I kissed my hand as I walked through it. I was always told it was bad luck if you didn't kiss someone when you went through a kissing gate. Reading some of the gravestones as I walked up the path that eventually emptied onto Disraeli's Manor, I stopped at the church doorway where most of our photos were taken to shelter us from the wind and rain. One photo sits on Mum and Dad's walnut sideboard in their dining room, and I remember our cheeks ached from constant smiling and the feel of Simon's hand around my hip that slipped and squeezed my bum when no one was looking. There are others on our chest of drawers in our bedroom back in Number 34.

Walking up past the cottages where we'd had our reception, at the back of the graveyard amongst the horse chestnuts, I saw a wooden bench. A carpet of mahogany conkers peeped like frog's eyes from their spiked, mottled green shells; they covered the ground like military flails.

Settling on the damp slats, I scanned the field where I had kept my pony when I was thirteen. Streams of silence slid in ghostly loneliness amongst the bare backs of the gravestones, placed a body's length apart. Some were well-kept with fresh white freesias and pink carnations. Some were with old cracked pots. Many were overgrown. Turning my face towards the sinking sun, orange burnt like a flame behind my eyes, I anticipated Dad's reaction. *I don't think he'll be so reassuring today*, I thought to myself as I practised telling him that I was going to move back in with Simon.

There was no doubt about my decision to move back home, but it was a big one to do it on my own without Dad's support. He'd been by my side for the past three years, assisting and guiding me with love and without too much judgement. In his eyes, he'd steered me to safety. And here I was going back down an unpredictable path, a bit like taking a battered boat back out to sea when a storm was still brewing. I needed him on my side, but I was prepared to go it alone if I had to.

As I opened my eyes, stretched my arms above my head, I noticed the back of one of the gravestones had a picture of a sun engraved on it, with the words, *Our sunshine after the rain.*

It struck me like someone had tapped me on the shoulder and had written it just for me. I felt I'd been sent a message. It told me things were going to be okay somehow. Slumping against the wooden slats like a crumpled bag lady, I inhaled the scent of fresh freesias laid on top of a recent burial. *Be grateful*, I told myself as I walked with purpose back to the car; *it could be a lot worse.*

It was teatime and they weren't expecting me. Reaching up, I rang the bell, my arms heavy, my back teeth grinding. My mind became worryingly empty. All I could do was pray that I would find the right words when Dad challenged my decision.

Flicking crumbs off her chest as she answered the door, Mum peered past me and said, 'Ooh. What are you doing here? You don't normally come at this time. And where's Bee?'

'She's at Phil's. I've come to talk to Dad,' I said as I peeked towards the gap in the kitchen door.

Dad was in his usual position at the head of the table. Pulling out his red and white chequered napkin that matched the tablecloth from his shirt collar, he stood and leant forward to greet me with a hug.

'This is a nice surprise, Tozzy. Do you want a cup of tea?' he said enthusiastically.

'I'll get it. You sit down and talk to your father,' Mum said, leaping to fill the kettle.

I explained that Simon's mood had levelled out. That he appeared calmer and less angry, and that I could see my Simon returning. Said that we'd had a heart to heart and that I thought it was fair to give him one more chance, and said that I felt it was safe to move back home. I'd been at Phil's for almost three months, and the sleeping arrangements hadn't been ideal. I'd needed that time to reflect and come to a decision. And following a pattern that I now recognised, it took Simon that long to stabilise. I'd waffled on and on like I was trying to convince a judge that I was not guilty of a crime.

'Drink your tea, dear. It'll get cold,' Mum said as I felt her squeeze my knee under the table. She did that when we were kids, usually when I told Dad about something that Phil shouldn't have done to get him in trouble. It meant *Stop right now. You've gone too far.*

The lukewarm tea relieved my parched mouth as I wiped my damp hands on the tablecloth rested on my knees, leant back and heaved a huge sigh. Pulsing like the thump in my chest, the kitchen clock above Dad's head ticked so slow that I could almost hear the space in between the seconds as I waited for his response. When finally, he turned to face me, his eyes were unyielding and frigid. His usual friendliness evaporated like summertime rain on the tarmac.

'Just listen to yourself. What on earth are you thinking of? And you're certainly not thinking about Bee, are you?'

He listed all the things Simon had done over the past three years: returned from Glastonbury in a psychotic state with trench foot; almost lost his job; smoked marijuana; turned his friends and family against me; spent our savings. The list went on and on. And he was right. He'd seen Simon's erratic behaviour for himself. Said it was unfeasible to reason with him at times. Listened as Simon had slagged me off on more than one occasion. Believed my marriage was irretrievable. And most of all, he believed that it wasn't safe for me and Bee to stay with him. He strongly believed that until Simon accepted the hospital's diagnosis of bipolar disorder in the previous year and took the recommended treatment of lithium, there wasn't much chance of my marriage surviving.

Phil had told me that Dad had been massively relieved when I moved in with him and Michelle. He'd also encouraged me to get the estate agent round and have the house valued. Make an appointment with a solicitor. Think about separating. I'd done everything he suggested. Had been completely and utterly guided by him. But now I wasn't. I was standing on my own two feet for the first time in my adult life.

'But he's my husband and I love him,' I blurted out.

Slamming his forehead with the flat of his hand, he said, 'I know you love him. But he's hardly shown you any love lately, has he? Can't you see that? This is the third year in a row that he's displayed this insane behaviour, each time getting worse. And each time he doesn't appear to give a damn about you and little Bee. You deserve better. Do you hear me?' He banged on the kitchen table with his fist and made the cups jump off their saucers.

The scrape from his kitchen chair against their imitation brick lino floor made my eardrums vibrate. His red and white chequered serviette landed on their white draining board as he threw it behind him. Storming out of the kitchen, he thudded up the stairs to his office and slammed the door shut.

I'd never seen him this mad – ever!

Cupping my jaw with both hands, I tried to stop my chin from trembling. The floodgates opened and I cried like I needed to break loose from my skin.

From her sleeve, Mum pulled one of Nanny's embroidered cotton handkerchiefs and stuffed it into my fist.

'Don't worry, dear. It will all work out in the end,' she said, patting my shoulder and straightening the tablecloth.

Many times over the past three years when I'd felt forlorn, Dad had been there to prop me up, reassure me. *Will I have the strength to deal with this on my own?* I thought as I pictured Simon still a bit high and unpredictable. Yet when I'd seen him in the last few days, I could see more of my old Simon was emerging. He wanted me back. I wanted to be back. I had to give it one more go. And despite everything, I hadn't fallen out of love with him. If I had, it might have been easier.

But what if it didn't work out? What then? Would I have to crawl back to Dad and admit he was right? But I was prepared to take that risk to save my marriage.

I exited my parents' house, bereft. I'd never departed without a hug and a kiss goodbye. Normally they both stood and waved from the lounge window. That day, even Sophie, their snooty Siamese cat, flicked its tail, turned its back on me and jumped off the windowsill. I had to stand on my own two feet for the first time in my life; like losing the stabilisers from my first bike, I had to balance and try to ride without falling off.

CHAPTER 26

The next day, my car overflowed with so much stuff that I couldn't see out the back window; a bit like my brain, I thought, as I struggled to reverse outside Number 34. Looking over my shoulder, I saw Simon on the doorstep with tears streaming down his face.

'Where have you been? I thought you'd changed your mind and decided not to come back home,' he sobbed with snot dripping from his nose.

'It took me longer than I thought to gather our things. I'm sorry, darling.'

'But why have you got so much stuff? I don't get it.'

'Because I've been away for three months. Bee and I needed clothes for work and school. I wanted Bee to have some of her things from home.'

Simon appeared baffled that I'd been away for so long. It was like he'd woken from a dream and had lost sense of time. When a person is in a full-blown psychotic episode, their memory is greatly affected. It is rare for someone who is in a deep episode to remember all that happened. This is why it's called a 'blackout'.

Many years later, not long after Michael died, the same happened to Brenda. She literally lost her mind. For several weeks she too became frenzied, aggressive, uninhibited and talked at speed. She was muddled about the past and present, disappeared under pages and pages she'd written about her life, things she wanted to tell people before she died. She was prescribed anti-psychotic drugs along with anti-depressants and a six-week stay in hospital, and we didn't believe she would return to herself; thankfully, she recovered. However, much of what happened during that time she was unable to piece together. Remarkably, she went on to make a full recovery. It left her sad and low for a spell.

I've since read that in some cases where the deranged episode is super intense, all memories can be lost; this is especially true if substance abuse or other drugs that can cause psychosis are involved.

Like an old man shaking with Parkinson's disease, Simon stood at the bottom of the stairs watching me lug everything past him. Gawping with his unshaven jaw wide open, he stared with drooping eyelids as I hung my summer clothes back up in the wardrobe, placed my sandals underneath and hung my handbags on the back of our bedroom door.

Sitting in the chair, pinching his chin, he stared out the window into the empty school car park across the road.

'I think you're right. I'm a manic depressive. I need help,' he whispered.

'What did you say?' I asked urgently, not believing what I'd heard.

'I said I think you're right. I'm a manic depressive.'

Hallelujah! Praise the Lord, I wanted to shout from the treetops. At fucking last. The penny's dropped. Equally, I wanted to rare up. Pummel his chest. Rant about what he'd put me through. But I could see from his bowed head and droopy demeanour that he appeared fractured, like the triangles of a fragmented mirror I'd laid in our mosaic garden.

It took all my strength to stay calm. Gain his confidence. Not judge him. Like a raging bull, he'd finally conceded.

Kneeling by his side, sliding my hand under his clenched fist, I took a deep breath and asked him, 'Why do you say that now and not before?'

'Because I'm scared. Shit scared. I can't control this demon that dominates my mind,' he said with a voice as small as a moth.

Patting his knuckles and looking in his eyes to reassure him, I said, 'It's okay, darling. It'll be fine. I'll look after you. We can get through this together. Really.'

He smelt of clean sweat as I rubbed his back, and I tried to kiss him, but he'd buried his head so deep between his knees that I couldn't reach his face.

I tucked him up in bed that night. Gave him a hot water bottle! I watched him from the door as he curled himself into the foetal position and tugged the covers over his head like a caterpillar in a cocoon. I felt a surprising spark of energy. Hoped that with him on my side, this could be a turning point and we would be able to battle his demons together.

I'd managed to get a 10.30 appointment with the GP the next morning. But although Simon had been keen the day before to ask for help, he didn't seem so enthusiastic in the morning.

'I'm not going back on lithium. That stuff's toxic. You know that, don't you?' he checked, spooning the milk over his Cornflakes.

'Of course. Yes. Whatever you're comfortable with. Let's see what the GP says, okay?'

Oh no, I thought to myself as I filled the kettle for another cup of tea. *He's having second thoughts. What if he refuses treatment altogether? then where will we be?*

Every six months at work I'd taken blood from a middle-aged man who came in with his wife to the surgery. He'd been on lithium for a few years. We monitored his liver and kidney function for changes and made sure he was on the right dose. They didn't know my circumstances, although I was desperate to tell them and get their advice and support, but it wasn't professional of me. He appeared balanced, smiling, said it had changed his life for the better; his wife agreed. *That could be us in a few months' time*, I thought as I closed the door behind them.

Cradling himself in the GP's plastic chair and answering in a monosyllabic fashion, like a hooded teenager when questioned about his mood by a locum GP, my heart sunk when Simon declined the offer of lithium. I believed it was the drug that could level him out. He complained to the GP that it took his personality away and refused to take it again. Lithium is still the main drug of choice for BPD today. And I have just read this on the NHS website:

'If a person is not treated with lithium, episodes of bipolar-related mania can last for between three and six months. Episodes of depression last longer, often six to twelve months. But with effective treatment, episodes usually improve within about three months.'

The GP didn't know Simon. Wasn't interested in his history, just agreed with what he wanted. And without looking up from his desk, he passed him a prescription for anti-depressants and referred him back to his psychiatrist. Just like that. No assessment. No offer of talking therapy. Six and a half minutes we were in there! 'Just take the pills. You should feel a bit better in a few weeks. Come back and see your own GP if you don't,' he said with his finger on the buzzer to call patient number twelve.

Thankfully things have improved for mental health patients since the 1990s. For a start: anti-depressants are more effective. GP's undertake mental health assessments to assess patients' level of depression and suicide risk. Talking therapies are available. And there are numerous charities offering help and support. And there are many twenty-four-hour phone lines available to help as well.

Simon insisted on going back to work that day despite me saying he didn't have to. Fortunately, his boss liked him and had been party to his rise and falls every day at work. He appreciated the fact that Simon was usually one of his best workers, and he allowed him time off to see the GP. Simon didn't want to let him down again.

131

He didn't look back as I waved him off. I was left feeling alone again.

In a matter of days, like going down the fast flume at the swimming pool, Simon dived into a deep depression. The worst I'd seen. His face contorted into a mask of pain. His eyes were dull and distant, like any hope he'd had had disintegrated.

Often on a Sunday morning, we'd take Bee for breakfast at McDonalds. We'd sit in and have pancakes with syrup and watch as the butter melted and dripped over them. Simon usually finished Bee's as it was too much for her. Sometimes he'd have an egg McMuffin as well, then finish it off with a large coffee. I couldn't even persuade him to come out the following weekend. So I took Bee on my own to get us out of the house.

I'd experienced his depression a few times by now, but this was on a different level. He barely spoke. Just stared at the ground. Smoked skinny peach tobacco roll-ups outside, sat on the kitchen step in the cold. He was a non-smoker before. Now he couldn't stop.

Bearing in mind we'd both been through a crazy summer, we'd had no time to talk about what happened or how we felt. I felt frustrated and humiliated for all the bad things Simon had said about me to everyone. He'd become close to one of our neighbours, Leslie; not a woman I liked that much as she was full of herself. Plus, her marriage was on the rocks. I bet she loved all the attention Simon gave her. Despite almost setting her shed on fire the previous year, our relationship with Joyce had recovered, mainly because she needed us to feed her cat and water her busy lizzies when she went away. Joyce told me how Simon had spent most evenings in Leslie's house smoking and drinking after I'd left. I felt humiliated, knowing she knew all my business.

Once Simon crashed down into a deep depression, she kept herself to herself, avoided eye contact with me in the street. Just like all the other hangers-on who'd surfed on Simon's wave of fun and energy when he was on a high who disappeared once he became depressed. We were left alone at that time. No one called by. We'd become boring and rubbish company.

All I wanted to do was talk about what happened, make sense of it. But Simon didn't. Couldn't. He'd disappeared into his shell, just like a tortoise. I couldn't even see his eyes as his head was bowed so low much of the time.

I became more worried as the weeks ticked by. Usually, there would be an improvement in mood after three to four weeks of taking anti-depressants, but there wasn't. I made a mood chart where minus ten was suicidal, zero was normal and ten was fabulous. He scored between minus eight and nine most days.

'Let's go back to the GP, Si,' I said, sitting opposite him as he poked his fork in his favourite scrambled egg and smoked salmon. He only took two mouthfuls and heaved, like I'd put too much pepper on it. He didn't answer, just turned his head sideways, gestured no.

In desperation I phoned the Community Psychiatric Team, a social worker and another GP, and they all said, 'Be patient, the anti-depressants will work.' When eventually his psychiatrist appointment came through, it was for ten weeks' time; the first week of December. Back then, although we had not long had a computer, Google didn't exist and there wasn't the same information about mental health as there is today. I confided in the senior partner, John, at the practice where I worked; he had met and liked Simon. He reassured me that it was just chemicals in his brain that would balance out once the anti-depressants started to work, a bit like getting the right dose of insulin for a diabetic.

I watched as he pushed peas around his plate like a toddler who wouldn't eat their veg. His weight plummeted.

The hems of his Levi's frayed on the floor. I had to cut new notches in his belt to hold them up.

At dusk one Sunday, I came home and found Simon gone. Earlier in the day, he'd said he might go for a walk. I'd been pleased as he hadn't been leaving the house much at the weekends, and I hoped he was feeling better.

I panicked. As it was late I asked Joyce to have Bee whilst I went out looking for him. I drove around the streets, then down by the river and walked along the towpath to where we often walked. Then along the edge of the woods. I peered down the gaps between the trees. Dusk quickly turned to dark. He still wasn't home when I got back. At 7 p.m. he appeared. He'd been walking for five hours and was surprised that I'd been worried.

'Oh my god, Si. Where have you been? I've been worried sick. I've driven around for the past two hours looking for you,' I said, stroking his face, holding his head.

'I just went for a walk, trying to clear my head,' he answered, puzzled by my concern.

And that's all he said.

Feeling frightened and fatigued, I phoned Jane the next day, told her how I thought Simon had gone off to kill himself. I asked her for help as I couldn't cope anymore.

It was coming up to October half term and she offered to take him down to Bantham Beach in Devon where we frequently went on holiday. She was going with Brenda and the children. He refused to go at first and said he was fine. But Jane and Brenda persuaded him, and kindly took Bee as well. They were shocked at how much weight he'd lost and how grey and gaunt he looked. They hadn't seen him for a few weeks, and I hoped they would realise how ill he was.

He came back a fraction brighter and then six weeks on, over a bowl of Cornflakes, I saw a further improvement. He scored minus six on my mood chart, and then five for three days in a row, followed by a consistent minus two to three.

I felt it was safe enough for Bee and me to have a much-needed break and stay with a friend for a weekend. I told Jane I was going away. She and Brenda jumped at the chance to look after Simon, but he insisted on being alone. He didn't want to be fussed as it reinforced what he saw as his shortcomings. I believe he self-stigmatiscd, like many men, and felt embarrassed to admit to his mental distress.

The Friday morning we got ready to leave for our weekend away, I stood at the kitchen sink, felt the warmth from the sun on my face as my thoughts bumped together like moored boats on a canal. In relative silence we worked side by side. I washed. Simon dried. Only the clink of the china against the sink could be heard until Bee ran in and wiggled between us. Scooping her up, Simon threw her in the air until she screamed. He gave her a big squeeze and said, 'Look after Mummy for me, won't you, darling? I love you.'

'I love you too, Daddy,' she said, smacking a wet kiss bang on his lips.

With the damp tea towel, I dried my hands, leant with my back to the sink and watched as Bee skipped back to the lounge. Simon stood in front of me, pulled me close, parted my fringe and kissed me on the forehead.

'I'm so sorry, babe. I know I've made you suffer. But you do know I love you, don't you?' he said with deep worry lines etched on his face.

'I haven't felt it lately,' I admitted.

'I'm so sorry. I'm fucked with remorse. Will you forgive me?' he asked, lifting up my chin, making me look at him.

I nodded *yes* as droplets of tears seeped down my cheeks. The pale ball of his face hung like a broken streetlight. Our lips quivered to meet like the first time we met. I wondered if we would ever be the same again. I could only pray that we would be reunited when he started to feel better about himself.

Breaking the moment, Bee ran in and said, 'Come on, you two. Can we go now, Mummy?'

A slow smile won itself across Simon's face as she pulled me away from him.

'Come on then, trouble, let's go,' I said, chasing her down the hall.

Simon carried our bags out to the car and strapped Bee into her booster seat. He gripped her hand and kissed her through the window. He held mine until it slipped like a silk glove into the breeze as I drove away. Like a guard waving off a train in the station, he stood out in the street. I noticed as I peered in my rear-view mirror that he had a waxy faraway stare, like someone gazing through the smoked glass windows of purgatory. He waved until we were out of sight.

CHAPTER 27

That weekend we stayed with one of my oldest friends, Pauline and her husband Tom, in Wood Green, London. They doted on Bee, as sadly they couldn't have children of their own. I slept until noon the next day whilst they took Bee to the park and played shopping games with food from their cupboards with real money. I chewed their ears off about Simon the whole weekend and tried to call him a few times, although he'd asked me not to. Despite doing our three-ring code, he didn't answer. I'd said to expect me home late Sunday afternoon.

As there was still a heavy November frost, Tom kindly scraped my windscreen before we left. As the dusk settled on the north circular like a mood, I turned up the volume and we danced in our seats to 'Gipsies, Tramps and Thieves' by Cher. Bee loved it. Knew all the words. They offered a romantic slant on Bee's beginnings, I thought. To make our journey more bearable, I played it over and over.

The house was in darkness. I closed the curtains in the front room. Switched on the lamp in the corner and fired up the gas fire as Bee trailed behind me like a new-born lamb.

'Where's Daddy, Mummy?' she quizzed.

'He must be at Nanny's, or with Auntie Janie. He won't be long, darling, don't worry.'

I thought it likely that he was at Brenda's where she would have cooked him his favourite roast dinner and made him a sherry trifle.

I went into the kitchen. The kettle was stone cold. One cereal bowl, one mug, soaked in the sink. The chump chops for his Sunday lunch were still wrapped in cling film in the fridge. The bed was made. The towel in the bathroom and his toothbrush bone dry. Neatly piled along the hallway were the photos I'd asked him to take down to prepare for the decorator. About forty of them, all in clip frames. Our families and friends had a special place there. I imagined him reflecting on all the happy times as he removed each one from the wall. A neat pile of small nails next to them.

I made myself a cup of tea. Put Bee to bed. Four times the answerphone said, 'No new messages.' He usually left a note to say where he was and when he'd be home. I sat for a while thinking about the times when he'd been psychotic and we'd argued. He'd spin on his heels and go and punch a hole in something. I was always left wondering.

I pondered and paced the hall for an hour. Called everyone I thought he might be with. No one had seen or heard from him, apart from Joyce next door who said she'd seen him drive off in the van early Saturday morning.

Sitting on one of our Van Gogh kitchen chairs with my hands under my thighs to stop them shaking, I rocked, staring at the black and white floor tiles and catastrophised about what might have happened, where he could be. There was no one left to call. But it seemed too dramatic to call the police, like I was overdramatising. But I had no choice. Pulling the receiver off the wall, I dialled 999 and reported him missing. They told me not to worry as most people turn up. Then I phoned Jane again, who came up straight away. We talked until 1 a.m. Cupped milky whisky coffees and cuddled hot water bottles in my bed. Me on my side, her on Simon's.

'Is there anywhere else you think he could have gone?' Jane asked, pulling her knees under her chin. She had the quilt puffed around her neck to keep warm.

'He did take me to a strange place in the woods just before I moved back home,' I said, pulling the quilt around my neck like her.

'What do you mean? You didn't tell me that?'

I recalled the tale of Simon bundling me and Bee in the back of his van amongst his tools and buckets just before we moved back home. He was driving like a lunatic and I had to hold Bee tight in my lap against the sides of the van to steady us. Like in the waltzer fairground ride, we were thrown from side to side.

'I've found this wonderful place. I've got to show you. You'll love it,' he shouted from the front.

I imagined a lake with wild birds. A sunset with a spectacular view. *It had better be worth it*, I'd thought as I questioned myself about why the hell I'd agreed to even get into the van. But he was in that agitated Sid phase, where I knew it was best not to argue. Plus, it seemed of such importance to him that I complied.

Being in the back of the van I couldn't see out and had no idea where we were and lost all sense of direction. We drove for forty-five minutes or so until he did an emergency stop. He pulled both the back doors open and said, 'Come on. Get out. Don't worry, this isn't it. We've got to walk for a bit now.' He spoke like a sergeant major.

Fucking hell, I thought, feeling car sick. Bee gripped my hand tight as we walked through fields of long grass. Marching ahead, he complained that we were going too slow. Field after field, it all looked the same. The slate-grey sky hung over us like a dome and made it feel much later than it was.

'Nearly there, nearly there. It'll be worth it,' he shouted over his shoulder, pacing ahead.

We walked through a meadow, along the edge of a small wood, under some barbed wire and into a dark wooded area that had a sign saying *Private* nailed to the tree. And there it was. A small murky pond, branches of willow tickling the water like hands hanging from a canoe. There was a rope swing on a thick branch of an oak tree for a seat. No view. No sound. Nothing.

'What do you think then? Amazing, eh?' He was swinging as high as he could like a child on the swing. I

139

heard the branch creak as if to say, *Get off me, I'm going to break.*

'How weird. All that way for nothing,' Jane said.

'Bizarre. I agree. But he is a bit crazy, isn't he?' I said, taking her mug, placing it on my bedside cabinet.

'And that's why we love him, isn't it, my darling friend?' she said as she kissed and squeezed my hand, then turned out the light.

When Bee saw Auntie Janie first thing, she wanted to stay home from school.

'When will Daddy be home?' she asked over breakfast.

Jane scooped her on her lap and said, 'Do you remember when we all stayed in Old Tiddly in Bantham, and you, Jess and Theo picked all the wildflowers from the hedgerow and made the butterflies fly off as we walked to the beach?'

Bee nodded and grinned.

'And do you remember how tired you all were because we made you walk back all the way from the beach, and you were only toddlers? Us grown-ups all had to carry you back home, didn't we?'

'And Daddy carried me on his shoulders and I hung onto his bald head, didn't I?' She giggled.

'That's right. Well, we wonder if Daddy has gone on a very long walk and laid down because he's a bit tired,' Jane said, rubbing Bee's back and kissing her on the head.

Totally absorbed in the tale, Bee appeared satisfied for the time being, but still wanted to stay home. Jane managed to bribe her to go to school with the promise of a Milkybar. Her favourite as she only liked white chocolate. I watched from the lounge as she skipped across the road, jabbering as she swung her Snow White lunchbox in one hand and held Jane's hand in the other.

Around the kitchen table we drank endless cups of coffee and dunked chocolate Hobnobs between phone calls to friends, who all gave their opinion of where Simon might be. A friend who had spent time with Simon recently was convinced he'd gone off to join the Druids. I thought it bizarre and didn't realise that Druids still existed. Having since learnt that Druidry, sometimes termed Druidism, is a modern spiritual or religious movement that generally promotes harmony, connection, and reverence for the natural world, I wondered if Simon was searching for peace, somewhere where he could be himself without responsibility or judgement.

Jane and I decided that he'd gone for a long walk, fallen asleep and was hypothermic in a field somewhere.

After being questioned by the police for half an hour, they searched the house including the loft and garage. They left with a photograph of Simon in his black leather jacket, taken on one of our holidays. His smile lit up the beach.

Jane and I have different accounts of what happened next. To this day I swear that Jane slept with me again the night the police came to search the house. She swears she went home and my parents came instead. Mum, with her now ninety-year-old sharp brain, confirms that she and Dad stayed the night. I have no recollection of that. I do, however, remember them being there the next morning. We sat around the kitchen table like we did when I lived at home. Dad at the end of the table, Mum in Simon's usual chair against the radiator, opposite me. It was cold in the kitchen that day, but we didn't want to move in case we didn't get to the phone in time.

I jumped in the air when it rang.

'Mrs Burdall?'

'Yes. Yes.'

'We've found your husband's van parked outside the Spade Oak pub, next to the forest in Bracknell. There's no sign of him yet, I'm afraid. We are hoping to get the helicopter to search the local area, but it's very foggy. We'll keep you informed of any news. Okay?'

141

Dad took the receiver from my grip and talked to the police officer for a minute to confirm what she said.

'They've found the van,' I mouthed to Mum, but no sound passed my lips.

'It could be good news, Tozzy,' Dad said, taking my hands, rubbing them warm with his as he knelt by my chair. 'Like Jane said, he's fallen asleep and got cold.'

Mum rubbed my back as I stared at the black and white chequered floor. Recently I found a photo of Simon sat in the kitchen chair, Bee standing on another chair behind him gripping the hair clippers in both hands, her tongue slightly sticking out as she concentrates on cutting his hair. I can remember the night we laid that black and white floor, both of us on our hands and knees. Simon cut the edges with a Stanley knife. I glued. Together we pressed down hard until it stuck. It looked like the dog's bollocks against our new white Habitat kitchen, with gold shell cup handles.

My focus was shattered. Thoughts danced in infinite directions. They both tried to raise my hopes and behave normally as we ate prawn cocktail sandwiches on brown bread. I only managed a few prawns as the crusts got stuck in my throat. We watched a bit of lunchtime news, followed by *Carry On Regardless* with Sid James and Barbara Windsor.

That afternoon, Mum made a pot of tea at three and we returned to the kitchen table. I couldn't face her coffee and walnut cake, so Dad had mine. With her fork, Mum squashed the walnuts left on her plate and brushed the crumbs off her navy and red tweed skirt.

Bang. Bang. My heart arrested when the Celtic knocker cracked twice on the front door. Dad leapt up, threw his napkin on the floor and bolted down the hallway. Two policemen in full uniform nodded at me over Dad's shoulder as he closed the door. Shaking his head from side to side and gripping his neck, Dad drooped down the hall like he had cement in his shoes. He reached his arms out towards me as if to guide me into a big Daddy bear hug.

All I heard him say was, 'Dead.'

Like a tall brick chimney being demolished by explosives, I dropped to the floor. Thumped my fists on the black and white tiles.

'No. No. No,' I wailed on all fours, curling myself into a tight ball, pulling fistfuls of hair from my head.

I don't remember much after that until I woke under a duvet on the settee. Mum stroked my feet with one hand and twisted one of Nanny's embroidered hankies in the other. Jane remembers driving up the hill towards my house, seeing a police panda car drive away and me standing at the door with my arms open to the sky, saying, 'He's gone. He's gone.'

She didn't collapse like me. She was more controlled and swiftly left to go to tell Brenda, Michael and Lizzy. To this day, I am still unable to recall that moment.

CHAPTER 28

As her school day came to a close, Bee was having story time at school across the road. She was due home within the hour. Mum and Dad wanted to stay whilst I told Bee, but I needed to tell her on my own. Glancing across to Bee's classroom, I pictured her cross-legged enjoying a story at the end of the day. Reluctantly, Mum and Dad hugged me goodbye. As the door closed behind them, I flopped like a ripped up Beanie Baby, slid to the floor and felt the prickles from the doormat under my fingers. There was a stillness in my chest as if my heart had ceased to beat. I stared. Just stared down our long, narrow hallway. As my eyes drifted in and out of focus, the bold black blooms on our slate-grey wallpaper swirled in a psychedelic fashion. And like rain flowing down drains, tears and snot gushed down my face.

Sitting in a bubble of time, I wondered how the fuck I would find the strength to tell Bee her Daddy was dead. God, I had to dig deep. I knew it would be the hardest thing I would ever say to her. I only had one chance. I had to get it right. She had to understand that he wasn't coming back. I didn't believe in telling children that dead people had gone to a better place or that she would meet him again in heaven one day. I couldn't give her false hope. Plus, I knew I would have to tell the real story in the future. So it all had to add up.

The Sleeping Dust Fairies, I thought in desperation. From when she could first talk, I made up stories about the Sleeping Dust Fairies. I told her that they collected different coloured fairy dust from the clouds for all the children to help them sleep. Each night she would choose a colour. I would part the curtains, open the window and pretend to call the fairies down, who would then give me a handful of dust. With closed eyes she would wait as I wet my fingertips

144

to make a gentle clicking noise, then I'd pretend to sprinkle it in her eyes. She completely believed the story, and still talks about it to this day.

Bee had already lost both her biological parents. She'd experienced grief before she was one. I couldn't make it okay. I could only comfort and love her. Oh my god, I loved her, adored her. She was my little ginger girl. My dream come true. She called me Mummy. I remember seeing my Mum cry with anger when I was about seven; it had terrified me. It made me feel insecure for days afterwards. In Bee's eyes, I was that strong mother person who didn't cry; I couldn't let her feel vulnerable.

Coldness had brought the synapses in my skull to a standstill. I felt frost on my feet. Ice in my blood. 'I must get a grip,' I said to myself as I crawled along the hall. Struggling to stand up, I dragged myself up the stairs on my hands and knees. Plastered my face with the green concealing cream that I'd worn on my wedding day that took away the red blotches and puffiness from my skin. I didn't know who I saw when I glanced at the mask in the mirror that day. A ghost. A wife. A mother. Not me.

I'd turned the TV on ready so she would go straight into the lounge and not look too closely at me when one of the mums from school dropped Bee home. In her usual spot in the corner of the sofa, like a puppy preparing for sleep, she bent her knees and curled her feet under her seat and rooted herself with Rabby Rab's on her lap. I watched through the crack in the door as she unwrapped the Milkybar Jane had promised. She smoothed the fine silver foil neatly to catch the crumbs and waited until she had taken her last bite.

Wiping my wet palms on my thighs, I clenched my teeth to stop them juddering. Knelt in front of her six-year-old frame and gently slid the remote control from her grip.

'Hey, Mummy. I'm watching *Blue Peter*,' she whined as she folded her arms with a huff across her chest.

'I know. But I've got something important to tell you, sweetie.'

Clutching Rabby-Rabs and thumbing his threadbare belly, she peered past me hoping *Blue Peter* would reappear. On her fingers, I smelt the fruity tang of white chocolate as I smoothed the pleats on her grey school kilt across her lap. Read *St Joseph's C of E Infant School* in gold silk on the front of her Cadbury's-purple sweatshirt. I prayed for self-control.

'Bee. You know Daddy's been missing for a few days, and the nice policemen have been trying to find him? Well...' I swallowed hard. 'They have found him, darling.'

Her eyes widened. Relief suffused her face.

'But he was asleep. A bit like Sleeping Beauty.'

Her forehead puckered. 'But he will wake up, Mummy, won't he?' she said, her eyes searching for hope in mine.

I hushed her lips with my trembling fingertip. Took an earth mother of a breath and said, 'Daddy died during the night in the woods. He got very cold and couldn't wake up.'

Her lashes fluttered as her eyes fixed on emptiness like an animal pausing on a forest track.

'Never wake up. Ever?' she blurted.

'No. Not ever,' I said.

'Not ever ever?' she echoed.

'Not ever. Ever. Ever. I'm so sorry. He's gone up in the clouds with the sleeping dust fairies. They will look after him up there.'

Her glowing cheeks turned porcelain white. A single tear seeped from her ultramarine glare and slid towards her quivering chin. I heaved her into my lap, and like a marble mould of a mother and child, we sobbed until we set.

PART 2

CHAPTER 29

The following day, I went to identify Simon's body. It was a Wednesday and I should have been doing my blood pressure clinic. I'd squeezed Mr and Mrs Jones in between other patients as a favour. They didn't like seeing the other nurses; said I lowered their blood pressures. I loved my job as a practice nurse, and being able to put people at ease gave me a sense of well-being.

They'll be wondering where I was, I thought, as I saw the sign for Bracknell Crematorium on that dank and bleak November morning. I'd worked hard to establish myself, and I felt appreciated by my patients. The surgery had become a place of sanctuary when Simon was ill, somewhere I could go and feel valued, where no one doubted my ability; where I was trusted and respected. I didn't want to jeopardise my position or let anyone down by going off sick.

Michael and Dad made small talk in the front as Jane, Lizzy and I stared out of the window at the steely sky. We were being driven by Dad in his red Renault people carrier, and it felt like we'd been picked up by a taxi and were going on a group day out. He'd bought it to ferry the grandchildren around and take his gardening waste to the dump.

Only yesterday Jane and I discussed our memory of that day. I swear Joe was there as well. But Jane said he wasn't.

As we turned up the long tarmac drive that led to the crematorium, pink and red remembrance roses appeared to bow their heads in respect as we got closer to the car park.

Linking arms, Jane, Lizzy and I followed our dads through the entrance and chatted about how relieved we were that Brenda had decided not to come. We thought it would have been too stressful for her. I believe the worst bereavement of all is the loss of your child, whatever their age. It was bad enough for Brenda to have suddenly lost Simon, without having to see him dead.

In my experience, we all react and behave differently to the loss of a loved one. I've since learnt there is no right or wrong way to react to death. It's personal. Any reaction is normal. What links us all in grief, however, is the shock, even if it is after a terminal illness. The sudden disappearance of a loved one is felt by the profound disbelief that you won't see them again. Ever.

The purpose of our visit was purely to identify Simon. Any one of us could have done it alone. But somehow we all went. Jane and Lizzy, like me, needed to see him to believe he was dead. I presumed Michael felt the same and thought it was a father's role to protect and support his daughters. And likewise, Dad would have wanted to support me. And being less emotionally involved with Simon, he would have wanted to take the pressure off Michael, who he imagined may not be in a fit state to drive afterwards. Not that any of this was discussed.

Having lived through months of unpredictability and insecurity when Simon was on a high and again when he was depressed, I'd forgotten what it was like to feel normal. When I say normal, I mean having an empty 'worry bag', where you wake up with a clear head, where all is well in your world and you can focus on the nice things in your life. Daily I worried about Simon. How he would be in his head when he woke up. If I could relieve his torment or take some of his sufferings away. I'd yearned for that clear head. I'd been living on the edge of a rumbling volcano. Yesterday, my volcano had erupted; the explosion was so loud that I'd stopped hearing others. Couldn't even fathom my thoughts. Hot lava had seeped into the folds of my brain, filling them with burning molten. Feelings of helplessness overwhelmed me.

Although we knew Simon was dead, we didn't know how, and Jane and I continued to fantasise that he had gone for a walk and died of hypothermia. The night he disappeared when Jane and I sat in bed, we talked of nothing else. We convinced ourselves that he'd lost track of time, had walked off the beaten track, fallen asleep under a tree or found an old barn to shelter in for the night. He loved being outside. All his working life he'd tolerated the burning sun on his skin whilst at work in the summer without sun cream or a hat. During the winter without any shelter he had been exposed to the ice, wind and snow as he laid brick after brick with cracked fingertips on building sites.

An eerie silence wafted over us as we entered the waiting room where you normally wait with friends and relatives anticipating the hearse to arrive. The heady smell of beeswax and air freshener clung to the burgundy plastic chairs. Floral boxes of tissues and faded fake flowers lined the windowsills below the net curtains.

Dad marched off to find the coroner, giving me just enough time to pop to the loo.

The hand-dryer still droned as I walked back in the waiting room to find everyone huddled around a short, stocky, bald man, who I assumed to be the coroner. In a strong Glaswegian accent, all I heard him say was, 'Tree.'

Barging in between them, I said, 'What do you mean. Tree? What happened?'

'There was a broken branch in the woods,' he said.

'What do you mean, a broken branch?' I urged, seeing the others avert their eyes, like they knew something I didn't.

'He hung himself from a tree. I'm sorry, pet.'

Like someone had slapped me on the back, I let out an almighty gasp and howled, 'No. No. No.'

Stomping my feet on the recently polished parquet floor, I paced up and down, clutching my head until Dad took hold of me. Forcing me to sit down, he pulled a handful of tissues from one of the boxes. Stuffed them into my clenched fists.

Deep down, I knew that there was a possibility that he could have taken his own life, but I never believed he actually would. Not being connected in those last few months, we didn't have meaningful conversations. Most days he was mute. He had become unreachable, even to Brenda and Jane. And when Simon was scoring 9/10 for risk of suicide, I've since learnt that he would have dealt with despair.

'Despair is the echo that emerges from the void. It's the rage at losing hope. It's an endless sadness that people who believe they've lost everything feels. Few psychological states can become as dangerous as that point when a person no longer knows which path to take or what they can truly believe in.'

This was not something I could ever imagine feeling, even in my worst times of grief. I do remember on more than one occasion, particularly when he was crazed, he would ask Jane and me to search for our demons. We giggled nervously around him, humoured him. Once alone, however, I did search inside myself. The only thing I found was the guilt I felt for taking someone else's baby, but nothing more sinister, like the demons he referred to frequently.

Often over the years, he'd ask questions like, 'What's the meaning of life? What's my place in the world? What can I do in this situation that doesn't make sense to me?' These

150

types of questions I've since learnt only feed the cycle of despair.

And of course early in our marriage, when he said he almost jumped from the top of the building that day, I can now reflect on many times he was troubled and I had dismissed it. But I was ignorant to the miseries of mental health. Not like now: I have a radar for it.

And although I was scoring his moods out of ten, I believed he was getting better, especially when he scored 3/10 and I thought he was well enough for me to have that break. But I had no experience of what I know now to be suicidal ideation (thinking about suicide or wanting to take your own life). I hadn't recognised the signs. Besides, I was alone. We were alone. There was no mental advice or support during that time in the late 1990s. Google was in its infancy and our GPs were not interested.

Jane came and sat down on the chair next to me.

'Come on, darling. Let's get on with it. Then we can go home and get warm,' she said, wiping tears off my cheeks and rubbing my thigh.

She was so much more measured. She wasn't a crier like me. Yet I knew her pain cut just as deep as mine. She took me in her arms like a big sister, even though I was the elder.

The coroner, who I later found out was called Bob, told us what to expect. He said Simon would be on a table, covered by a cloth. Said we would be able to look at him through a window once he'd opened the curtains. I don't remember much more than that.

Dad leant in close to my ear and said, 'You don't have to do this, Tozzy. The others can do it.'

'I know, Dad. But I have to see him. I have to know what he looks like,' I said, blowing a copious amount of snot from my nose and wiping my hands with the tissue.

I had to see for myself that it was Simon. I needed to see his face. His expression. Touch him. Smell him. Hold him. Needed to ask him what the fuck he'd done. Why he'd left us. Check that they hadn't made a mistake, otherwise I wouldn't have believed he was dead.

Filing out, we formed a queue. Michael in front, Lizzy next, holding one of Jane's hands and me holding the other like little girls in the playground at school. We left Dad in the waiting room, and in a stilted fashion we followed Bob down a gloomy and cold corridor. Coming to a halt outside the infamous door-sized glass window, like you see in TV dramas, we linked arms side by side like we were forming a human barrier and waited for Bob to pull the curtain on the other side.

Jane's nails cut deep into my palms as our fingers linked into fists. My adrenaline surged so fast that I had to fight the urge to run back to Dad.

I held my breath as the words *Fuck. Fuck. Fuck, I'm going to see him* repeated themselves in my head. And then, like the curtain going up at the beginning of a West End show, Simon emerged. Laid on the slab like a monarch in a mausoleum. He was draped in a deep purple velvet cloak, the same colour as our front door. Only his head was exposed.

Rather elaborate for a tradesman, I thought, wondering for a moment if someone knew that was one of our favourite colours. *Or he'd chosen it knowing I'd be impressed*, I thought as I gawped through my tears at his shell. He always did try and impress me with what he wore, and here he was, draped in a fine robe looking regal. All he needed was a crown and fur collar and he could have gotten away with being one of the royal family. He would have laughed at himself. We would have laughed together.

'Can we come in?' I asked Bob.

Nodding a reluctant yes, he let us file in one by one. Scenting the pungent odour of formaldehyde, I walked into what felt as cold as a butcher's freezer.

With shaky hands, I cupped his cheeks. Kissed the dimple in his chin. Smelt his bald head. Lingering on his rigid rubber lips, I was stunned by the sense of his flesh. It was cold and firm like Madam Tussaud's waxwork dolls. I ached to see his electric blue eyes, just once more. Somehow, I thought seeing them would reassure me that he was okay, like he might be alive in there somewhere.

As I was about to look below his neck, Bob jumped around the slab and said, 'No. No, pet. I think you've touched him enough.'

I wish I could have stayed longer, on my own. In silence. Without distraction. Talked to him. Said goodbye properly. I would have scanned his face for longer so that I could draw on his image in the future. I would have told him I loved him over and over. Stroked his eyelashes. Traced the contours of his face. Felt for breath in his nostrils. Peeped at his teeth. Held both hands in mine. Of course, he was dead. Stone dead. But somewhere inside I believed he was in there. *If only I could see him smiling one more time*, I thought, feeling the pressure of the others waiting to see him.

I walked out, and I have no recollection of the others even being there. Dad collected me. He sat me on a hard wooden pew as we waited for the others. I felt the warmth from his hands as he cupped them over mine in my lap.

There and then, we booked a double slot for the cremation. The normal time of twenty minutes wouldn't have been enough for everyone to stand and say their tributes. Jane and I wandered up and down between the empty pews in a daze. We needed to make sure they had a decent music system as music had been so important to Simon. Dad said they did, and he made the final arrangements.

Ushering us along, Dad shimmied us back to the car, like a head teacher making sure all the kids got back on the bus. The rest is a blur.

Feeling like I'd been hurled into a TV drama where I was playing the grieving widow, I experienced an out-of-body feeling, like I was watching myself a few feet in front of me. I was now experiencing first hand shock, denial and disbelief, the emotions I'd explained to numerous patients. I don't remember anything more about the day and was gobsmacked when Jane told me years later that we all went for a pub lunch.

That evening Dad moved in. He balanced his chunky red tea mug with his razor inside and his Old Spice shaving foam on the edge of my porcelain, bathroom sink, bang next to Simon's eucalyptus foam and silver-handled razor. *How strange*, I thought as I sat on the loo. Their razors touched. Jostled for one space as though competing for gold on a podium. I stared for some time, deciding whose to move as there wasn't room for two.

The most sensible thing was to place Simon's shaving attire underneath in the vanity unit. But it was too soon. So I moved Dad's underneath and walked away. Faltered and retraced my steps and returned it to the sink. Sitting back on the loo, I rocked with my head on my knees. My head was so blank I couldn't blink. I had no tears left to lubricate my eyes. For a moment I thought I'd left myself back on the slab with Simon. I was incapable of making a small decision, yet it was also huge. Who stays on the sink? My dad? My dead husband? I left them both. Simon's leant on Dad's, where they balanced like that until Dad moved out three weeks later.

All my life Dad propped me up, rescued me, jumped in in a crisis. Like the night we sat around the kitchen table with the GP when we waited for Simon to return to encourage him to go to the hospital to get help. I've learnt that when you are deeply embroiled in a crisis, you are unable to see objectively and rationally, mainly because you are firefighting, trying to find ways out of danger. And that's where we were. As Dad wasn't emotionally involved in the same way as me, he was able to see clearly what needed to be done.

My family were, and still are, very controlled, precise and punctual; they leave nothing to chance. Dad is always ahead of the game, predicting what may or may not happen, always having something in place to deal with the worst. Unlike Simon's family who are laid back, spontaneous. Although they genuinely liked and respected Dad, they found him controlling. He was a problem-solver and acted fast when things needed sorting. He didn't have time for emotions. Not that he doesn't feel, because he feels deeply, and he cries easily these days recalling emotional tales. It was during this crisis that we bonded. Although I didn't tell him the true extent of Simon's behaviours, the drug-taking for example, as he would have disapproved, he was a good listener and didn't judge things how I thought he would.

At the peak of Simon's mania, I had not known who to listen to. My heart and loyalty lay with Simon, and I wanted to believe, like Brenda and Jane, that he was just a little florid and that it was the stressors we'd faced in our marriage that made him behave as he did. But deep down I always knew he was ill. Dad saw it. And as a father, he only had mine and Bee's interest at heart.

CHAPTER 30

The following morning after Dad dropped Bee at school, Paul, a local police constable, took us to the woods to see where Simon ended his thirty-nine years. Joe had had a conversation with Paul and had asked him if he could show him where Simon died. And once Joe mentioned it to us, we all decided to go as well. It seemed natural to see everything related to Simon's ending, as if we would understand more about what happened. It was like pulling evidence together in a crime drama to find answers to why he'd done it.

As I bumped in the back of Joe's jeep and leant between the front seats talking to Jane, the car jolted my head from side to side as the wheels tackled the grooves in the muddy track, back and forth like one of those nodding dogs on the parcel shelf in the 1970s. As we followed Paul in his Panda car down the side of the woods, I checked behind to see if Michael and Lizzy had kept up.

'Oh god. There's the pub where Simon left his van,' Jane said, pointing to a bland brick building with only one car in the car park. It's not the kind of pub Simon would have been attracted to, as nothing was inviting about it. It looked a bit derelict. But I suppose he wanted to have a pint. Gather his strength. I've wondered many a time since what would have been going through his mind. What would he have been feeling?

I believe that his desperation to escape, what he often referred to as his demons, drove him to that decision. I've given up trying to imagine what that must have felt like because, unless you have had those feelings, I think it's impossible to experience that level of anguish or despair.

I've since read that the pain of existence often becomes too much for severely depressed people to bear. The state of depression warps their thinking, allowing ideas like 'Everyone would all be better off without me' to make rational sense. Of course, that's not true, and I often wonder if they could see the devastation they leave behind that perhaps they would think differently.

The charcoal-grey sky mirrored our mood, and a cruel cold breeze nibbled at my bones as we climbed out of the car. Pulling my fur hood over my head and my zip up to my chin, I tucked my face inside my coat and breathed hard to warm my face. *At least it's stopped raining*, I thought as I searched for Simon's Timberland boot footprints in the tracks. Edging slightly ahead of the others to get a clear view of the path, I searched for the two diamond patterns present in each sole, but because of the rain making the mud sludgy, I found nothing. With every step, I prayed I was walking where he'd walked that day.

Gastric juice grumbled in my gullet and brambles jabbed at my thighs as we crouched to enter the woods. Pine needles carpeted the ground, making it sponge-like to walk on, and the spicy smell of the pine trees standing close together like soldiers on parade reminded me of Christmas. *A hint of comfort*, I thought as the creepy silence wrapped around us and the light dimmed, as if someone had turned down the light. An area cordoned off by yellow and black police tape loomed ahead in the heart of the forest like a crime scene.

Blimey. I hadn't expected that. Why was it taped off? Was it a crime? Was it being investigated like murder?

Twelve years after Simon died, I worked as an occupational health nurse for the police. I've had answers to the many questions I didn't ask. I learnt that suicide has to be investigated to rule out foul play and to help the coroner reach a verdict.

And I've since looked up the definition of 'suicide'. One dictionary described it as 'Self-murder' or 'self-killing', as

157

it was referred to in the eighteenth century. I shuddered when I read that. I didn't want to be associated with anything macabre, but I was. It felt like something you would read about in the papers, something that happened to other families, not ours. It felt shameful. Dishonouring. Like I'd be tarnished and people would look at me in the street with disdain or cross the road to avoid me.

When revisiting the scene in my head, I still find it chilling. Everything about it was lonesome, remote and creepy. It disturbed me to think of him walking down the track, planning his exit, and then being there on his own for a few days until he was found. I can picture him now, wandering in the woods, choosing the tree, touching them, testing their strength. He loved the woods. Could name the trees. Loved going deep inside until the daylight dwindled. Being scared of the dark, I didn't like it. I prefer to walk in open spaces with a view.

Paul lifted the plastic tape for us to crouch under a small area about thirty feet square.

'What, that's it? That's the tree?' I quizzed, raising my eyebrows at Jane who looked equally perplexed.

It was slim and petite. Like the baby of the grown-up trees, not tall and strong like the others. It was broken, and its foliage brushed the ground, appearing to have snapped off in the wind. Splintered bark stood up like broken glass. I'd imagined a sturdy oak tree. Broad and brawny like in a western film where cowboys are left dangling after their horse has bolted.

I gripped its girth between my palms. Pressing my face against the abrasive bark, I hoped to feel where Simon last touched it. Pacing around it several times, I pictured him there before he died.

A gargantuan growl that had built in my belly belched out of my mouth as I wailed and wailed, stomping around the tree.

'Why? Why? Why?'

I honestly didn't understand it. Why would he do such a brutal thing to himself? Why would he want to leave me? Leave Bee? Leave everyone who loved and adored him? And after all we'd been through. All the nurturing. I genuinely believed we'd turned a corner. The anti-depressant had started to work. He'd appeared more motivated and his psychiatrist appointment was coming up in the following week.

As I kicked and punched the tree, my fury rose. Marching out under the tape needing space, I freed myself. Feeling like I wanted to run, I fell to my knees. As I picked up and threw dead pine kernels like throwing grenades in a war scene, the sudden shriek of a crow stopped me in my tracks.

'Muack. Muack,' it squawked overhead.

'The souls of dead bricklayers calling for muck,' Simon always commented whenever he heard the shrieking of a crow.

Oh my god. He must be calling me, I thought as I caught my breath. Searching the sky for a sign of Simon, I fumbled in my pocket for the black rune stone I'd bought from the hippy shop in town to place at the site. The symbol of Odin. A god in Norse mythology who hung from a tree thousands of years ago. Pressing it against my heart, I gave it a prolonged kiss. Then hung it by its leather choker at the break of the tree. It symbolised courage, strength, precision and aspiration.

The first time we went for a walk in the woods near to my parents, Simon stopped in his tracks. Looked heaven-bound. Put his finger to my lips to shush me, and said, 'Listen. Listen.'

High above the trees, I heard a raspy rattle sound repeated several times.

'An old bricklayer at the end of his career taught me on my first day on a building site that whenever you hear a

159

crow calling, you must salute it as a sign of respect for all the dead bricklayers who've gone before you,' Simon said as he nodded and winked at me.

I didn't take much notice. But every time I hear them sing, I salute them and like to fantasise that Simon's calling to me.

CHAPTER 31

At thirty-eight, I hadn't expected to be organising Simon's funeral, or anyone's for that matter, and didn't know where to begin. Looking through the Yellow Pages, I found Pimms & Son Funeral Directors and chose them, as Simon made a wicked jug of Pimms with copious amounts of apple and cucumber, topped off by mint that ran wild in our garden in the summer. So he would have appreciated it.

In a state of shock, and anxious about going to the undertakers alone, I took Jane and Lizzy with me. Nervously, we giggled and rolled our eyes at each other before going in. We were probably suffering from PTSD – post-traumatic stress disorder – but didn't know it. Not much was known about PTSD back then. It was something you heard about when people suffered serious trauma like having their legs blown off, or being involved in a traffic accident for example, but not in ordinary folk like us. Now I know that it is an anxiety disorder. It can develop when people are severely harmed, or experience something extremely upsetting.

A brass bell jangled above the door as I pushed it inwards. A strong smell of surgical spirit reminded me of the church hall where I went to Brownies when I was seven. Photographs of funeral cortèges were displayed along the walls, together with framed certificates saying *Best Funeral Directors of the Year* from 1987 to the present. Glass cabinets contained ornate wooden urns in different shapes and sizes – all waiting to be filled with someone's ashes.

We were greeted by Sylvia who was dressed in a navy-blue pencil skirt and white and navy polka dot silk blouse. Her dead-straight line, painted red lips and charcoal eyeliner slanting down showed a false sadness. We sat in a row like on a church pew. Leant against the cold plastered wall at the back of her office. It felt like we'd been summoned by the headmistress at school for misbehaviour. She started her pitch with the coffin. There seemed little point in spending hundreds of pounds for something only for it to be seen for a few minutes before vanishing behind the infamous curtains to be reduced to dust on the other side. We'd already agreed to keep the costs low as we'd heard that if you weren't careful it would end up costing thousands of pounds, and I didn't have the budget for that. But when we were shown chipboard, it felt disrespectful and cheap. We settled for Parana pine. It had a pinkish wave-like grain running across the lid and down the sides. For a moment we could have been choosing kitchen cupboards from Magnet or IKEA.

Making notes in her little black book and without changing her expression, she slid back a door behind us to reveal a real glass coffin on the sidewall.

'Oh my god!' We gulped as one.

It revealed the inner workings of a coffin: snow-white, silk and cotton quilted linings and pillows. I wouldn't have been surprised to have seen a waxwork man lying in it. Fuck me, I thought, I had never imagined what it looked like on the inside of a coffin. You're too busy finding a hankie to mop your tears to give it a thought. But when faced with it, suddenly it mattered. The thought of Simon's head being framed with white-flowered lace made my toes curl. He was a geezer. A big bloke. He didn't suit white silk. Black at a push. We chose cotton. No frills. And then from the top drawer in her desk, Sylvia pulled out a tray of ornate brass, gold and chrome handles, as though she was showing us taps for a bath. We could contain ourselves no longer and laughed out loud like schoolgirls caught out in naughtiness.

Finally, Sylvia mentioned transport. From her bottom desk drawer appeared an antique-looking photo album with dog-eared edges that had been viewed by many grieving relatives over the years. Lizzy laid it on her lap. Jane nudged

162

my elbow with hers and I had to dig deep not to laugh out loud, and so did she. It was full of tank-like black polished chauffeur-driven hearses. There was one image of the funeral director pointing to the room for the body in the back, just like a car salesman. All for a further few thousand quid, it appeared. Enough to pay for a new conservatory and have money left over to tarmac your drive. We declined. And if Simon were on my shoulder he wouldn't have wanted that much fuss. Being a master at DIY, having made the panels for the bath and doors for the vanity unit, he may have suggested making his own coffin. He would probably have sent me off to get test paint pots for colours, and we would have spent hours choosing the right shade of cream.

Then just as we got up to leave, the word 'embalming' made my head twitch. The thought of Simon being tampered with, a stranger prodding and pulling his body, infusing him with toxic chemicals, distressed me. He was my Simon. I felt possessive of him and wanted to protect him from more bodily distress. But Sylvia assured us he would look natural. No fake tan or plumped up lips. And like all the decisions we made that morning, there was no time to think. Being in such an emotional state, we would have agreed to anything. *We should have bought Dad with us*, I thought. Someone with experience of at least one funeral under their belt to guide us.

As I've grown older, I've become more cynical of these things. And unless you are going to see your loved one in the chapel of rest, there's absolutely no point in having them done. And let's be brutally honest, however much embalming fluid you fill them with, or however much make-up you apply, they look stagnant and blank. I know that sounds harsh, but it's true. And most of all, they can't appreciate how good you made them look. You're better off spending your money and treating yourself to a facial or a make-over, as that's what you need at the time.

It gave me comfort, however, to know that Simon's sturdy skull was cushioned and comfortable for his last excursion. And after a nanosecond of a discussion, we agreed to have him preserved. Sylvia finished by asking me to return the next day with Simon's clothes and advised I left his shoes and socks behind. That made me sad as I didn't think he'd have felt fully dressed.

Pressing his maroon moleskin shirt, flattening his sea-green stripped boxers and straightening his faded and hem-frayed Levi's jeans, I remembered the last time he wore them. It was to take Bee to the local fair on the village green. I can picture him now with his arm around her in the bumper cars as she screamed each time they got bumped from behind.

I'd made up a simple family symbol like a kiss with a circle between the two lines to represent Bee safe in between us. I drew it in a turquoise felt pen on a small piece of white card. Placed it in the back pocket of his jeans. *Only he will know it's there and what it means*, I thought as I folded his final outfit neatly and took them back to Pimms & Sons the next day.

As a family, we held no strong religious beliefs, and the Humanist Society could offer a secular funeral service, without mention of religion. The focus was on the celebration of human life and nature. The ceremonies are simple, sensitive and personal. A member of the Humanist Society, David, known as an officiate, met with us beforehand to coordinate the ceremony for the day. Simon would have liked David, as he was young, a bit trendy and had a similar taste in music to Simon. He sat in Michael's chair and listened to all our anecdotes and described the kind of person Simon was. Despite Brenda's sorrow, she rallied round in her usual style. Didn't sit down for long. Made tea. Lined one of her mother's antique plates with oozing chocolate éclairs and placed it on the coffee table.

Several times, Jane and Michael said, 'Come and sit down,' but she never did.

That was her style. Refilling mugs with coffee or tea. Knocking up a shepherd's pie or chicken curry, she'd busy herself in the kitchen. Even on that day when her input was important, she busied herself in the kitchen.

Those last few years hadn't been easy for her either, wondering what Simon would do next and whether she could support him. Trying to keep the peace between him and Michael. She told me many years later how she dreaded the calls he made to her at random times and how sometimes she'd wake at 4 or 5 a.m., creep out of the bedroom so she didn't disturb Michael and be up, dressed and ready in case Simon phoned or called round. She said she did whatever he wanted her to do, just to console him. She knew he was ill, but she didn't realise the extent of his illness. And like me, she wasn't able to reach him.

She was there when we chose the music though. It was difficult as Simon had been a music buff, and each member of the family wanted something different. In the end, we chose Vaughan William's 'Fantasia on a Theme' to walk in with, 'Born Free' by Andy Williams to reflect with and Jeff Buckley's 'This Is Our Last Goodbye' to walk out to. Friends and family took turns to share stories about his colourful life.

I've been to several funerals since. I ask myself the same question every time as the clergyman tells the tale of what a wonderful person they were. How they had been exceptional husbands, sons, fathers, brothers, best friends and colleagues. And this is my question: Were they told this when they were alive? I doubt it! But Simon was. He was told often. He just didn't believe it. I have since learnt that to be a common trait of people who suffer from depression. They don't believe they're any good. You can tell them. But they don't believe it.

Self-esteem issues can be exacerbated by episodes of depression. 'People who feel depressed feel worthless and have a sense that everything they do is not as good as it could be. They can feel inadequate in their work and their relationships – even though these perceptions are not true reflections of their abilities or worth.

A chronic mental condition such as bipolar disorder can affect how well someone can function and, in turn, that person's quality of life. The emotional ups and downs related to bipolar disorder affect a person's lifestyle and behaviour and can have a very negative impact on interpersonal relationships with family, friends, lovers and jobs, and this can lead to feelings of rejection and damaged confidence. Everything Simon felt on and off for much of his adult life.

I set a marquee over the patio, draped it with deep purple ribbons, vases of red gladiolas, orange gerbera and multi-coloured red, blue and yellow glass beads on the white linen table cloths. Jane and Lizzy set up a cocktail corner with Bloody Marys, White Russians and Noilly Prats, one of Simon's favourites before he died. He'd cut the zest of the lemon into a strip, twist it and pour over ice into tall stemmed glasses and make them for us all.

The house overflowed with people like a party. Simon would have loved it. The kind of party we'd always said we'd have, where all our friends and family would gather. I can picture him shrugging his shoulders, waving his arms in the air, raising his eyebrows and chuckling out loud as he turned the music up, doing a crazy dance with a cocktail in his hand. He would make everyone feel special. He would have been thrilled that so many people turned up to his farewell party.

A week later I called back to Pimms & Sons, where Sylvia had slipped some of his ashes into the emerald-green silk drawstring bag that was lined with tango orange. I had spent hours searching for something that was both practical and beautiful for his final journey. Sylvia appeared more relaxed that day, gentle and caring. She wasn't out to sell me anything, I thought as I waved goodbye and thanked her. Said I'd be back another time to collect the rest. It seems strange now to think that I separated his ashes. I wouldn't do that today. In fact, I wouldn't have anyone cremated either.

I don't remember any conversation about cremation versus burial. In both of our families, cremation was assumed, so I didn't give it a second thought. It wasn't until I buried my second mother-in-law ten years later that I gave it any thought. I found it personal, and more peaceful. The beauty of woodlands and a natural burial is that when we visit the grave, we can picture her there. In one piece. Exactly as we laid her out. It's now that wish I could sit by Simon's grave, imagine him whole in body and soul, not lost in space, out in the ether. I also regret separating his ashes, spreading a bit here and there. I didn't give it a thought and neither did the others as we were all in a state of shock.

I placed Simon's ashes in my tan leather handbag, and he sat on the passenger seat next to me and I talked to him all the way home! I felt for him in my bag as we sat waiting for the traffic lights to turn green. Was I really doing this, telling him we were on our way up the hill and nearly home? It's a miracle I didn't crash on the drive home, as every few seconds I'd look at my bag and feel inside to check he was still there. The silk felt velvety. The ashes inside like sand. I ran my fingers over them. Took the weight of them in my palm. Pretended he was holding my hand.

Pulling up outside our house, I peered across the road into the playground, hoping to catch sight of Bee in her lunch time, but I was a bit too late. Throwing my coat over the banister, I rested Simon on the kitchen table whilst I made a cup of tea.

Pulling the strings of the silk bag loose, I peeked inside. Examined the grey ash that remained. Only a few white crumbs stood out. I wondered if it could have been one of his pleasing white teeth. Slowly I sipped my tea, shook my head in disbelief. Not wanting to touch the ashes as such, I spilt a handful around the apple tree and mosaic garden, and the remainder around what we called Bee's tree. The tree with leaves like baby elephants' ears that we planted to celebrate her arrival. Each year it grew a bit taller, a bit like her. Glancing up at Joyce's back window, I was relieved to see she wasn't there.

CHAPTER 32

The first morning I had to take Bee to school on my own, my deaf alarm clock vibrated under my pillow at 6.30 a.m. Automatically, I reached across to Simon's empty side of the bed. Hugged and smelt his pillow! Couldn't believe he wasn't coming back.

Dad pretty much took over looking after Bee when he moved in. He gave her Coco Pops for breakfast. Stood her on the edge of the bath to do her teeth. Helped her dress. Brushed her hair and just about managed a ponytail. Having just turned six, she could do it all herself; she just needed a little finessing, particularly with her hair as it was now waist length.

By stroking my hand and talking directly into my ear, he'd been waking me on his return from school with a cup of tea.

'Come on, Tozzy. It's time to wake up now,' he'd say.

Being deaf in one ear himself, he knew I wouldn't respond any other way.

With my eyes still half closed, I found my way to the hook at the back of my door and slipped on my fleecy grey dressing gown and sheepskin slippers, the ones Simon bought me for my thirty-seventh birthday. Zombie-like, I drifted towards the bathroom and splashed water on my face. Practised a smiley face by stretching my mouth wide into a clown-like grin. I thought I'd better pull myself together and appear to be capable of looking after my child.

Dad's face was in yesterday's shrimp-coloured *Financial Times* spread across the kitchen table as I walked into the kitchen. Like a raven, his Brylcreemed black hair shone in the sunlight, slicked back off his face. Even today at ninety, he's not fully grey. Wearing navy checked trousers instead of his usual jeans and a clean navy crew

169

jumper with a pale blue work shirt underneath, he'd looked business-like to see his GP. He wasn't chatty first thing in the morning like Mum would have been. Didn't even look up as I clinked my cereal bowl and tore open a new box of Frosties.

'Do you want another cup of tea, Dad?' I asked in an upbeat tone.

I knew the answer.

'No thanks. I'm leaving at seven fifteen to miss the traffic,' he said, turning the page.

Pushing my Frosties around the bowl, I soaked each one with milk. Waited for him to ask me if I'd be okay taking Bee to school for the first time. He didn't. He was too busy studying the opinion and analysis page. Only able to manage a few mouthfuls of my Frosties, I was still there half an hour later when he shouted from the front door, 'I'll be back in time to pick Bee up from school as usual.'

By now everyone will have seen the article in the local paper and know it was my *husband who'd hung himself,* I thought as I wandered into the lounge, wrapped my dressing gown tight around my waist and watched as one by one the teachers parked in front of the school. Dad had warned the teachers I'd be taking Bee that day. He'd told me that the night before and said that every day Mrs Moore, Bee's teacher, had asked how I was. I was relieved and grateful that they were prepared.

The neighbours had all gone to work. Joyce and Ian as usual had placed their orange and white cones in front of their house to make sure no one parked in their space. Nothing had changed for the rest of the world. They went about their daily routines without a thought, like I used to.

The local gazette was still on the floor by the fireplace, where I left it last night. I read it each night as I knelt to turn off the lights. Seeing it in black and white reinforced it was real and that I hadn't imagined it. Picking it up, I read it for the twentieth time:

The body of a London man who had been reported missing was found in Great Hazes Wood, near Shurlock Row, on Tuesday. The man, who has been named Simon Mark Burdall of Rutland Road, Maidenhead, was reported missing by a relative on Sunday evening.

A police search, headed by Inspector Dennis Sharp, was mounted on Monday after Mr Burdall's van was reported abandoned outside the Pines Restaurant, in Crow Lane. The search was started in the early evening and officers used dogs and thermal imaging to help them. Officers wanted to use the police helicopters but were unable to because of fog.

The search was suspended before midnight and resumed just before dawn on Tuesday. Mr Burdall's body was found in woodlands just before 11 a.m. by a man walking his dog.

An inquest has been opened and adjourned to Tuesday 17 December 1998 at the Guildhall, Windsor.

I wore the navy beret Simon had bought me from Camden Market, and the biggest pair of sunglasses I could find, and we walked across the road to school. Bee was thrilled that I was taking her. As I lifted my sunglasses to see my eyes as I knelt to do her top coat button up, she said, 'Don't worry, Mummy, everyone will be very kind. They have been to me.'

And the teachers were very kind that day. When they asked how I was, I replied with a few lines that I'd rehearsed over and over.

'I'm fine, thanks. Getting better every day. Thank you.'

Trapped in my grief, I cruised around in a trance. Lost my identity. Stopped being a wife. Stopped being a family. My new title was Widow. *What the fuck does a widow look like?* I wondered one day. Widows used to wear black for the rest of their lives to signify their mourning. In places like Greece and Spain you still see women dressed from head to foot in black. I wished it was the same here, then

I'd know what to wear and how to behave. I was tempted to resort to a black band on my arm so people would understand and give me a wide berth.

On my first day back at work, a mask of nude foundation covered the dark circles under my eyes. Rose lip liner curled my lips up into a sham smile. I'd blow dried my hair to curl it back off my face. In my bedroom mirror I talked to the person who looked back at me. I told her she looked normal, just the same as she had on her last day at work. I stood up straight and from a distance looked just like I used to, like the other nurses in my team.

In the early weeks, I was only given admin to ease me back in. One by one I faced my patients. I had to focus on their needs, not mine. I vaccinated the babies. Smeared women's cervixes. Dressed leg ulcers and removed stiches and was comforted by many of my regular blood pressure patients who themselves were widowed and understood my status. Squashing their arms as I pumped up the cuff on my blood pressure machine, I watched in silence as the mercury oscillated down the tube and measured from the systolic to the diastolic blood pressure. I didn't talk about myself. Always focused on them. There were some, however, like Frank and Peggy, who knew me well and asked me lots of questions and hugged me goodbye each visit.

Once I'd seen them all once, the next time they didn't ask how I was. The odd one did, but generally most didn't. Like I was meant to have healed. But I wasn't. I'd become Mrs Grief, shrouded in a shower of silver ash. It clogged my pores. I tasted it on my tongue. It caught in the back of my throat when I muttered the word 'Simon'. My clothes were covered in it. Every day.

Standing in the queue in my local supermarket with negative, destructive thoughts drenching every pleat in my brain, I heard a mother say 'No' several times to her toddler as repeatedly he grabbed the chocolate buttons off the shelf, and I noticed an old lady squeeze all the oranges until she found two she liked. Two women in white tennis attire waved goodbye to each other as they skipped back to their cars. Everyone went about their daily lives, like normal. I felt entombed, sealed in a glass compartment where nobody could get to me, like a dummy in the window who stares out at the world as everyone walks past. I yearned to shatter the glass and shout, 'I'm here. I'm still me. Please don't forget who I was. I was once that fun person you enjoyed being with.'

CHAPTER 33

The following spring of 1999, as the purple crocuses circled the apple tree in the garden, I organised a small memorial at Brenda's church where she sang in the choir and arranged the flowers. I had a small plaque made and we placed some of Simon's remaining ashes in the local graveyard by it. It was somewhere Brenda could visit close to home.

We met at Brenda's before the memorial one Friday afternoon; it was only for the immediate family, plus Mark, one of Simon's closest friends. Every few weeks Simon would get together with Mark and they'd chat about philosophy, art and politics. They joined a philosophy evening class and went to art galleries and music events in places like The Marque or Ronnie Scots in London.

I had grown fond of Mark over the years, although I didn't like him when we first met at college. He was aloof with a big ego and barely acknowledged me when Simon introduced me to him as his new girlfriend. Most people found him a bit awkward when they first met him. He could be intense and didn't like small talk.

Over the years we'd become close. I'd got used to his funny ways and he'd confide in me about his girlfriends, who never quite worked out. Not long after he'd helped build the extension on the side of Number 34, he went travelling to South Africa. I felt his absence as we'd spent day after day talking in the garden. I tried several times to talk about Simon's low moods, but he wasn't interested. Preferred to talk about himself. And when I think back, he was never a great listener. I didn't mind as I enjoyed his company, as Simon had been low around that time.

I remember lying on my hospital bed looking like Pudsey Bear with my head and ear wrapped up in a large white bandage and still wearing a hospital gown after one of my many ear operations wondering when Mark would return from his travels. Then out of the blue, the nurse popped her head round the door and asked if I was up for a visitor.

He appeared with his arms full of about twenty bunches of daffodils, so many that I couldn't see his face at first, and his smile popped out from behind the yellow petals. Chuckling and charming, Mark handed the flowers to the nurse who slipped off to find enough vases for them. He leant over my bed and his thick blond hair tickled my shoulders and smelt damp as he kissed me on both cheeks. Pulling up a plastic chair, he shared tales of his adventures. The nurses told me afterwards that they thought he was my boyfriend.

I'd worn Simon's favourite tangerine cable knit polo neck jumper, short black corduroy skirt and charcoal-grey tights with my chunky black suede biker-like boots. Brenda busied herself in the kitchen having made a huge chicken curry for afterwards.

Before we all left for the church I cornered Mark in the garden. Face to face on the garden path, we stood under one of Brenda's bras dangling on the washing line. Each cup was large enough to fit on our heads like a baby's bonnet. For a moment the familiar scent of her blue Comfort fabric conditioner gave me strength to challenge his recent absence. His shoulder-length, bounteous, buttery blond hair stood out against his black polo neck and black denim jacket that he wore with the collar up. I'd asked everyone to wear bright colours, which wasn't something Mark ever did. He usually wore his hair in a ponytail. Only wore it down on special occasions.

Looking up into his eyes, I said in a jokey way, 'Been too busy to call in then?'

At first he grinned, that cheeky attractive smile that had reassured me about different things over the years. Then he frowned. Tipped his head to one side and went to get past me.

'Mark. I need to understand. Why haven't you been to see us? We both miss you,' I said, moving so he couldn't get past me.

I'd seen him once in four months, and that was a few days after Simon's funeral. He'd popped by for a brief chat and said that Simon's loss would be far worse for him than me. He went on about how I'd meet someone else, but he could never replace his only friend. And that turned out to be true, but it wasn't what I needed to hear.

Running his tanned builder's hand through his hair and looking over my head, he stepped closer to me, flared his wide nostrils and bore his steel-blue eyes into mine. In an almost threatening way, he said, 'Just let it be. One day it may be okay. But not for now. Okay?'

'But why? I don't understand,' I begged him, fighting my tears.

'Just leave it,' he said, shaking his head with an exasperated expression. Pushing past me, he went back to join the others in the house. Dumbstruck, I stood facing the reservoir that backed onto the house.

Fuck me. He must blame me, I thought. I felt condemned, like I'd been dumped. And that's exactly what happened that day. Mark discarded me. Right there under Brenda's J cups, flapping in the breeze.

Blame is a word you hear a lot after a death by suicide. And I certainly experienced an underlying sense of being blamed. I believe that by his actions, Mark blamed me for Simon's death. For years I tried to come to terms with it. He abandoned me at a time I desperately needed support and reassurance. I had expected him to be there for me and Bee, especially as he had been such a close friend to us all for twenty-plus years. I only heard about him via Jane, and I have a recurring dream where he welcomes me with a beaming smile and a huge bunch of daffodils, and he gives me a hug and we make peace.

And there were others like Mark, who I believe blamed me for Simon's death. Those people who'd experienced Simon's psychosis first hand, colluded and helped him organise his own music festival. They hadn't realised he was ill. They'd enjoyed him when he was high as he was such a scream. Even when Simon had hung me out of the bedroom window and he told Mark the next day, Mark laughed out loud and said, 'What is it with you two?' like we enjoyed a drama.

I don't believe that Mark understood Simon's depression either, as when he was depressed, he never wanted to see Mark during that time. And if Mark rocked up unannounced, Simon put on a brave face and livened himself up; he was good at masking his true self to others.

In my experience, men don't talk about their feelings the same way that women do. So I don't know if Mark understood that Simon was even ill at all; whether he was on a high or low. I believe that Simon would have slagged me off to Mark much of the time when he was manic. I can see why Mark might want to blame me. In his eyes, I caused his friend to leave his life.

At Michael's funeral, twenty-three years after Simon died, I saw Mark. Briefly we talked about what happened. He admitted that he *had* blamed me for Simon's death and believed that Simon's mania was caused by his drug-taking alone. Although it was painful to hear him say that, I felt lighter after seeing him. I put his blame down to the pain he was experiencing at the time. We had a hug and made peace, and I have since resolved things in my mind. Phew!

Jane has also told me that her and Brenda didn't believe Simon was really ill either, even when they experienced his psychosis and desperate depression. They just thought he was a bit stressed. And even in the month before he died, thoughts of mental health weren't there for either of them. Jane has since explained that when she was a student nurse and worked on a psychiatric ward, the patients would say things like they were pregnant with Elvis Presley's baby, they were about to give birth to a python, or they'd report hearing voices telling them that the police were waiting outside to arrest them. That is what Jane thought was *serious* mental health. They were in fact the patients suffering from schizophrenia. She, like Brenda, thought Simon was a 'little florid'. It is only since his death that she can now say that her brother had bipolar disorder. And she still doesn't think that Brenda has ever believed that Simon was suffering from *serious* mental health issues. Yet in a conversation with Brenda many years later, she told me that she knew he was full of anguish, and despite her working with mental health clients in the community, didn't associate Simon being ill in the same way.

I didn't stop crying after the memorial until I got home that evening, as I realised that I had lost Mark as well as Simon. I woke the next morning unable to get a grip. I sobbed in the car. Sobbed at work. And continued to sob until one of the doctors sent me home. But my car didn't drive me home that day; it took me into Maidenhead town centre and parked itself.

Drifting around town in a trance, I found myself in Contessa, a lingerie shop in the high street. The last time I was there was when we were living with Phil in the months before Simon died. I'd gone there with Martin, my brother's friend, to exchange a bra that was too big. He was going through a divorce himself, and like me, he also found refuge at Phil's. So he helped me find my right size. I'd insisted I was a 34B, but he, who appeared to know all about women's breast sizes, insisted I was smaller. *How dare he*, I thought. I had lost half a stone with the stress of everything, so he was probably right. He'd coined the phrase that he repeated often, 'More than a handful is a waste.' He showed me his hands that were enormous and grinned. I'd grown up with Martin, who was more like a brother – hence the familiarity.

Like most women, I'd never been measured and assumed I was a 34B and usually bought the same size. I'd gone with his girlfriend to buy some sexy bras a few weeks before, in the August before I moved back home. We'd both bought the same Lovehoney Love Me Lace push up fun sets! She bought pink and I bought deep purple with a black lace edge. I was estranged from Simon and not sure if we would make it back together. I'm not sure what I was thinking. Perhaps I thought I could allure Simon back into loving me again – who knows.

Shivering, I wafted aimlessly between the silk nightdresses, fluffy dressing gowns, large nan pants, tiny string thongs and bra sets. I wish I'd worn my coat on top of my uniform, or at least a vest top. I was freezing. My bras had gotten too big. I knew I'd lost weight but didn't know how much.

'Can I help you?' said the plain middle-aged assistant.

Oh fuck, I thought. I didn't know what I was doing in there let alone whether I wanted to buy anything.

'Can you size me?' I said, looking down at my shoes.

'Of course. Go into the dressing room. Take your top things off and shout when you are ready.'

Like a grey manikin, I drifted into the plastic cubicle and obediently undressed. I was determined not to tell her my tale as I'd let myself down a few times recently; I'd seen a couple of old school friends in John Lewis and blurted out my macabre tale when they asked how I was. Bereavement by suicide is like no other. 'Suicide' is an unpleasant word; a bit like 'murder', it's macabre and portrays something gruesome or ghastly. It's not a word you say out loud when talking about how someone died, unlike cancer, heart attack, dementia or road traffic accident.

It's interesting because only the curious or nosey people ask *how* he did it, and that's when they wished they hadn't. And even when on numerous occasions over the years I've choked on the word 'suicide', some still have the audacity to ask *exactly* how. And then I've had to go into detail, and each time I recite the story I relive the trauma that goes with it.

I appreciate that we all have a morbid curiosity, like when we rubberneck on the road when there's been an accident, but when you're the victim, the last thing you want is to share your tale with someone unable to support you appropriately. It's such an intimate and private predicament to share out loud or in a public place whilst having a chit chat. A counsellor on a course once told me never to ask a person the details of how someone died, however desperate you are to find out, because it doesn't benefit the victim. It only compounds their suffering. If they want to share it, they will.

When I did tell them, they didn't know how to respond and usually regretted asking and would hastily excuse themselves, leaving me reeling from the pain once again. I'd got to the stage that I wanted to put a sock in my mouth to stop myself from spewing my tale. Even now, twenty-four years later, the reaction is the same, but I've learnt to skim over it and change the subject, unless, however, I believe the person is genuinely interested.

Whizzing open the curtain when I called, the assistant came at me with a stiff, cold tape measure. Wrapping her arms around my back, I could smell one of those cheap body sprays and see the creases in her pale green eye shadow. With squinting eyes, she stood back and sized up my tits like I was an artist's model she was about to draw. Above her head, I counted the curtain rings on the faded candy-stripped curtains until she stood back and said, 'You're 32A, dear.'

'I'm a 32A? Are you sure? I haven't been that since I was twelve and got my first bra,' I exclaimed, a bit shocked.

'I've been sizing women of all shapes and sizes for twenty-six years next month. I'm sure. What is it you're looking for – exactly?'

Cupping my breasts with both hands, I thought for a moment. What did I want? Something comfortable, soft and stretchy. I certainly didn't want to be hard-wired, trussed up like a Christmas turkey with metal cups sticking into my thirty-two-inch ribcage, for sure.

'I'll get you a selection, shall I?' she uttered, as I was obviously taking so long to answer that her patience ran dry.

Returning, she handed me a selection: plain, soft white cotton, floral padded, underwired, and a red and black push up bra. In a trance, I tried them all on. I'm not sure why, out of curiosity, perhaps. I needed the push-ups to give these little poached eggs a lift, but I couldn't be bothered with any of it. I was exasperated and I hooked them all over my arm to give back to her, and when she appeared she said, 'Which one would you like then, dear?'

Gripping my chin and without thinking, I said, 'The widow bra, please.' The words slipped off my tongue like honey off a spoon.

Both our mouths fell open as her pale skin flushed pink.

'Oh, no, I'd promised myself not to tell anyone anymore. I'm so sorry,' I said.

Sadness clouded her features and, looking past my shoulder, she whispered, 'Shall I wrap the soft comfy one up for you, dear?'

Often I recall that tale to people because I was at the peak of my grief. I wasn't myself. I'd lost my way, completely and utterly. I wasn't sure if I'd find my way back. I'd not only lost Simon, but I'd also lost Mark, Jane and Joe, and Brenda, Michael and Lizzy. Lost everyone on Simon's side. Not only because the word 'blame' was flying around, but also because they were all grieving like me. And when

181

you're grieving, you are temporarily unavailable. Unavailable to connect with others. But equally you don't want to feel invisible; you want to be asked to things, to be included. But everything is such a massive effort; it feels like you have concrete in your shoes. If you are lucky like I was, I had my family and good people around me, who understood and continued to care for me. They got me through.

CHAPTER 34

Simon died at the end of November 1998, and once the coroner had declared his death as an open verdict in December, a few days before my thirty-ninth birthday on Christmas Eve, I hoped things would settle. As in, I'd seen him in the mortuary, been to where he'd died, had the inquest and survived my first Christmas without him. Plus, I'd gone back to work and faced everyone. It was the blackest winter I'd known. I counted the days towards the clocks going forward. Yearned for the lighter, longer days and to see the first daffodils show their yellow faces.

Approaching what would have been Simon's fortieth birthday in March 1999, just after I'd just dropped Bee at school and was about to curl up on the sofa, the Celtic door knocker banged three times. Opening the door, I was surprised to see Bob, the coroner, holding a buff A4 envelope under his arm.

'Your sister-in-law, Jane, asked me to drop this to you, pet,' he said with a flush across his cheeks.

Oh fuck. I'd completely forgotten. In a previous phone call, he'd asked me if I'd wanted it. Categorically, I'd said no. The thought of seeing what Simon had used to end his life made me shudder and recoil. It felt uncomfortable, a bit like I was going to witness a weapon used in a murder. I didn't want it. But apparently, Jane had asked for it. And here he was, handing it to me on my front doorstep.

'You'd better come in. It's cold out there. Would you like a cup of tea?' I said, walking through the hall in front of him towards the kitchen.

'I'd rather have a coffee. Black, no sugar. I've been working all night.'

I dangled a peppermint teabag by its string in the boiling water and savoured its fresh smell as it infused. Plonking

183

the mugs on the kitchen table, I watched as Bob surveyed the garden through the patio doors.

A heavy frost lay over the lawn like a lace tablecloth. Silver cobwebs glinted between the conifers, and the sun lit up the dream catcher hanging from the apple tree at the bottom of the garden.

'Your Simon build all that?' he said with one hand in his shiny, worn trouser pocket.

'Every single brick. In all three walls. Plus, the ornate one at the edge of the patio, by himself mainly. Sometimes I handed him bricks. A bricklayer friend helped him lay the patio, and together we laid the mosaic deck at the bottom of the garden,' I said without drawing breath.

'And what have you done to that drain cover, pet?' he quizzed, pointing to the edge of the patio.

'It's meant to replicate the modern artist Mondrian; he worked in bold colours like red, yellow, white and blue. And loved abstract shapes,' I said like an art critic.

'It's certainly different, pet,' he said, rubbing his chin and grinning.

'Do you want to see our mosaic garden?' I asked, keen to distract him.

Without waiting for an answer, I unlocked the patio doors and led him across the circular steps to the back corner of the garden. I'd spent months gathering coloured tiles from car boot sales and junkshops. I smashed old teacups and saucers, blue and white willow patterned plates and much of Grandpa's mismatched china. Spending weeks on my hands and knees, I laid each penny-sized piece, one by one. It had been hard to get bright colours like orange or red, so I bought modern mugs and smashed them up too. I even fashioned a navy-blue snake with an orange tongue. And when the mosaic was complete, Simon finished the patio with deep rust old stock bricks. It had been a real joint effort. Sitting outside with friends and family in our brand-new sky-blue director deck chairs, we drank tea and scoffed

Brenda's lemon drizzle on sunny afternoons. I felt immensely proud of what we'd both achieved.

'Wow. What a talented bloke Simon was to build you a walled garden. And you too; he couldn't have done it without you. At least he's left you something to remind you of him, pet,' Bob said.

As I look back to those early years, it was incredibly hard. For five years we lived on a building site, inside and out. We both worked tirelessly in the evenings and weekends and didn't go on holiday apart from weekend breaks in the UK. I have numerous photos of Simon in his work clothes covered in cement and bending over to pick up bricks, then sloshing muck between them. Standing up and rubbing his back with yet another cup of tea in his hand. It makes me sad when I think about how hard his life was during that time. And despite his early breakdown, he always went to work and managed to build us a home that we could be proud of.

Once back in the house, in a fatherly way, Bob patted my shoulder, pointed at the envelope sat on the kitchen table, and said, 'Well, here you are then, pet. The reason I came to see you.'

One of my overwhelming feelings, apart from my shock and grief, was the macabre nature of Simon's death. I'd describe it as ghastly, grisly and gruesome. Horrifying and repellent. The kind of thing you hear on the news and associate with other people, not with yourself. It left me feeling tainted, and I didn't want to be associated with it. I wanted that feeling to fade. But it never has. Whenever I meet new people and exchange biographies, I rush over the bit about my first husband killing himself and change the subject back to them so that I don't have to go into it.

Picking up on my distress, Bob said, 'I know this is tough, but you can ask me anything. I've dealt with lots of young lassies like you in my time.'

On one hand, I felt sick and wanted to disassociate myself from *it*, yet on the other, I needed to know how Simon died. I thought it might help me to make sense of it all. Macabre in itself, you might think, but I believe that the more knowledge and facts you have, the less you are likely to speculate; plus, I thought it would help me process it.

'Perhaps you could tell me exactly how he did it,' I said, digging my nails into my clenched fists and holding my breath.

Bob crossed his legs and made himself comfortable at the kitchen table. I continued. 'Some people have said that it could have been a mistake, like Simon could have changed his mind at the last minute. Something to do with how his hands were placed. Is that true?'

What I now realise is that apart from with Jane, I've not had deep discussions about the details of how Simon died with anyone else. And why would I have had? Everyone has their own narrative about the events. And much of the time, without the facts, we make up what we believe to be true. Jane told me that Brenda still doesn't know exactly how Simon died. So I must apologise to anyone else who doesn't want to know – skip the rest of this chapter!

'There was no mistake, pet. He meant it all right,' Bob said, rubbing the back of his neck.

'How can you be so sure?' I quizzed.

'How about I show you?' Bob replied.

Before I had the chance to answer, he'd picked up the envelope and tore open the seal. I was stuttering, and my internal remote control switched itself to pause until *it* was fully out of the envelope. Floppy, textured, army-green strapping, two inches wide, three-feet long, slipped out like a silk toy snake. Stumbling back, I sat on the kitchen chair and watched as Bob stretched it out and wound it around both his fists, as if to show me its strength. Feeling light-headed, I gripped the sides of the kitchen chair until my fingers hurt and my chest tingled.

'You okay, pet?' Bob asked.

'I think so,' I said, shaking my head to clear my vision.

I couldn't believe he was sat right there in my kitchen on a normal school morning, describing how *my* husband, Bee's daddy, had taken his own life. *Surely he's talking about someone else*, I thought, taking a deep breath to calm myself.

That scene is as clear to me today, as if it had happened last week. And part of me wonders why I put myself through such torment. But I was being swept along. Things happened to me that I didn't choose. There was no guidebook. I could have said no, but I'd lost my strength, like a daddy longlegs trying to escape the water in a bath or shower.

'I'd imagined a piece of rope. Something chunky,' I squeaked.

'Oh no, pet. This is the real thing. It's called Paracord. It holds five hundred and fifty pounds. It holds up parachutes,' he said boldly, like he was lecturing a soldier, and like I should be impressed.

Then, in slow motion, he demonstrated exactly how Simon had killed himself. Simon hadn't jumped or dangled from a tree, how I imagined people did. He'd made a noose with the cord around his neck, then attached it to the horizontal, fractured branch of a baby pine tree, a few feet above his head. Wedging his knuckles, with his fingers pointing outwards inside the cord against his carotid arteries, he'd crossed his ankles and bent his knees. And like a ballerina doing a pirouette, he dropped. Just like that.

I sat stock still. Dazed. Numb. Mute. Like someone had pulled out my plug. Like I too had dropped dead. Propping my head up with my fists, I thought that if I'd let go, my head would have fallen off and rolled under the table. Then everything went black. A loud ringing in my ears overwhelmed me, yet I was aware of a faint voice in the distance, like I was dreaming. When I came to, Bob was crouched on the floor by my knees offering me a glass of water. I'd fainted. Uncurling, like a new-born lamb, I steadily came back to life.

Strangely, Simon's end sounded less brutal than the hangings you saw on TV in old films. Almost dignified. Like bending to sit in a chair, and the chair being taken from beneath you as a prank.

'Would it have been quick? Would he have suffered? I couldn't bear him to have suffered,' I asked.

'Yes. It would have been quick. He didn't suffer. His knuckles would have crushed his blood vessels and stopped the blood from going to his brain. He would have lost consciousness and died within a few minutes,' he said.

Heaving myself back onto the kitchen chair, I said, 'But there had been a lot of discussions around if he meant it or not because of the way he placed his hands inside the cord. People said he could have changed his mind at the last minute. Is that true?' Frantic questions were falling like dribbles from my mouth.

Refilling my glass from the tap, Bob continued. 'Oh no. He meant it all right. In my experience, men are more likely to succeed in killing themselves, compared to women, as they generally use more lethal means.'

'I desperately tried to get him help, you know. He even showed signs of improvement. That's the most dangerous time for them to do it. Isn't it?'

'Indeed, it is. It's said that they have a bit more energy and can see a way out of their misery.'

'The problem was that not everyone thought he was ill. To others he appeared flamboyant, charismatic, foolish. Fun to be around. That's if you didn't get in his way. And when he crashed down and became reclusive, he hid away. So people didn't get to see his depression.'

188

Bob made me a cup of coffee, as though I was in his kitchen. Gave me two sugars, although I didn't usually take sugar. He sat opposite me as I poured my heart out to him. He didn't rush me; he just nodded here and there and reassured me that I couldn't have done any more than I did. Counselling me, he explained why 'death by misadventure' was given for the cause of death. In most suicides, the death is attributed to an accident that occurred due to a risk that was taken voluntarily.

An hour or so later, giving me a bear hug as he left me on the doorstep, he made me promise I would call him if I had any more questions.

My body weighed heavy against the door as I pushed it shut. It was all I could do to drag myself to the sofa where I collapsed in a heap on top of my duvet. It was ten past three when I woke with what felt like a hangover. It was the first thing I saw when I went into the kitchen. It was half in and half out of the envelope. All the morning's events came flooding back. Without touching it, I scooped it up, folded the envelope back on itself and stuffed it in a plastic bag and put it in the cupboard under the stairs. Pulling my coat on, I was only just in time to walk across the road and collect Bee from school.

Many years later, I asked Jane to remind me of how the envelope had come to me. She said she'd wanted it because it was the last thing that Simon had touched. I understand that now. We still talk about him every time we meet to keep his memory alive.

Recently I told Dad about writing about the coroner calling for this book, and he told me that he found a rope with multiple knots under my settee after Simon had died. He threw it away and had never intended to tell me, until now!

It's obvious to me now that Simon had been contemplating and planning his death for some time. Trying different ways of doing it. Like the day within his three-year hypomanic phase when he shouted at me, 'Have you ever had a plastic bag over your head and a noose around your neck?'

CHAPTER 35

Four months after Simon died, November 1999, Jane called me and talked so fast that I couldn't catch what she was saying.

'Slow down, slow down,' I urged.

'They've found a note in Simon's van. It's on its way to you now,' Jane shouted.

'What? Oh my god. What does it say? What does it say?' I spluttered.

'I've no idea. It's addressed to you. They wouldn't let me see it,' she said, panting.

The guy who had bought Simon's van had handed a note in at their local police station. She said that Paul, the policeman, would bring it round before lunch.

'Call me as soon as you get it. Promise?' Jane begged.

'Of course,' I promised.

'Thank you, Si. Thank you,' I said, blowing a kiss to the air above my head as if I was thanking him personally.

My mind flitted back and forth. I wanted to skip and shriek. I wanted to phone everyone to tell them I had a note.

I'd been baffled and troubled that he hadn't left me a note. I felt resentful on top of my multitude of haunting emotions. Plus, I felt it was the least he owed me for all he'd put me through. It didn't fit with his true thoughtful nature – pre-illness, that is. Often he would leave me silly notes. Like our family symbol written in red biro on a piece of kitchen roll, left on the worktop for when we came home. It was an affectionate way of saying 'I love you'.

I now realise that it didn't help my grief. I was struggling enough with the shock and horror of events. A note may have given me a tiny fragment of peace in my tattered head.

Simon's writing was distinctive. I'd recognise it anywhere. All the family would. And the spooky thing is

191

that Lizzy's handwriting is identical; neat, loopy and leaning to the right. I hold my breath sometimes when a birthday card from Lizzy lands on the mat, as I think it's from Simon.

I felt a quickening of my pulse and lightness in my chest as I sprinted up the stairs. Scrubbed my teeth. Brushed my hair. Lined my lips with coral lip-gloss. A sparkle appeared in my eyes when I peered in the bathroom mirror, like someone had polished them clean. Chucking my old trackies and baggy T-shirt on the floor, I slipped into my jeans and my favourite jumper, and stroked the chunky cable knit as I hugged myself warm.

I waited for Paul in the fold of the bay window in the lounge biting my lip. I couldn't stand still, hopping from foot to foot. Balancing on the arm of the sofa, I noticed the only black rose out of all red ones we'd painted around the perimeter on the varnished floorboards. With my forefinger, I traced the outlines of its shape. First the green leaves, then the black petals. I could see Simon as he leant back on his knees, his builder's bum showing over his blue candy-striped boxers, waving a thin paintbrush in his right hand, a tiny black pot of paint by his feet. Grinning back at me with one eyebrow raised, he winked, his teeth radiating white like the perfect Colgate ring of confidence. Chortling, he raised his hand and made the peace sign with his two fingers in the air, and said, 'This one's for me. The nihilist.' Then he went back to painting the petals.

To this day, I am not certain if he said 'the nihilist' or 'the narcissist' as both would fit with his character at different times. He painted it before he was ill, so I like to believe he meant nihilist as it means anarchist and rebel, as opposed to a narcissist who would be a boaster or egocentric, although these were the traits he had when he was crazed.

A bang on the door broke my thoughts. I jumped up, sprinted down the hallway and tugged the door open with such a force that it banged against the wall and made a dent in the wallpaper. I cursed Simon for never putting a rubber doorstop against the hall wall. One of the smallest of jobs that Simon never got round to finishing, yet it wound me up every time the door opened. I placed one of Bee's beany babies there in the end, to stop it from happening again.

At six feet six, Paul, the PC dealing with the case, towered above me. A stereotypical gentle giant of a policeman. He bent down and kissed the air beside my left ear and wiped his size twelves on the mat as it had started to rain.

Half smiling, he said, 'Has Jane told you why I've come?'

'Of course,' I replied.

In truth, I just wanted to grab the note and push him out of the door.

'Come in. Come in. Would you like a drink?' I said as the cold breeze shook my bones.

'No, don't worry. I expect you are keen to see the note,' he said with one hand on his heart, tilting his head sideways.

'Just a bit. It's come as a massive shock. I'd given up hope,' I said, putting the kettle on anyway.

'You're lucky to get a note. The stats say that only twenty-five to thirty per cent of people leave one.'

I've been grateful ever since that I was one of those people.

Paul then went on to tell me a bit more about Simon's last few hours from what he'd been able to piece together. He believed that Simon went to have the van serviced on the Saturday, maybe for me to sell it.

'Why would he bother to do that; do you think?' I queried.

'Some people like to put things in order before they die, so as they don't leave things in a mess for their family,' Paul responded.

How thoughtful, I've since thought, and puzzlingly rational, given his state of mind. And that fitted with Simon's considerate nature. For years I've assumed that when someone is contemplating ending their life that their thoughts would be irrational, jumbled and chaotic. We likely think of them as desperate and bonkers. But now I can see how rational and level-headed he was. I can only conclude that he found clarity, certainty and a way out of his misery.

The post-mortem revealed that he had a pint of beer, presumably at The Pines pub where they found his van. In all the years we'd been together I'd never known him to go into a pub on his own, so I tried to imagine him sitting in the corner alone, sipping his pint of lager, contemplating his next move.

Paul imagined that Simon sat in his van, wrote the note and tucked it in the driver's sun visor. Often he'd tuck things up there in the pocket. On Thursdays, when I was doing my evening clinic, he'd tuck a comic and a Milkybar up there for Bee. When we talk about it now, it makes her feel special. She likes to think that she was the only person who would have known that's where he may have left a message. A comforting thought for her all these years later.

Reaching inside his uniform pocket, like reaching for a gun, Paul pulled out a slightly squashed, white, long envelope with *Mrs Burdall, Private & confidential* typed in the top right-hand corner. As I stared at the lines in the pine kitchen table, my body stiffened in anticipation. I must have worried Paul as he turned his head to one side, trying to look down in my eyes, and said, 'You okay? Shall I go so you can have some time?'

Very perceptive, I thought, as I said, 'Would you mind? I'm sorry, but…'

'Call me if you need anything. Anything,' he said, ducking to get in his small Panda car parked outside in Joyce's spot.

My heart throbbed as I took the phone off the hook. Closed the lounge curtains. Sat with one hand cupping my mouth, the other clutching my waist. I wanted this so badly. Yet I was fearful of its contents, a bit like waiting for exam results that could change your life.

With Grandpa's fine silver paperknife, I sliced through the envelope and pulled out a small scrap of folded lined notepaper, the everyday kind you get for a quid in a newspaper shop. The ones with a spiral metal edge. It started in blue biro. And as the ink ran out, he'd finished it in pencil. I turned it over. Kissed it several times before reading it. I wanted to relish and examine every word, every letter, every trace:

Dear Ginger and Bee,

What you must have realised by now is the fact that although we all love each other, I don't love myself. The effect of this is to destroy all the people around me with my negativity. I know that you are both worthy of far greater things, and to be around someone like me is soul-destroying. Everything I become involved with I can't see it through to any conclusion. I have no drive or energy to motivate myself.

Ginger, you are a classic case of a woman who loves too much. You are innocent; you try so hard to make things ok. My family and my friends I know are realising this is all about me and not for a second about you.

I have been a burden you have had to carry around with you all of the time. This is coming clearer and clearer to me. You will be a free spirit without me to fulfil yours and Bee's life together. I will never be able to change. I am only able to go a couple of months without things all feeling all too much. This won't be the case for you once I have gone.

195

You will be able to grieve, but this will end. You will meet another man who will love you in a way that I haven't been able to.

Say sorry to everyone for me.

There were no kisses. No signature.

Rubbing my eyes, I read it again and again and again. Traced his bold swirly symbols. Smelt the paper. Folded it as he had. Tried to imagine how he felt. Was he lucid? Resolute? Or afraid? As slow desolate tears spilt from my unblinking eyes, I ran my finger around and around a penny-sized, dark brown knot that looked like an eye on our pine kitchen table, expecting it to answer my questions. Admittedly, there were times in the last weeks of his life when I'd felt exhausted and drained. I had wondered sometimes how the future would look if his depression didn't lift. But I didn't agree that he held me back in my life – far from it. And I didn't see him as a burden. But that must have been how he saw himself.

Did it have to end like that? All on his own. And did he wait until I had gone away? The worst thought of all. Did he do it to set me free? Oh fuck. That would be the worst. Like a swarm of wasps, these thoughts swirled around my head. I couldn't catch them. Desperately, I wished to go back and change what had happened. But I couldn't.

I crawled up to my bed, although it was only 1 p.m., and phoned Jane, who was desperate to see the note and know what it said. We didn't have mobile phones or email back then. She asked if she could come and get it. I copied it out for myself and gave her the original. I'm not sure who read it. They copied it out for themselves and somehow it came back to me. I sometimes wonder what Simon would make of his letter being published for the world to see. In my heart, I believe he would be proud that I have told our tale, but I'm sure when he wrote it he had no idea where it would have ended up. And I've asked myself if it's okay to share such a private and personal letter. But by showing it, I hope it will help others.

That afternoon, with salty tears in my mouth and my chest full of lead, I set off southbound on the M4 to ask him if he'd done it to set me free. I didn't know how to get to the spot where he died using the back roads, but I remembered that the path between the forest led to a barrier that came out on the M4. Jane had pointed it out once when we passed by on the way to Swindon.

As I parked on the hard shoulder, juggernauts shook me in my little green Polo as they whizzed by at 80 mph, like shaking a dice onto a board of Snakes and Ladders. My thumping heart made my silver locket, with a photo of Simon and Bee inside it, sway against the cable knit on my Jaffa jumper. As I clung to the steering wheel for support, my palms slipped as I blubbered out loud to myself, 'What the fuck are you doing? You could get yourself killed. You stupid bitch.'

But I'd moved past rational thinking. All I could think about was getting to Simon to ask him questions. Nothing else mattered.

Between a fuel tanker and a caravan, I jumped out of the car. Throwing myself against the buckled barrier, I felt the metal cut into my palms as I hung on to catch my breath. Colours merged into browns and blacks. Dust billowed behind me like a horse had galloped away in a cowboy film as I slid down the track that parted the forest. Too scared to go in, I squinted into the darkness. Rows and rows of trees, their shadows like people, made me jump as every tree moved in the breeze, poised to attack me. Like a tramp's overcoat, the clouds covered the trees as I forced myself under the bracken. But fear found me and spoke in its crackled voice: 'Go home. There's nothing here. You've gone mad,' it said.

I shat myself as a pinecone the size of a tennis ball dropped on my shoulder like someone had thrown it at me.

With shaking legs, I scrambled and ran. Stumbling, I almost fell. Unable to swallow as my tongue stuck itself to the roof of my mouth, my Polo appeared like a matchbox toy car in the gap in the trees above the barrier. Clawing up the desiccated soil on my hands and knees, I clambered back up the bank. Flung myself in the car. Banged the dashboard with both fists. Rocked back and forth in my seat. Watched as snot dripped in strings on my steering wheel.

What an idiot. I could have got myself killed. Left Bee an orphan. And still, I had no answers to my recurrent questions: had he done it to set me free? Could I have saved him? Would he still be alive if I hadn't gone away?

I've since read much about suicide and one thing I learnt was that a suicidal person can truly believe they would make the world a better place by removing themselves from it. They are not being selfish; in fact, they believe the opposite. But they don't realise that they leave a well of pain for their loved ones that go on for years afterwards, which for some is unresolved.

Suicide is the most extreme action taken by desperate and vulnerable individuals. It is my belief that it is pure desperation that drives them to do it. Nothing else. And that's why we can't blame them, and more importantly, blame ourselves or others, for their death. It was their choice to end their life. No one made them do it!

Suicidal behaviour is quite frequent amongst people with BPD, and up to 4 to 19 per cent of them ultimately end their life by suicide. And 20 to 60 per cent of them attempt suicide in their lifetime, with the risk of suicide being ten to thirty times higher than the average population.

Only through my research for this book have I been able to understand why he took his own life. Although Jane and I still talk about it frequently and I talk to other friends about it, I still haven't talked to another 'survivor of bereavement by suicide' like me. And although I worked in the field of mental health and with other medical professionals, it's not a conversation I've had. I've worked it all out for myself.

CHAPTER 36

The night I received Simon's letter, I struggled to sleep and I drifted back to a holiday in Bude where, during the second year into our relationship, we spent a weekend with Simon's family and his cousins. It was one of those rare summer days when the sky framed a caramel beach with a canopy of aquamarine, and the sun reddened our shoulders and knees. Simon and I lazed around Grandma and Granddad's pastel pink beach hut with Jane and Joe, waited until the waves had calmed and it was safe to go in the sea. Unlike most people who had left the beach and were on their way out for their evening meal, we stayed until the sun had slipped halfway down the steal-streaked sky and the red flag had been swapped to green.

The sea had been unpredictable that day with waves as high as a house, and a riptide as quick as a Formula 1 driver at the start of a Grand Prix. There had been a fatality the week before, and two weeks before that. We skipped like six-year-olds down the beach, past the lifeguards practising their drills. They wore lemon-yellow polo shirts and wound safety ropes around their elbows. Excitement raced through me as Simon ran ahead with his white wooden board. He'd painted a red go-faster stripe down the centre and was determined to stay up for at least a minute – a long time in surfing terms.

Jane and I didn't want to get our hair wet, as later we were going out for a Chinese meal. We hadn't intended to swim as such, just prance about in the spray like the beach babes in *Baywatch*. We jumped higher and higher as the waves reached our necks. The weight of the water tugged our skimpy bikini tops down as we screamed to cover our pert little B cups, just in case anyone saw.

In the bubbling surf, Simon flew past. Flailed his arms to catch our attention as he teetered and caught a wave. For about twenty seconds, he stood upright before he disappeared into the water. I was puzzled as he walked out of the sea and back towards the beach huts. I called after him but the roar of the waves drowned my sound. Like jumping on pogo sticks, we bounced over the top of the waves, still trying to keep our hair dry. Joe chuckled at our frolicking frothy display. Being over six foot, his feet stayed firmly on the ground. Like a yoyo on a string, he pulled us back each time the rip plucked us out.

Colossal, mighty waves one after the other as the tide surged to the shore. *Bang. Bang. Bang.* And then *whoosh.* The rug of the ocean was wrenched from beneath my feet. I churned in acrobatic summersaults. Swimming wasn't my strength and I always avoided going out of my depth. Jane caught Joe's outstretched hand. But I was out of reach.

Like buckets of wet concrete, waves crashed over my head. Each time I caught my breath and tried to swim, another ton of water bashed me down. Saltwater rushed into my mouth, my nose, my throat. I gasped for breath. Tried to swim. An inch forward. Three feet back. Through the haze, I saw Simon wading down the beach. As he dived in the sea, his bricklayer biceps thrashed and crawled towards me.

Oh, thank god. He's going to save me, I thought as he swam behind me and clutched my crutch with his hand. And like a shot putter, he hurled me forward.

'Swim. For fuck's sake, swim. Fucking swim,' he roared again and again.

But I couldn't. My power had gone. The figures on the beach bleached out. The roar from the waves changed to a high-pitched ring. I sank. There was no white light they talk about when death calls you forward. No time to see my life flash before me. There was no choice. I glimpsed Simon swim past my left shoulder. *Has he given up? Lost his strength? Chosen his life over mine?* I thought, pulling one final gasp for air. Then joy. I felt the floor. My tiptoes clawed the sand like an excavator digs the earth. I was saved.

That night between the yellow nylon sheets in the old-fashioned bed and breakfast, I nestled on Simon's furry chest, counted his heartbeats under my fingertips. My limbs tingled with warmth and I sunk into his body with gratitude.

'I was about to let you go,' he whispered. 'I had to decide to save your life or mine, as I too had started to get pulled out by the riptide. So I used all my power to hurl you one more time. And thank god as I swam next to you, I saw you'd touched the ground. I saved your life, babe. I saved your life,' he whispered. I fell asleep with the warmth of his arms wrapped around me.

Each person who dies by suicide leaves behind an estimated six or more 'suicide survivors'. All are left struggling to understand what the hell happened. A suicide loss is like no other. Several circumstances set death by suicide apart and make the process of bereavement more challenging because it's sudden, sometimes violent, and mostly unexpected. We were all left with mixed emotions and unanswered questions that, for me, were self-punishing.

I've heard that those who have attempted suicide and lived to tell the tale say that the primary goal of suicide is not to end life but to end the pain. Apparently, their corrosive thinking reduces optimism, the hope of possibility, and increases their feelings of helplessness. The depressive illness itself makes it virtually impossible to hold on to any semblance of the pain going away. And this is what people don't understand. They are not being selfish. They have no space in their head for others, as they are consumed by misery. They are desperate to be free from their torment, just like someone at the end stage of cancer or motor neurone disease, for example.

Apart from the time in the kitchen on the Friday before he died when he pulled me by my belt loops and engulfed me in his powerful arms, I hadn't believed he had any love left for me.

As I smelt his coffee breath and felt his bristles when he buried his head in my shoulder, he murmured, 'I'm sorry, babe. You do know I love you, don't you?'

Pulling back, I saw a glimpse of his old self when he'd looked at me with a whisper of love in his eyes. I could see that he was genuinely sorry. If not for that moment, I would have believed that any love he'd had for me was long gone.

But I now know that it was the love for himself that was lost. And without self-love, how can you love another? To this day, I am grateful for that moment. At least I heard him apologise and say he loved me. Without that, and his letter, I would have found it even harder to come to terms with my loss.

CHAPTER 37

Almost a year after Simon died, foolishly I'd promised Bee a dog for her seventh birthday in October. I thought it would be good company for us both. We'd seen a small one we liked, a Patterdale Terrier. They came in different colours and were intelligent, confident and friendly. I found a breeder in Wales who had one puppy left. It was wirehaired and sandy-coloured.

Jane and I set off down the M4 with all three kids in the car. What should have been a three-hour journey from Jane's became a five-hour one. As the M5 came to a standstill, we remembered it was October half term. Hills became mountains and roads became tracks. I navigated with a large road map. It was normal for us to get lost during the last mile or so. It happened every time. All I had was a scrap of paper I'd written on in pencil from the breeder with directions.

'Are we nearly there yet?' whined the kids in turn.

'Turn left at the Pit Pony Sanctuary,' I said.

'Ponies, ponies. Can we stop?' squealed Bee and Jess.

'No. They've all gone on holiday to see their friends as it's half term,' Jane said.

'Now take the second left.'

A pub appeared on the grey horizon.

'If you get to the Farmers Arms, you've gone too far,' the note read.

'Oh my god. Why do we always do this?' said Jane, struggling to do a ten-point turn in a gateway.

Three times we went up this same road.

'Let's turn up here. Come on, there's no choice,' I urged. We were irritated and wound up by now. With no mobile phones back then, I could only rely on the notes I'd made. These generally got us lost at some point or other.

'Excuse me. We are looking for a Patterdale dog breeder,' I said to a large man with straw-like hair sticking out of a flat cap.

'Yep. That's us, me duck. It's my wife you want to see,' he said, pointing towards a run-down house and outbuildings.

The kids bounced out of the car as the door opened. The woman was far from friendly. She didn't even offer us a drink or ask how far we had come or anything. Plus, we were all parched and needed a wee.

The puppy scurried under the table into the corner of the room. The kids all scrambled underneath and tried to get him out. The man picked him up by the scruff of his neck. At thirteen weeks old, he was all that was left and was far from what I had expected. Too timed. A bit scruffy, but not in a good way. More like a rat. Not what I was used to. Our previous dogs, Otto and Lutz, were healthy with shiny coats. They couldn't wait to greet anyone and wiggled their bodies and wagged their tails like propellers. Not like this little thing that shook and wouldn't come out.

'Right then. You paying cash?' said the grey-haired woman.

'Yes. Okay,' I said, counting my £20 notes before handing them over.

I wasn't sure about taking the puppy. But things moved so quickly, there was no time for discussion. The man produced a cardboard box, picked him up and plonked him in. The woman gathered a carrier bag with food and feeding instructions. And then we were on our way. I had the dog in the box on my lap. It shook and puked all the way home.

Jane dropped us off at home, and once inside, we puffed up his new bed and he went straight to sleep. I was disappointed to say the least. Bee was delighted. Her dream had come true. Her own puppy and she didn't have to share him with anyone.

205

He looked sweet with a scruffy wiry coat, but he was terrified of anyone who came to the house, particularly men. He would scurry to the back of the kitchen and cower under the table and bark at everyone. Even snarl at times. He'd lunge at and bite the broom and hoover. I had to put him in another room when I did any cleaning. However, Bee would curl up on the sofa after school with him on her lap and talk to him when I wasn't there. He got me out twice a day which was good for me, rain or shine.

He was the worst dog I've ever had, everyone said so. He nipped at people's ankles, and barked and wrestled with anything with wheels, including the dustbin. Ran off and wouldn't come back. I'd chase him and just as he was at arm's length he'd dart off again. Several years later when we got another puppy, I gave him to my new mother-in-law whose own dog had died. She fed him beef stew and dumplings, fattened him up so much that he could barely walk.

On the plus side, Bee loved him. She was good with him and he was good for her. Fizzy, she named him, because he behaved like a firework and kept going off like a rocket.

As he sat on the floor under the table when he wouldn't come out, she'd coax him with Bonios and titbits until gradually he'd sit in her lap. She carried him around, even put him in her toy pram and pushed him up the street to show him off. And being so small, he was easy to pick up and put in the car.

I encouraged Bee to be responsible for feeding him and ensuring his water was topped up. At the weekends he gave us a purpose, like we were a family again. We got into a habit of walking along the Thames in Cookham to a riverside pub. I'd have half a lager, she'd have a Coke, and Fizzy would share her pork scratchings. We would bath him together and laugh at how rat-like he looked when all his fur was wet.

Fizzy has become her companion, I thought one day when I peeped in the lounge and saw her talking to him on her lap watching *Blue Peter*. Simon would have been contented to see us moving on and to see me enjoying another dog.

CHAPTER 38

Despite being stuck in my grief, I'd noticed a shift after reading Simon's letter and going to the woods. His words *My family and my friends are now are realising that this is all about me and not for a second about you* went round and round in my head, giving me comfort, like he'd spoken to me. Reassured me that I wasn't to blame.

One Monday lunchtime during the September ten months after Simon died, Finn, the counsellor at work, peeped his head around my door and said, 'How you doing, you free?'

I'd just finished my diabetic clinic, so I moved patients my notes off the patient's chair and invited him to sit down. Closing the door behind him, I caught a whiff of cheesy feet. I'd been examining feet all morning as part of my assessment, so I prayed he didn't think it was me who smelt.

'How are you?' he said in his sympathetic southern Irish accent.

'Glad to be busy and distracted, you know,' I said, pretending I was okay.

Being a counsellor, however, he saw straight through me.

Even though he was a familiar face in the surgery and I referred patients to him regularly, we'd only ever talked on a professional level or exchanged small talk in the kitchen over coffee.

'Come on. Tell me the truth. Think of me as a friend,' he said, dipping his head to meet my eyes.

Letting out a deep sigh and slumping in my chair, I began to speak.

'Well, I expect you've heard that my husband killed himself in the local woods? It's getting on for a year now. And to be honest, I still feel shit and I can't see how I will ever feel normal again,' I said, spewing out my tale, trying hard not to cry.

Nodding in all the right places, he didn't say a thing until I dabbed at my tears.

'For sure, you're gonna feel crap. But you'll be fine. You will. This is all normal,' he said, placing his ivory and recently manicured hand over mine as he leant across my desk. I caught a lemony-lavender floral scent that pleased my senses.

His voice alone soothed me. I'd heard flattering reports about him, particularly from the female patients. Plus, a couple of the receptionists fancied him and fought to type his letters after the clinic; I understood why now.

His blue-black hair, snowy skin, yellowish-green eyes and the way he looked at me were charming. And his wit amused me. However, I only ever saw him as a bit square in his slim plain navy suit. Each week he wore a different coloured plain pastel shirt with the same thin plain tie, like they'd all been bought as a batch from Marks and Spencer. My impression was that he was a square, middle-aged family man with lots of children. From that, I aged him in his mid to late forties. I later found out he was three years my junior.

Placing his cool hand over mine and leaving it there until I shifted in my chair and felt uncomfortable, I swiftly changed the subject to him and asked, 'What about you? I know you're married, have loads of children and drive a big black people carrier to ferry them all around. I see you in the car park sometimes.'

He went on to tell me that his wife had had an affair. She'd moved out around the same time as Simon had died and left him with their four children. Anger and sorrow showed in his eyes as he looked down at his thin gold wedding band and wrung his hands together. He stood up and said, 'I'd better let you get on. I'll catch you next week.'

I'd been touched by his genuine concern and felt that we'd connected, even though it was to share our grief.

From then on, each Monday when he was at the surgery, he'd pop into my room during his lunch break and eat his cheese and pickle sandwich on white bread.

After a few weeks, he asked me out for dinner. Not knowing any babysitters who'd come for only a few hours, I asked him to come to me for supper instead. I regretted it as soon as I said it, as I couldn't decide what to do with Bee as Friday night loomed. I didn't want her in the house when a strange man came visiting. I wanted to keep that separate. I heard of women introducing their kids to lots of different men. I didn't want to unsettle her further. Fortunately, my neighbours a few doors down, Matt and Mandy, whose children Bee had become friends with, offered to have Bee for a sleepover. When I told them about Finn, they teased me about having a first date. But it wasn't a date. I didn't even fancy him. I reinforced the message that we were work colleagues. Nothing more.

I burnt sandalwood incense and placed tea lights on the windowsills. Cleaned the house from top to bottom. Cooked a small tarragon chicken to go with a Caesar salad and homemade garlic bread. Thought that was a safe choice, not knowing his taste. I laid the table with my best white and silver-rimmed wedding china, tall-stemmed wine glasses and bone-handled cutlery. A bit over the top as I look back, but I liked the table to look nice. I chose background chill-out tunes to create an atmosphere. It was a long time since I'd cooked for anyone apart from Bee.

Many a time before Simon was ill, we'd plough through Delia Smith and Sophie Griggson's cookbooks, regularly made tarragon and lemon chicken, dauphinoise potatoes followed by bread-and-butter pudding made with soft rolls, Simon's favourites. A hobby we shared in the good times.

Marvin Gaye sang 'Let's Get It On' through the CD player in the corner of the kitchen. For a moment, I was taken back to the first time Simon and I made love in the hotel in Bath. He'd taped Marvin Gaye's album and bought his cassette player to play it to me. Tipsy on one bottle of Muscadet wine, he'd dimmed the lights, held my waist as we smooched on the spot losing ourselves in each other's eyes. I can remember the intensity of that tingly feeling. As I'd looked up at him with my arms around his shoulders, I was in heaven and couldn't believe he felt the same way about me.

Barely blinking, we went round and round on the spot like a long-playing record to 'We're all sensitive people,' singing the words close to my ear to ensure I heard. Our clothes dropped to the floor. Eyes locked like magnets. Between the crisp white sheets, he caressed my cheeks, my eyelids, my nose. Kissed my fingers, my breasts, the insides of my legs. All the time he looked back to see I was okay. Despite just turning twenty, he knew what to do. Took his time. Waited until I was ready. Slickly, he slipped himself inside me, moving with the rhythm of elfin waves at a shallow tide. I thought I heard him say 'I love you' when he came, his head buried in my neck. Entwined in a figure of eight, we held each other until we slept. We woke in the same position and continued to coo and smooch like we'd been cast in a love movie like Clark Gabel and Scarlett O'Hara in that famous scene from *Gone With the Wind*.

Bringing a strange man into the house felt disloyal. But nothing was going to happen, I told myself. We were just two lost souls in need of company. I imagined what Simon would be thinking if he looked down on me: At least this bloke appears gentle and genuine, I thought, as I hurried down the hall as I heard the door knock.

Clutching gifts, Finn handed me a large packet of Minstrels for Bee, a bunch of yellow roses and two bottles of wine.

'Wow. You look grand,' he said, kissing me on both cheeks.

Admittedly, I'd made a big effort. Bought a new white V-necked ribbed jumper to go with my black jeans. Wore the large turquoise stone pendant Simon bought me back from Glastonbury the first year he went. I almost felt like a woman again.

I couldn't say the same for him in his tweed jacket, chocolate-brown cords and crinkly brown lace-ups that were the same as Dad's. I preferred him in his work suit; he'd looked sharp. I couldn't place his fruity and floral scent. I didn't dislike it, but it wasn't something Simon would have worn.

'I didn't know what you liked, so I bought both,' he said, waving a bottle of Merlot and Chardonnay in my face.

'Thank you. That's so generous. I prefer white,' I said, smelling the roses. I handed him the bottle opener as I rummaged for the black and yellow vase Simon had made at one of his pottery classes.

As the wine flowed, we exchanged biographies. He'd started his career as a psychiatric nurse in Ireland, and had met his wife during their training. She was a pharmacist who he described as the one who wore the trousers. They had four children, two of each; the youngest had not long turned four. She'd gone off with the builder who'd extended their house. Finn wanted to punch the bloke's lights out, but he was bigger than him. Being a passive man, he said he wouldn't stoop to that level. The children had stayed in the family home with him.

After a bottle of wine each, far more than I usually drank, I asked him if he wanted to stay the night or take a taxi home. He jumped at the chance to stay over. And as the evening hotted up, he removed his jacket, rolled up his sleeves and undid three of his shirt buttons to expose a tuft of chest hair. In a Pierce Brosnan kind of way with slicked-back hair, tall and slim, he appeared a smidge more handsome. Plus, his seductive accent and alluring wit pushed him up into the bracket of attractiveness.

Noticing that I was viewing him differently, I started to imagine him in a sexy way. *The wine must have opened channels in my brain that have been closed for some time*, I thought, sitting on the loo with the room spinning a bit. *Do you fancy him, Ginger? Do you?* I asked myself three times. But he wasn't my type. He was too refined. Delicate. Usually, I went for edgy, stylish, creative men. I had to connect with them and want to shag their brains out.

Strolling back into the kitchen, finding him looking through my CD collection and deciding that I did fancy him a bit, I changed the music to a dance compilation. I was taken aback when Finn leapt up from the table and twirled me up and down the kitchen like we were barn dancing. Feeling dizzy, I had to stop and straighten my top and tried to appear less pissed than I was. I couldn't keep up with his drinking. He'd had three vodka and Red Bulls to my one.

He'd planned to get a taxi home, but in the early hours I ended up showing him to the spare room where I had a king-size bed pushed against the wall as it was too big for the room. After cleaning my teeth, I went back to say good night and was gobsmacked to find him lying naked with the lights full on and the duvet pushed down towards his waist. Lying back with his hands behind his head in a not-so-cool Pierce Brosnan pose, his lily-white skin matched the pasty pillows. A few wiry black hairs walked towards his naval like daddy longlegs. Wiggling his eyebrows and winking, he patted the bed next to him, and in his soothing, seductive voice said, 'You getting in then?'

Fucking cheek, I thought. Yet despite a lack of foreplay my clothes peeled themselves off, and before I started seeing two of him I'd turned out the main light, and as ladylike as I could I climbed over him, being careful to avoid his gusset and not to tread on his legs.

I hadn't had a good shag for months. One of the last times was when Simon was wild and Sid was in play. Four months before he died when I was living at Phil's, I'd gone

213

to ask Simon to sign the estate agent's papers agreeing to put the house on the market. We were in the lounge, sat next to each other on our low contemporary black leather sofa. He was unpredictable. One-minute laughing and joking, the next threatening me.

'Do you fancy a shag?' he'd said, slapping my thigh.

I gasped out loud.

'What? Are you serious?' I quizzed.

We'd practically been hating each other and fighting each time we met.

'Come on. I know you wannit,' he said with a smirk.

The next thing I knew we were ripping each other's clothes off like we were having a steamy affair. I was slightly scared because this wasn't Simon's usual style of lovemaking. Yet we were hungry for each other. I'd missed him. Wanted him. And him me. Within seconds I was on top in that familiar position we both preferred. Straight in. Like driving home. I knew the way. Knew his body as well as my own. My hands gripped his strong tanned biceps. I smelt that clean, soapy space I loved in the middle of his soft hairy chest. I kissed and gripped his warm bald head. Safe in his strength as he gripped my butt. I knew his rhythm. His rhyme. Knew what he liked me to do to enhance his joy. Knew the sound of his tune when he was about to come. Like I'd come home, I buried my head in his neck. Smelt that familiar odour that I loved. And when he came, he breathed, 'I love you, babe.'

Lying in his arms, I watched as he stared up at the ceiling. Stroking his chest, I could feel his heart slowing and sensed that perhaps we might be okay. The next minute, he'd leapt up and shredded the papers. Then ordered me out of the house.

And the final time we tried to make love was when he was depressed a few weeks before he died. It hadn't been good. I'd instigated it, but he had nothing left to give and apologised. I said I understood, but I hadn't. I felt hurt and rejected.

After Simon died, I craved the intimacy you feel when you have sex with someone familiar. That feeling afterwards when you are in love and your bodies fill with warmth and your limbs lay heavy over each other like you've both taken the same drug. But now, almost a year after Simon died, I lay flat on my back in my guest bed, arms by my sides, legs tightly shut. Thank god I wasn't in my marital bed; I would have felt unfaithful. That sacred space in our antique high oak bed, with Bee's cartoon stickers on the headboard, represented trust, faith and family. An intimate place where married couples make love, make babies if they're lucky and then become a family.

I'd forgotten how to behave and felt like a virgin in a period drama, where the lady is a vessel for her husband's pleasure. I vaguely remember Finn kissing me as he climbed on board. He was a good kisser, but it didn't last long before he fumbled in his trouser pocket for a condom. I hadn't used condoms since I was sixteen with my first boyfriend. I was glad though, as I was terrified of HIV, which had only been around for ten years back then. I couldn't risk putting Bee through losing another parent.

Finn was gentle and respectful. Had the rhythm of a professional racehorse who usually came in last. It was good to feel him inside me and pull his butt towards me. But it wasn't deep enough. And I only knew he'd come because he rolled off as quickly as he jumped on, like falling off at the last hurdle. Or he fell off in a drunken stupor, more like.

It wasn't until the morning that I remembered what had happened. I leapt up, got dressed, cleaned my teeth. Found him as cool as a cucumber in the kitchen like nothing had happened, making himself tea and toast. By 10 a.m., he'd gone to collect his kids.

That night I reflected, and I felt lonelier than before. That was not my memory of making love. Had I just lost a bit more of Simon in letting a stranger play where only Simon had played for twenty years? Finn didn't even hold me. Caress me. Kiss me for very long. I was craving comfort as well as sex, and was desperate to have the familiar feet at the end of my bed when I woke.

Finn was safe. Kind. Amusing. We were both nurses, counsellors, caring for others. He had an abundance of empathy and gave me time. Our situations were similar. We'd both been dumped. Despite our circumstances being different, the losses we experienced were similar. We shared the loss of status, home, friends, time with children, extended family. Without warning, something familiar and trusted had been ripped away from us both. We had both experienced pain and a shift in our identities. Our hearts were broken. The sensation felt physical. No analgesia could relieve that pain. We connected on this level. We were both seeking to fill a void and found comfort in each other around the same time.

I believe that recovery from divorce may be worse than being bereaved. I'm able to talk about Simon with pride, love and respect. Have his photo in a prominent place on the mantelpiece. Reminisce with those who loved him. Most divorces are acrimonious; few end with friendship. Most photos get shredded, and spouses are spoken about with acid tongues and resentment.

I asked my friend Rose, one of the receptionists, if Finn was in on Monday morning; she checked his list and said he had no clients for an hour. I crept across the corridor in my lunch break, as he hadn't come over to my side as he had been previously. I found him in one of the GP's rooms across the other side of the building. I refreshed my orange scandal lipstick; checked there was none on my teeth. My heart fluttered a little as I felt nervous about seeing him. I checked no one was in the corridor. Gently knocked and pushed the door inwards. His head was bowed as he wrote up his notes.

'Hey. You okay?' I said, crossing my legs as I sat in his patient's chair.

'Busy,' he said, barely looking up. My jaw tightened. *Oh no. This is embarrassing*, I thought. It felt like he didn't want me there. He put his narrow-tipped navy ink pen down, leant back in the chair, ran his hand through his hair, then covered his eyes with his hand like he was going to say something profound, but didn't. He leant forward, picked his pen back up, resumed writing. His body language spoke volumes.

'I'll let you get on then,' I said. 'You're busy.'

I was confused and felt rejected. *Is that it then?* I thought. I didn't want a relationship as such, but I expected a bit more familiarity. It annoyed me that he could dismiss me like I was one of the receptionists telling him his next client was there. But I couldn't get him out of my head, which was ridiculous. He had given me a bit of what I needed. He'd listened to me. Flattered me. Made me feel alive again.

A couple of weeks later he popped his head round my door and said, 'How's the craic?'

What he meant was, *Do you fancy getting together again?* And of course I did. I was needy. Grateful. We slipped into a routine where after supper, wine and too many vodkas and Red Bulls, we danced around my kitchen to 'Mambo No. 5' by Lou Bega, then we shagged most Friday nights.

He made it clear from the start that there was nothing in it for him and even encouraged me to go out with other blokes. That was the first time I'd heard of the term fuck buddy. It describes a slag, if you ask me, but it appeared to be all the rage and still is. Internet dating was starting up.

But one was perceived as being a bit of a loser if you weren't able to find a partner in the normal way. Not like today where it appears to be the *only* way of meeting someone. Each time I'd hoped the shag would last a bit longer. But it was the same each time, missionary position, me on my back, him on top.

With fondness, I look back and laugh to myself. Laugh, because we did have fun. Occasionally we went out dancing, but most of the action was on my black and white tiled kitchen floor. For many months, I hoped it might be going somewhere. But we had nothing in common. We were not suited. He was looking for a nice Irish Catholic lass, and I, a lively, creative arty type. But most of all we both craved to be a couple and to be loved again.

Is this what Simon meant in his letter when he said *You will meet another man who will love you in a way that I haven't been able to?*

I hope that's not it, I thought as I read it again.

And although Simon hadn't shown me much love when he was ill, I was comforted by all the love he had given me over the years.

CHAPTER 39

The first anniversary of Simon's death, 23 November 1999, loomed upon us like Concord coming into land. Jane and I talked about what we'd do on the day. After deliberating going to the woods or driving down to Bantham Beach, neither of us had the energy for either. In the end, Bee and I went down to Swindon. Brenda, Michael and Lizzy stayed at home. After consuming too many gins and crying much of the evening before, I woke with a dreadful hangover. And when I walked into Jane and Joe's bedroom the next morning, they were sat up in bed as normal, drinking a cup of tea. Throwing me a pillow, Joe moved his legs out of the way to let me in the bed. Our normal position when we had stayed there was them up one end, Simon and I up the other. It was our early morning adult time before the kids woke up and climbed in as well.

'You okay?' I asked, lifting the quilt and climbing in.

They nodded.

'You okay?' asked Jane.

'I think so. Do you think this is it now then? Like, we are gonna be okay?' I responded.

'Who knows, darling. Who knows,' Jane said, stroking my feet.

'Joey, do you want to go and make me and Ginger a cup of tea please, darling?'

'If I must,' he said, scratching his head and reluctantly getting out of bed.

Once he was downstairs, I jumped in his warm spot and cuddled up to Jane. With her arm around me, she said, 'I've got an idea. How about we have a girlie night out for your birthday. Go clubbing like we used to?'

'What, for my fortieth?' I questioned.

'Of course your bloody fortieth,' she said, pulling me close.

I sat back and looked at her, asking, 'Are you sure?'

'Why not? It would cheer us up. And Simon would have liked that. Seeing he missed his own fucking fortieth birthday,' she said with a smirk.

Simon would have been forty in March that year. If things had been normal we might have had a party at home. We'd talked about it when he was depressed between his manias; I'd tried to cheer him up by talking about the music we'd play and who we'd invite. And becoming forty is a significant milestone in one's life, I believe, as usually one is settled, you've found a partner, had a family, bought your house, built a career. And one certainly shouldn't be dead at forty!

Having her permission and beginning to believe that my grief was behind me, I went to town. Invited another four close friends. Told them all to bling it up, like they were going to a ball.

Preparing the house for their arrival, I placed red gerberas on the kitchen table and on the sideboard. Washed our crystal wedding flutes ready for bubbles. Filled my essential oil burner with geranium and rosemary, and my daisy design ceramic bowls full of nibbles. I allowed myself three hours to get ready to include a long soak in the bath.

I'd been to the beautician and treated myself to a manicure and tan, and bought myself a posh frock. When I eventually emerged, the transformation took me by surprise. My honey gloss lips were plump. My skin was caramel, and my lashes were long and lush. A tingle of anticipation fluttered in my tummy as I tried on my gown, buckled my sequined stilettos and searched for a back to my topaz vintage dandling earrings.

Catching myself in the mirror with a flirty grin like my dad, I remembered seeing a photo Mum showed me that she kept in one of her many diaries. It was taken at Dad's work

Christmas do at The Dorchester in London. Mum wore a full-length black velvet off-the-shoulder ball gown; her neck was draped in pearls that rested on her ample bosom. The chain of her black patent clutch bag swirled across the white linen tablecloth amongst the champagne flutes as she leant against Dad, who posed like Clark Gable. *How lucky they've been in their forty-three-year marriage*, I thought. The only trauma they'd ever faced was me and my drama.

Jane was the first to arrive with more flowers and bubbles. In her usual glamorous style, she wore a slinky black dress with a diamante collar. Her pale pink-fuchsia lips and naturally long eyelashes made her look as stunning as always.

'Fuckin' 'ell. You've gone to town. Let me look at you,' she said, inspecting me like I was an art exhibit in a museum. 'You've even had a fake tan. And I love the pixie hair cut, darling. It makes you look young again!' she said, tweaking the hair around my cheek.

'Promise me I don't look like an Oompa-Loompa from *Charlie and the Chocolate Factory*, or a Jaffa orange?' I said, rubbing a small streak on my arm.

I was just about to return the compliment when the knocker went again.

'Oh my god. Have I come to the right the house?' shrieked Theresa as she looked me up and down like a nodding dog.

'You look bloody gorgeous, gal. Good on ya!' she assured me.

I fluttered my new fake lashes like Gertrude the cow on the *Magic Roundabout*.

'Omg. You've even got fake lashes.'

'I'm not sure though. Do you think I've overcooked it? I feel like a drag queen,' I said, stroking the velvet fabric downwards on my thighs.

'You look perfect, love. Absolutely gorge,' she further reassured me.

Her gold ruched sequined bodycon mini dress rubbed on my bare arms as she pulled me into a bear hug. The familiar smell of her Eternity perfume always reassured me.

Theresa, known as Trees, was Baxter's wife, one of Simon's best bricklayer friends. She was a bit of an Essex girl compared to my other friends and had always been ahead of fashion like most hairdressers were. She was the first person I knew to have a fake tan, false nails and lashes.

Diana came next, a recently qualified district nurse who was originally Jane's friend, but we had become friends as we went on holidays together as couples. She too shook her head in disbelief as she gawped at me.

'Blimey, Ginger, I'd have walked past you in the street. You look exceptional.'

'Good exceptional. Or bad exceptional?' I quizzed, starting to feel a fool.

'Good, of course. Come on, let's get the drink going,' she declared, following me to the kitchen to join the others.

Celeste and Pauline, my oldest friends, were last to arrive.

'Right, girls, we need to down this one as the taxi will be here in a mo,' announced Trees, sharing the last drops of bubbles in each glass.

'Let's do a toast. Here's to Ginger. Happy fortieth birthday, darlin', and let's hope next year will be a better one.'

Diana put her arm around Jane's shoulder and said, 'And to you too, Jane.'

Chinking glasses, I noticed Jane take a big breath in, then she excused herself to the bathroom. I chased her up the stairs, and as she touched up her lips, I asked, 'Are you okay?'

'Yeah, course I am. It's just that it's the first time I've been out properly since Simon died. I feel a bit guilty if I'm honest.'

'What do you mean, guilty?'

'You know. Guilty for having a good time.'

That hadn't occurred to me. I was desperate to have a good time and feel like my old self.

As the front door banged downstairs, it stopped us in our tracks and Trees shouted up, 'Come on, you two, the taxi's here.' Scurrying like ants, we pouted our lips and flicked our hair in the hall mirror. I grabbed the keys and locked the door. I was gobsmacked as I turned around and squealed. Blocking the street sat a white limousine. As they beamed back at me with their glasses raised, Jane gave me a wink; she'd ordered it as a surprise.

Guiding me down the pavement towards the open double doors, the chauffeur steadied me by my elbow. I hadn't walked in these shoes before, or worn a full-length dress since my wedding. It wasn't easy. Shuffling like a Geisha girl, I could barely part my legs to climb in and I had to hitch up my dress to my knees in a most unladylike fashion. The limo smelt of Christmas – cedar and cinnamon. Peacock-blue neon lights the same colour as my dress sparkled in the mosaic-mirrored cocktail cabinet. Navy velvet walls and a mirrored ceiling made the inside look twice the size. Unbelievable. I felt like Cinderella going to the ball. And like hens in a coup, we clucked and squawked all the way there.

Huddling around the bar and larking about, Trees passed me a vodka and Red Bull and ordered me to 'Get this down your neck, gal.'

So when 'Mambo No 5' came on, I was off, dragging Celeste, Pauline and Trees with me.

Whooping to myself in my head, I felt groovy. Gyrating in time to the music, and in the usual girl circle, we danced around our diamanté clutch bags. Hijacking my brain cells, the music pumped itself inside the seams of my gown, thrusting my arms high in the air like you see at a rave.

But when I opened my eyes, I was on my own and felt a bit of a twat. Unsteady on my feet, I stumbled back to the bar to find the girls all huddled around Jane.

'Jane. Jane. Come on. Come and dance. It's my birthday. I'm fucking forty. Trees, come on, love. You come and dance with me,' I slurred.

Even in my drunkenness I could read the situation. They didn't want to dance. But I hadn't gone to all this trouble for nothing. I wasn't going to waste it on more fucking grieving. *Not tonight, anyway,* I thought as I stumbled against a few people at the bar.

'Come on,' I shouted over the music to Jane. 'It's our song, Gloria Gaynor, "I Will Survive".'

Like pulling material that was stuck under a table leg, I dragged Jane with me onto the dance floor. We'd always danced together at clubs. Jane would thrust her arms and hips back and forwards in a sexual way, and I would twirl my arms and snake my hips in an equally sexual way. It wasn't uncommon for us to attract attention, particularly from black guys who we both had a penchant for. Simon and Joe liked to watch with amusement.

Trees tried to liven everyone up by using her hairbrush as a microphone, making us all mime to the song.

Pulling Jane close, I shouted in her ear, 'We will survive. We're okay now, aren't we? I'm not doing this grieving shit anymore. I've had enough.'

She humoured me with a nod, as the music was so loud we couldn't hear each other speak anyway.

I twisted and twirled like an uncoiling rope, reeling and stretching as far as my dress would allow as Gloria sang to me. She told me it was going to be okay.

A squeeze around my waist jolted me out of my trance. I turned around and there was Vernon, a super cool, well-built black guy I had known before I met Simon. His hands curled around my frame as I toppled like a weakly spun spinning top into his chest. Wearing a short sleeved Hawaiian shirt and black jeans, he smelt of Paco Rabanne, a citrus aromatic scent, one of Simon's faves.

Without saying a word, I coiled, twisted, whirled and weaved. And like a peacock attracting its mate, I spread my iridescent tail feathers and made a rattling noise. As he took my weight in his toned gym forearms, I melted into his arms.

Just as I was getting in the groove, I felt a tight squeeze on my elbow that startled me back into the room. Diana was telling me it was time to go. *But I've only just got going*, I thought as Vernon spun me around. Lifting my palms upwards, shaking my head, I signalled to Vernon that our time was up. He held me for a while and whispered, 'Call me,' tucking his business card down my top!

Staggering back to the bar, the girls all looked like they'd had a hard day at the office.

'What's going on then, girls?' I slurred above the music to Jane and Diana who had their backs to me. 'The night's only just begun,' I said.

Before they even had the chance to answer, Trees, Pauline and Celeste ushered me to the toilets. Stumbling against the wet sink, I caught sight of myself in the mirror. One of my lashes had lifted on the inside of my eyelid, making me look cross-eyed, and a white streak had appeared on my previously sun-kissed face. As I tried to reattach the lash, I could see the girls in the mirror making faces at each other, as if to say, *What are we going to do with her?*

'Right. What's going on then?' I said, propping myself against the grey, fake marble vanity unit.

Trees explained that Jane wasn't having a good time.

Mortified, I pulled myself up straight like a soldier about to go on parade and said, 'We can't have that. She's my One

Brain (our knick-name for each other). And what would Simon say?' I thought.

Even in my pissed state, I felt blameworthy and couldn't bear it when Jane and I were out of kilter. Rarely it happened, but when it did I felt it profoundly. And like me, she could usually rise to any public occasion, however bad she felt. *This is big shit*, I thought as I barged past them and confronted Jane.

'What's going on? Don't you like the music? Come and dance. It will make you feel better. Come on,' I pleaded, tugging her sleeve.

She stared past me. Her arms folded tight across her chest. As I turned towards the bar to order another drink, I felt Diana grip my wrist.

'The taxi's here, Ginger,' she insisted.

The taxi's here. Fuckinell. That's the end of my party then, I thought as Whitney Houston's 'I Wanna Dance with Somebody' banged from the speakers.

'Okay. Okay. I'm coming. Give me a minute,' I answered back.

Stroking the velvet of my dress down both my thighs, I clutched my bag under my arm and in a bit of a strop, I strutted like a bridezilla walking down the aisle towards the exit. The others fell in line behind me like they were my bridesmaids. Tripping out of the door almost falling flat on my face, two burly doormen caught me. The girls were falling about laughing, but it broke the tension and when we got in the taxi everyone chatted as though nothing had happened. And by the time we got home, we were chilled. Or so I thought.

Kicking my shoes off in the hall, I shouted instructions to the girls.

'Trees, you get the glasses and shampoo out of the fridge. Pauline, you top up the nibbles. Celeste, you choose some music. I've got to get out of this dress.'

Barefoot, I scrambled up the stairs to my bedroom. Unzipped my dress. As I hung it back under its designer bag, I stretched out the creases and picked at a couple of stains with my chipped false nail. I noticed a small rip under the arm where the green lining had come away and the velvet had frayed. I could see the seams inside. The fibres were flat and the space was dark. A bit like the state of my mind.

Musing about it as I have since, I can't believe the effort I went to. False nails. False lashes. Fake tan. A ball gown to go to a club in town. What a sham. All that effort for a few moments of joy where I was able to lose myself in Gloria's melody of 'I Will Survive' and escape from the hymn of woe.

Pulling on my old trackies and tugging a polo neck over my head, I caught one of my eyelashes with my nail. It tore right off. *A drag queen transitioning back to a young widow*, I thought as I stared in the mirror. Like separating a butterfly's wing, I pulled the other one-off. Wrapped them both in tissue and flushed them down the loo and headed down the stairs.

Trees, Celeste and Pauline were huddled closely together on the sofa, their heads in one of our many photo albums. Trees pointed to her three boys wrestling with Simon on the floor one Christmas.

I was still pretty pissed and hadn't initially noticed that Jane and Diana weren't around.

'Where's Jane?' I asked the girls.

'I think she's having a fag outside with Di,' said Trees, not taking her eyes off the photos.

'What? Outside. But it is freezing.'

Oh shit, I thought. This is so unlike Jane. She's usually the Queen Bee buzzing around others making sure their drinks and bellies are topped up, putting others needs before her own.

Grabbing a coat and blanket off the rocking chair, I met Diana coming back in through the patio door.

'What's going on? Is Jane okay?' I asked.

'Not really. She wants to be close to Simon. She believes he's out there somewhere,' she said, rolling her eyes. 'I've tried to get her to come in, but she won't.'

'Is she down the bottom of the garden then?' I queried.

'Yes, darling,' she said, rubbing her arms as she shivered.

When Simon first died and the wind blew, all the wind chimes that hung from the apple tree above the mosaic garden swayed. I believed Simon's breath had moved them. Even when it was a still day, as soon as I walked outside, a breeze would come and make music as the chimes tinkled together. Jane and I clung to that idea. We believed he was talking to us.

At first, I couldn't see her. I switched on the fairy lights to light up the tree. Hunched like an armadillo, wearing Simon's old donkey jacket, she was sat on the edge of the mosaic garden. With one hand she stroked the shards of willow pattern tiles and flicked her ash at the base of the tree with the other. She was never a smoker. Neither of us were. But after Simon's death, and after a drink, we would share a fag. Usually ponsed from a proper smoker.

'Oh, darling, you shouldn't be out here, you'll perish,' I said, throwing the blanket over her shoulders.

As I crouched close to her, she didn't respond. Stretching my arm over her shoulder, I smelt her familiar fresh floral sunflower scent. Then the sun and moon, blue pottery chimes, tinkled above our heads.

'He's here. Listen. He's with us. Watching us. Saying, "What the fuck are you two doing sat out there freezing their tits off?"' I said with lightness in my voice.

'Do you think he knows it's your birthday?' Jane said, leaning into me.

228

'Maybe he's wishing me happy birthday, as he missed his fucking birthday, didn't he? Wanker,' I answered.

We sniggered and rocked with our heads locked together and stared at the mosaic snake lit up by the fairy lights.

This was the first time Jane allowed me to comfort her. We'd comforted each other along the way, and I believed I needed her more than she needed me. Throughout Simon's illness, she'd been there for me, despite her mixed loyalties. She tried to convince and reassure me that he wasn't as crazy as I thought he was. Many a time she'd smooth things out between us and acted as the adjudicator. And when he died she took on the role of intermediary, liaising between all parties, making her enquiries behind the scenes, piecing things together for herself. As well as supporting Brenda, Michael, Lizzy, Bee and me and Joe and the kids, just like Brenda, she put others needs before her own. I'd leant heavily on her, and that night, after a few drinks, she appeared not to be able to take on the weight anymore.

'Do you think tonight was a mistake?' I asked, taking a drag from Jane's fag.

'I don't know. I thought I was ready, thought I'd be able to muster the energy, but I felt guilty that we were having a good time, like he should have been with us having a good time too. I'm sorry it all turned out a bit shit for you, darling,' she responded.

'At least I got to see all my special friends and dress up like a tranny and make a twat of myself,' I said as our teeth chattered and our bodies shook.

'Come on. Let's go in. I'll make us all a whisky coffee like Simon used too,' I beckoned.

Welcoming us back in, the girls wrapped Jane up with a blanket and hot water bottle, whilst I made Irish coffee in tall glasses. Sitting around the kitchen table, we cupped our drinks. Trying to cheer us up, one by one, the girls talked about the first time they met Simon. They all said the same, that his wide American-style smile lit up the room, and how

229

he made them laugh. After a few more tears, the girls tucked us both into my bed like a pair of grieving twins. And that's what we'd become. We grieved together. Talked on the phone for hours most days, trying to make sense of it all. But we never did. Not until now – that is, twenty plus years later.

CHAPTER 40

Approaching our second Christmas, 1999, I reflected on what a strange old year it had been. I'd been wearing my comfortable widow bra for several months, and despite Fizzy the dog being a pain in the arse, he comforted us and made Bee laugh. I'd become fond of my regular fuck friend Finn.

We were at the end of the autumn school term and we'd established a good routine. My alarm clock vibrated me awake at 7.00 a.m. I would snooze it twice and surface by 7.15 a.m. Making myself a cup of tea, I'd scoff lime marmalade toast on the move, I'd shower and do my make up sat at our antique, marble-topped washstand in our bedroom, dress for work, give Bee her first nudge by 7.45, and allow her to unravel. Then give her a final call at 8 a.m. Once dressed, Bee sat between my legs on the floor to brush her beautiful ginger hair. It was almost waist length, and it was radiant and glossy. Most days she would make a meal of choosing hair bobbles before deciding on a style: bunches, French plait or plain ponytail.

It reminded me of brushing Nanny's fine silver hair after Mum and I had bathed her on a Sunday morning. Once she'd sunk back into her fresh brushed cotton sheets, she'd let me put her silver strands into plaits to dry. She insisted on closing the metal pin curl clips herself, like she didn't trust me to do it properly. They'd always fascinated me as a child as I could never fold or clip them the right way round.

I'd thought about my nan a lot after Simon died as our lives had followed similar paths. Nanny hadn't been able to get pregnant until she was forty, and her husband, who was in the First World War, died when Mum was only four. She too was widowed and left with one child to bring up on her own. They became homeless when their flat in Elephant and Castle was directly hit by a bomb. She remained single and I often wondered if that was how it was going to be for me, always on my own. *At least I have a car, my own house and a job I love. I have nothing to complain about in comparison*, I thought as I smoothed down Bee's hair until she decided how to wear it.

'Mummy, do you think I could be chosen to play Mary in the school nativity play this year?' she asked, looking through her hair bobble box.

'I don't see why not, do you?' I said.

'No, but Rosie and Hanna said that Mary had blonde hair, and that I can't be Mary cos I'm ginger.'

'I have a feeling Mary had brownish hair. But it doesn't matter these days. They could have a ginger Mary for a change, couldn't they? And you would make the best Mary ever, my darling,' I said, turning her to face me and kissing her on the nose.

Later that day and full of beans, she ran out of school jumping on the spot, and said, 'I'm going to be a wise man, Mummy.'

Hannah, her blonde friend whose parents were practising Christians and who frequently had the vicar round for tea, was chosen to be Mary.

Bee was thrilled, however. And as usual, it was my job to make the outfit and provide the accessories.

'So what does your wise man carry then, darling?' I asked as we bashed the heads off our boiled eggs that teatime.

'So we've got to find some myrrh and put it in a bottle. And Mrs Moore said we mustn't drop it,' she said, dipping a bread finger into her runny yellow yolk.

'Do you know what myrrh is, Bee?' I said, clearing the table.

232

'No. But Mrs Moore says it's very important that we keep our heads still when we are walking with our gifts for baby Jesus.'

I had such a pang of love for her at that moment. She appeared adorably cute. I felt a deep sadness at what Simon was missing. He would have melted seeing her little face light up when she described how important it was to be a wise man. Jane felt the same about Jessie and Theo and would often get angry about Simon not being there to see the little things that melted our hearts.

To make an authentic costume and appear like a perfect parent, I checked out what the three wise men carried and what it meant.

This is what I found:

'The three gifts had a spiritual meaning: gold as a symbol of kingship on earth, frankincense (an incense) as a symbol of deity, and myrrh (an embalming oil) as a symbol of death. This dates back to Origen's book in Contra Celsum: "gold, as to a king; myrrh, as to one who was mortal; and incense, as to a God".'

How bizarre. My little Bee has been chosen to carry embalming oil as a symbol of death, I thought as I tucked her in bed that night. I wondered if this was a mystical message from the spirits up there somewhere, helping her to process her grief in some way.

Around the time of Simon's death, Sylvia, the undertaker, had asked if we wanted to see Simon after he had been 'embalmed'. Jane and I went together to the chapel of rest, a room at the back of the undertaker's. Giggling and cringing, we didn't know how to behave. It became serious when Sylvia shushed her lips at us and told us to go in separately. I stood for a long time looking at Simon's face. Stroking his stiff fingers. Saying goodbye.

Afterwards, we discussed his lips.

'Did you notice his top lip?' I asked, reversing out of the car park.

'Oh my god. Of course I did. It was puckered, wasn't it?' she replied.

'Yes. I tried to straighten it out. But it was set, a bit like clay. It wouldn't budge,' I admitted.

'Oh my god. So did I,' Jane squealed. We laughed out loud, making me nearly crash the car.

Often we thought and behaved the same. I named us 'One Brain' after that. We still sign our text off today at 1B, followed by a kiss.

Where we did differ, however, was about the kids seeing Simon in the chapel of rest. Jane wanted to take the kids, but I declined. The thought of Bee seeing Simon dead freaked me out a bit. I wanted her to remember him as he was, not lying on a coffin having been pumped with embalming fluid and looking like a wax replica.

Like Jane and me, Jess, Theo and Bee did everything together. They'd become our three toddlers. Like we were one family. I didn't want Bee to feel left out if she didn't go, so I asked her.

'Darling, do you want to go and say goodbye to Daddy in his coffin in the chapel of rest?' I said casually over her Frosties at breakfast one morning.

She screwed up her face and said, 'Oh, no, Mummy. I don't want to see him dead and not talking.'

I consciously didn't push it either way, and was relieved when she said no. And all these years later, she doesn't regret her decision.

Her last image of him was on the day we last saw him. We'd bought Bee a disposable camera for her sixth birthday in October. That morning, as we got dressed to go away for the weekend, she insisted on taking photos of the three of us. One of me and Simon where I'm leaning against him, his hands tucked in the front pockets of my jeans. One of

Simon on his own, his hands linked below his belt as if in prayer. His denim shirt was bright against the cream wardrobe doors. One of him holding Bee on his hip, her legs curled around him like a crab's claw. He gave the bravest smile, like you would give in the rain outside a crematorium.

As I look through my tortoiseshell glasses at them now, I see the distant stare of a Belsen survivor who had returned from a concentration camp. His skin was sucked into the hollows in his cheekbones like dried leather. His electric blue eyes were scuffed like a doll discarded at the bottom of the toy box. In my experience as a nurse and having looked after many dying patients, I would have assumed from these images that he was at the end stage of a terminal illness.

In my opinion, some serious mental health conditions are like terminal illnesses as there isn't always a cure. They would fall under the category of long-suffering, where individuals suffer daily emotional pain and yearn to be free.

Jess and Theo did go and see their Uncle Simon and Jane was pleased that they did. Jessie had just turned eight when Simon died, and being the first-born of the three, had been close to Simon. Theo, being the youngest, was indifferent.

Finding one of Simon's almost empty Aramis aftershave bottles, it still smelt of him: woody, floral and spicy. I still associate that smell with him. In our early years together I'd buy him a bottle every Christmas. It reminded me of the nurses' home and falling in love with him. He'd worn it on our first date when he took me in his Mark 2 Cortina to the cocktail bar where we sat around the pool, drank White Russians and listened to Frank Sinatra singing "You are all I long for. All I worship and adore."

Washing it out, I tied a green, gold and red ribbon around it. Filled it will extra virgin olive oil. Placed it on the kitchen table next to the salt, pepper and tomato sauce. When Bee sat up for fish fingers at teatime, she noticed it immediately and crinkled her eyes and mouth, grabbed it and bellowed, 'Oh, Mummy. You found some myrrh. Real myrrh.'

Closely inspecting the bottle, she swished it from side to side like a Genie was going to pop out of the top, then jumped off her chair and gave me a massive hug that brought tears to my eyes.

Bee appeared to deal reasonably well with her grief. She'd have an occasional angry outburst if she got frustrated with something she was doing, for example, and at parents' evening her teacher showed me a self-portrait where she'd drawn herself with wide eyes, bright red cheeks and huge teeth like a lion with a drooped down smile. But she didn't cry very much. Often she said, 'I miss Daddy, Mummy.' We'd talk about all the fun things they did together and look back at all our holidays with Jane and Joe, Nanny and Papa.

The morning of the nativity, I wrapped her in a deep-purple piece of silk material that I had made into a full-length tunic. Tied it together with a wide gold sash that almost dangled to the floor. Determined to keep Simon alive in any way I could, I found the authentic black and white bandana that Jane had bought him back from her Kibbutz trip, the one he wrapped around his head and tucked into his collar like an Arab on exceptionally cold days. Being able to wrap it around her head, it felt like I was wrapping her in his arms, keeping her safe. White ballet pumps and a few pairs of my old pearl beads around her neck finished her off a treat.

Wanting a good view, I got to the church early so that I could sit near the front. Most of the mums had brought their husbands. I can't remember why my mum or dad weren't there with me. I have a feeling I was trying to appear like I was over it and could manage on my own. Plus, I'd arrived to meet up with Max and Mandy from a few doors down, who I'd become friends with this past year. People I would never normally be friends with. They had lived there for about ten years, but we only ever exchanged small talk in the playground or a wave if I was in the front garden weeding. After Simon died, they called for Bee to take her to school and left a basket of homemade soup and bread rolls on the doorstep. After a few months, they persuaded me to join the Parent–Teacher Association (PTA) where they did lots of events for the school. It was a distraction from my grief and gave me a sense of community.

I felt out of place at the first PTA meeting in the school, bearing in mind that I looked out at it every day and could sometimes see activity in the staff room, so it felt strange sitting in there with other parents who I had only seen from afar and never talked to. Looking out of the window, I could see my bedroom window and wondered if the staff had ever been party to any of our ups and downs and Simon's erratic behaviours. They were planning a Summer Ball. It was hard for me to get my head into it all. But I went along with faux enthusiasm. I helped Max and Mandy who both worked in hospitality with the table arrangements. I couldn't face selling tickets to parents in the playground; that felt like too much of an effort.

Despite playing at being a waitress and taking food to the tables on the night of the Ball where everyone was dressed up to the nines in tuxedos and ball gowns, I didn't feel a genuine part of it. A bit like I was going through the motion. In retrospect, I was amongst strangers. Another tribe. Not the people I would naturally socialise with. Yet, Max and Mandy became my friends as they nurtured me in my day-to-day life. I saw them more than my original friends and family. We became familiar with each other. We'd walk to and from school together and they invited me for supper and drinks. Their house was cosy and full of knickknacks and embroidered tablecloths and place settings. Bone china plates were displayed in an antique pine dresser in their dining room resembling a doll's house.

From their handpicked sloe gin, they poured perfect gin and tonics with lashings of ice and lemon, and even an olive on occasions. Mum and Dad had been delighted that they were keeping an eye on me.

Awaiting the nativity to commence, I observed the couple on the opposite pew as they admired the red, blue and yellow stained-glass windows. I felt a pang of envy as she peered up at his eyes, brushed flecks off his black jacket collar. They held each other's gaze and squeezed hands on his lap, like Simon and I would have done before he was ill. A wave of widowness engulfed me like a witch's cape. I turned off my hearing aids to shut out the sound of happy couples. A black blind rolled down in front of my eyes as I pretended to be in prayer. I drifted back to the day Simon had taken off work to go to Bee's first nativity. We had often fantasised about our child's first school play; we had waited fourteen years to see her come out as a sheep. We both dressed up, as it was going to be held in the church at the end of the road. Simon even wore his only jacket and tie, the one he'd worn for Jane's wedding. We didn't know anyone back then and felt we stood out as brand-new parents, especially of an adopted child. Word soon gets around in a small local community.

I'd saved seats for Max and Mandy, who arrived just as 'Mary's Boy Child' echoed round the church and the three wise men walked stiffly out from behind the front at the back of the church. Bee was last, clutching her myrrh tight to her chest, and not moving her head. I tried several times to catch her attention and give her an encouraging wave, but she was dead set on being the best wise man she could, and like one of those human statues you see in most cities, she stood for half an hour until they finally laid their gifts by Baby Jesus's crib. Like monks in an abbey, they walked back the way they'd come.

Tears seeped from the corners of my eyes. My heart hammered in my head and made me feel hot. So hot, I had to take my jumper off. I tried to control my mixture of joy and pride, sorrow and loss. I held my breath, counted to ten before I let it out to still my body and not let Bee or the whole congregation see my tears. She'd taken it so seriously and hadn't faltered. Despite her difficult year, she'd pulled it out of the bag. I imagined how Simon would have burst with pride. He would have picked her up and thrown her in the air until she screamed, then told her how much he loved her. But he wouldn't this year, or any other year, ever again. Max handed me his clean ironed hankie, squeezed his large hand over my clenched fist. Together we all stood as the head teacher called for an encore. Clapping and cheering, most of the congregation dabbed their tears.

Being a year or so after Simon died, I thought I'd done my grieving. I imagined I'd have been okay by then. I'd got used to arriving home and no one being there. Been to parents' evenings on my own, grown accustomed to not being invited to couple things. And after signing off my twentieth Christmas card, writing *Love from Ginger and Bee*, it flowed just the same as *Love from Ginger, Simon and Bee* had, although I hated it. I had to get over it. Not having experienced trauma or grief before, I had no idea how long it would last. Studies have shown that for most people, the worst symptoms of grief – depression, sleeplessness, loss of appetite – peak at six months. As the first year continues, you may find these feelings ebb. But it's normal to still feel some grief years after a death, especially on special occasions and anniversaries. It is still Simon's birthday and the anniversary of his death that stands out in my calendar.

CHAPTER 41

January 2000, the millennium year. I decided, being a naturally loving and tactile person, that I was not designed to be without a partner. I'm also solution-focused and believe that there is always a way out of a problem. Hence I took action, that I now cringe about!

With Vernon's business card in my hand, I'd curled the telephone cable into a tangle by the time he picked it up after four rings, and I said, 'Hello, is that Vernon?'

'Yeh. Who's that?' he answered quietly.

'It's Ginger. Remember? We met at the club on my birthday last year,' I replied.

'Course I do. How are you doing?' he asked brightly.

Blimey, he sounded pleased to hear from me. It had taken a huge amount of courage to make the call, but as I said to myself every time before I did something uncomfortable, *What's the worst thing that can happen?* The answer came back and said, *He can only say no. And if you don't try you may have missed an opportunity.*

A few days later, we met for a drink. Standing up as I entered the pub, he greeted me like an old friend, kissed me on both cheeks. He smelt of Aramis, Simon's favourite aftershave. For a moment, I felt comforted, like he was familiar. And he was familiar, as around the same time I met Simon I'd seen him when I was out with the girls at a bar or club. He'd throw me the odd wink and nodded hello. It turned out we didn't live that far from each other either. We chatted easily about the past and all the old places where we used to just wave at each other. He was gentle and attentive and wanted to know about what happened to Simon. He insisted on buying me drinks and opened the door for me on my way back to my car. I'm an old-fashioned girl, and he impressed me and made me feel respected and cared for.

On the second date, we went to the Cinema to see *The Matrix*. Not in a million years would Simon have gone to see a film like that. I had no idea what it was about and was just glad to be taken out by a kind person. Someone from my past, from the same era; it felt comfortable somehow.

Picking me up from home in his new bottle green Range Rover, he held the door open as I climbed up and slid across the cream leather seat. Sade singing 'Smooth Operator' drifted out of the speakers. *What would Joyce next door think if she saw me driving off with a man*, I thought as I adjusted my safety strap.

Linking his arm as we strolled towards the cinema, I pretended I was normal, like he was my regular boyfriend. He paid for my ticket and popcorn. *What a gent*, I thought as the lights dimmed and we settled in our seats. I hadn't even thought about the film and was almost sick in the first half when Keanu Reeves climbed out of the pod in all that goo. I had to snuggle in Vernon's armpit until it was over. *What am I doing?* I thought as I struggled through the rest of the film. We had absolutely nothing in common apart from the fact that we fancied each other. And I craved comfort. I'd lost my self-esteem. No longer felt attractive. Had become invisible under my widow's shroud. Vernon, being attentive, smelling like Simon and treating me well, was just what I needed. He was nothing like Finn. He was more my physical type, but not my intellectual type. But that didn't matter. Nothing mattered that early in my grief as long as I had company; it helped me feel less alone.

A couple of weeks later we went back to the club where we met on my fortieth birthday. Vernon was a great dancer and our rhythm matched, a bit like John Travolta and Olivier Newton-John in tune, both together and apart. As we smooched towards the end of the night, he pulled me and whispered in my ear, 'Do you fancy coming back to mine?' I didn't hesitate. Bee had gone to stay at Phil's for the night and I didn't have to pick her up until teatime the next day.

In a small cul-de-sac not far from town, the cab dropped us off outside his modern semi-detached. The kitchen was immaculate. A bit clinical for my taste. From his wine chiller, he poured me a large glass of Chardonnay and lit scented candles strategically placed around the house. Lounging on his cream leather sofa, we made small talk, and then he reached out and placed a small multi-coloured Rasta Man silver-hinged tobacco tin on the coffee table, followed by a small cellophane wrap and a rolled £10 note. *Oh blimey*, I thought.

'Do you fancy a line?'

'Ooh. I don't know,' I said, leaning forward to inspect the wrap. 'Is it cocaine?'

He grinned, amused by my naivety.

'Yeah. It's Charlie.'

'I don't know,' I said, giggling. 'Will I pass out or die?'

'Of course not. It will make you feel relaxed. Just try a bit.'

What the fuck, I thought. I was already pissed and it wasn't going to kill me, so why not?

Following Vernon's lead, like in a scene from the film *Wall Street*, I flattened one nostril and snorted the white powder up the £10 note into the other. The hit was quick. A tingle rushed from my thighs to my groin to my head. Stretching my arms above my head, and pointing my toes, I slumped back into his slippery, smooth sofa. Vernon rolled a spliff and placed it between my lips. I pulled a drag and blew smoke back into his open mouth. Gripping his shaved bald head, my pelvis ached as the familiar Aramis woody scent seeped into my cells. For a moment he smelt and felt like Simon as he pressed his spongy mouth over mine. Pulling him on top of me, I hitched up my dress and

242

opened my legs. Any fear I had left me as our bodies pushed and pulsed. Pressed and thrust. I drifted in and out of a blissful state until Vernon whispered in my ear,

'You okay? Wanna go up to bed? It's more comfortable.'

After another quick draw on the spliff, I climbed the stairs after him. In his minimal white and grey bedroom, he handed me a fresh white towelling robe with a toothbrush in the pocket, like I had arrived at the spa for the day. *More like I'm another notch on the bedpost*, I thought as my head spun. Anticipating what was to come, doubts seeped into my mind until another rush of cocaine crushed my doubts and my 'fuck it head' took over.

Candles danced and the sandalwood scent solaced me as I entered the bedroom. Glowing like a Greek god in a museum, his silhouette played tricks on me. *It must be the drugs*, I thought. Then, as if reading my mind, he said, 'It's okay. Come and lay down. Chill. I'll give you a massage.'

As he dripped warm oil down the ladder of my spine, his hands were gentle and warm, caressing my back, my buttocks, the insides of my thighs. He rolled me onto my back and I felt a sweet spasm seep through me and goose bumps gladdened my skin. Hooking his knees inside mine, he drove himself deep inside me. Thoughts of Simon slipped away as I steered him in and out of that hungry place.

He woke me up the next morning with a plain white mug of milky tea. I preferred my tea strong but was grateful for the fluid as my head throbbed. He'd also bought up the *Sunday Times*, plus the *News of the World*. A strange combination, I thought.

'I didn't know what you would like to read, so I got you a bit of both,' he said.

'Oh, thanks. I like reading the papers in bed on a Sunday morning,' I muttered as I pulled the sheets over my chest.

'I'm going to get my car. I'll only be about half an hour. Make yourself at home,' he said, leaning round the door.

'Okay. I will. Thanks,' I replied.

Once he'd gone, I jumped out of bed to inspect the damage in the mirror. It wasn't a good look; mascara and lipstick smudged in the creases of my skin. My hair was stuck up like Ken Dodd's. I jumped in the shower, found some wet wipes and erased last night's stains. I felt dirty, like a slut. *Was this a regular Saturday night for him, where he seduced and drugged vulnerable women, then had sex with them?* I thought. But I hadn't refused. Had I? I'd enjoyed it. Encouraged it, I thought as I scrambled to find my tights and pants in a tangle under the bed. My dress was crumpled in the corner on the floor.

I was sat on the sofa in the lounge pretending to read *The Times* on his return.

'Vernon, I need to get home for Bee. Could we go now?' I said, looking down and picking fluff off my dress.

'Sure. Don't you want any breakfast?'

'No. I never have breakfast, thanks,' I lied as my stomach grumbled with hunger.

Again, I'd placed myself in new territory. It was fine whilst I was pissed and stoned, but a false reality hit once daylight broke. I think I liked the idea of these new adventures, but once I'd tried them, I felt even more out of my comfort zone.

We barely spoke on the way home. He kissed me on the cheek as I climbed out of the car.

'That was great, Ginger. You're a special girl. Let's do it again?'

'Of course. Yeh,' I lied again, slipping off his cream leather seat towards the comfort of my front door.

Smiling, I waved him off. I rushed up the stairs, ripped off my clothes and shoved them into the dirty bin. I climbed into my bed and buried my head under the covers. Darkness came like strong protective arms, and I felt safe under the shield of my duvet.

I didn't care for myself. I searched for something to replace Simon. If I had that time again, I would stay home. Puff myself up. Allow myself time to heal. Write more. Not try so hard to get over it, because it's impossible. You can't rush grief. But I tried all the same. And that's all with the benefit of hindsight.

I was traumatised; in crisis. I'd lived through three years of manias and depressions. My Simon had killed himself. I'd seen him on the slab at the mortuary and in the chapel of rest, clung to the tree where he hung for a few days alone. Watched as the coroner demonstrated in graphic detail how he'd ended his life. Fuck me, it's amazing I survived myself as I look back. And perhaps that's why they call us 'survivors of suicide'. And I have lived to tell the tale. I am still working on making a full recovery, despite having no therapy. I needed to go a bit crazy to find myself again, find out who I was and what I needed.

CHAPTER 42

The Vernon experience had an unexpected impact on me, and I became even more reckless. It was the beginning of February 2000 when I found this new 'fuck it' poise. It felt like I'd peeled off my own skin, like a reptile renewing its body's coating.

I placed an advert for men in *Time Out*. I wanted to see if I got a response.

Single, fiery red-headed female, 5'6" (exaggeration), *a curvy size 12, loves the arts, poetry, travel, all that stuff. Seeking similar. Must have a sense of humour*, I wrote.

I was gobsmacked when thirty-eight men responded to my ad. 'Wow,' I said out loud to myself. How flattering. But they haven't seen me yet. I'm barely pushing 5'3" with short, crispy ginger hair and hearing aids!

I left messages asking some to call back. Talking to strangers on the phone, and within the safety of my own home, gave me a thrill. And of course this was long before emails, chat rooms and online dating. It would have been equivalent to swiping left or right on Tinder today. I'd just poured the last glass of Pink blush wine when the phone rang.

He introduced himself as 'Malcolm from Margate', and we talked for two hours. My inebriated motor mouth told him everything. He appeared to understand me. Empathised about Simon, like he'd known him. Said he was psychic and would love to do my star chart. I woke up in the morning with a vague recollection of the conversation.

As I settled to watch *Blind Date* after I'd dropped Bee off for a sleepover down the road, Fizzy barked at the front door. A stout middle-aged man with greying hair sticking out in different directions like a mad professor stood in a black three-piece suit, swinging a black briefcase. With pale watery eyes, he beamed at me.

'Hi, I'm Malcolm. We spoke last night,' he said, reaching his hand out to shake mine.

Oh, fuck. Where has he come from? How does he know where I live? I thought, picking Fizzy up against my tense stomach.

'Aren't you going to invite me in then? I've had a long journey, you know.'

Pushing past me, he marched down the hall towards the kitchen and threw his case on the table. Fizzy wriggled to get out of my grip. As I dropped him, he bared his teeth at Malcolm's white socks standing out below his short trousers.

'Aren't you going to offer me a cup of tea then?' he said in a jolly but pushy tone.

'Oh, of course,' I said, filling the kettle.

With his unnaturally thin fingers that looked like clematis tendrils, he spread what looked like a large map across my kitchen table.

'You're very attractive, Ginger, you know. Much better than I imagined. Much younger too. Isn't this marvellous? We've met at last. My chart said I would meet you this year. Come and have a look at this. It shows Taurus tipping the scales in Uranus and stinging Scorpio's tail. It means we're meant for each other.'

Oh fuck. What have I done? He's such a creep, I thought as he covered my kitchen table with his chart, like spreading a map to plot an attack in World War One.

'You don't appear as thrilled to meet me as I am you. You were most forward on the phone last night,' he said, looking me up and down.

'Oh, I'm a bit shy in real life. It takes me a while to get to know someone,' I lied.

There was something in the way he looked at me; his eyes bore into me and his fixed smile watched me like a vendetta mask, like he was doing much more than just taking in my form like other men did. I sat opposite him with Fizzy gripped to my chest for protection, and he told me how he wanted to take me to a special secret underground club he went to in London.

'You'll love it. I'll find you the right outfit. You'll look fab on my arm,' he said, standing up, taking a step towards me.

My pulse quickened as I clutched Fizzy's ribs. Lurching around the table at speed, Malcolm tried to grab me. Snarling, Fizzy snapped and caught his tie with his teeth, shaking it like he'd caught a cat in the death roll. Malcolm tried to fight him off, but Fizzy didn't let go. As he stumbled backwards, Malcolm turned grey. He landed with a bang against the sink and wiped his brow with a crumpled cream hankie. Leaping up, and holding Fizzy out towards him like a weapon, I grabbed the phone as adrenaline flooded my system and in a shaky voice said, 'I'd like you to go now please, or I will call 999.' I pretended to dial the numbers.

'Hey, calm down. There's no need for that now, is there? Come on. I think you've led me on, don't you? The least you can do is feed me. Then I'll go,' he said with a chuckle, talking to himself as he folded the chart away.

Putting Fizzy on a short lead, I scrambled in the freezer and found a small pizza and some chips. Chucked them in the oven on high. Watched him fill his face until he was satisfied.

Still rambling rubbish about us being meant for each other, he stood up to go.

'Can I use your convenience before I go?' he asked, looking down the hall.

'It's at the top of the stairs,' I said, giving him a wide berth to get past me.

Opening the front door, and standing on the doorstep hoping the neighbours wouldn't see him, I was ready to push him out.

'I sense a strong spirit upstairs,' he said, strolling past me out of the gate to his beaten-up old Vauxhall Astra. 'Perhaps your husband's in the loft!'

'Really,' I said in a sarcastic tone, not wanting to appear scared.

But I was shitting myself. He completely freaked me out. He appeared to know things. They say that about spiritual people, don't they? And part of me likes the idea that our spirits live on, but not in my loft.

Dropping Fizzy from my grip, I banged the door shut behind him, then ran to the back of the house and bolted the patio doors. I shut all the curtains and put all the lights on in the whole house. Peering up the stairs, I saw a shadow of what looked like a man hanging on the landing wall. Too scared to go upstairs to bed, I slept on the settee that night. The loft hatch was on the landing just outside my bedroom. Having a vivid imagination and a fear of the dark, I imagined there might my something in there. And the police had looked in there for Simon. It's not uncommon for people to hang themselves in the loft. And the house was Victorian, built in 1919, so who knows what stories it held.

Regret washed over me in the morning like long slow waves on a beach. Each wave was icy cold and sent shivers down my spine. I'd been drinking too much lately, especially on my own. I'd start after Bee had gone to bed on a Friday or Saturday night. I used alcohol like medicine to cover the cracks. I'd have a cigarette as well, or even five if I was pissed. I recently read that the reason we can't remember much after drinking in excess is because the brain stops making memories. It's not that you were so drunk that you can't remember. That's what must have happened when I told Malcolm my address. My body went cold and bile rose in my throat as I thought about the consequences of what could have happened. Thank god I had the dog. He saved me. I felt ashamed of whom I'd become. Simon would have had a fit, to think that I'd laid myself bare. He'd been protective of me when he was well; he even walked on the outside of the pavement to protect me from the traffic. That sounds mad, doesn't it. But that's what gentlemen did back in the day.

Recollecting back to that time, it's like I'm looking at someone else's life. I'm horrified at the risks I took. I was wearing the weight of the past few years on my shoulders. Dragging an imaginary ball and chain around my ankles. I'd dodged the bullets of blame and guilt. Been emotionally attacked and dragged down by Simon, particularly in the last year of his life. Felt vulnerable and insecure. My self-love tank was empty. I ached for the warmth and comfort that I believed only Simon could give me.

CHAPTER 43

Despite my near-death experience with Malcolm, I picked myself up and continued down the road of self-destruct. My daytime life remained stable. Those around me were unaware of what I was getting up to. Mum and Dad thought I was having a nice time, going out with new friends, coping at work etc, because that was the picture I painted. Bee appeared to enjoy doing sleepovers with the neighbour's kids and her cousins. Jane of course knew what I was up to as I'd share my stories in her bed and make her laugh. Occasionally she'd suggest I pull my reins in a bit. But I was running wild.

I started going out with Dawn, one of my regular patients at work and her friends. I'd dressed her wound when her boob job went wrong. They were a group of divorcees who, like me, were grieving, and I joined their pack. But I didn't quite fit in. Being hairdressers or beauticians, they fashioned fake tans, false nails and teetered on biro-thin stilettos heels that you could break your neck on. To fit in, I tarted myself up in tight titty tops and skimpy short skirts. They took me clubbing to tacky 'divorced and separated' venues, where we downed vodka shots and smoked Marlborough Lights. With our arses in the air like baboons, we'd strut our stuff.

My behaviour was out of character. I'd spent the past twenty-odd years as a married woman with a child, had built a home and was at the top of my career as the senior practice nurse. I was behaving in an unprofessional manner. One didn't fraternise with one's patients as it went against the Nursing Code of Conduct. I'd taken on a new persona, and I think I enjoyed it at times. I liked the dressing up, buying new clothes and teetering on spikey heels.

I'd heard of these nightclubs being like a cattle market where men of all ages stood round the edge of the dance floor and scored the women out of ten! With our self-esteem shot, we didn't give a shit, as our loneliness drove us to attract a mate. Drinking more wine than I ever had before, I acquired a taste for smoking. Regularly bought a packet of twenty Marlborough Lights for my nights out.

Initially, I liked the thrill of pulling men. I even pulled a twenty-six-year-old once! But I had nothing in common with any of these beer-drinking men, who only talked about football, golf and cars. I'd seen their Mercedes, Porsches and BMWs in the car park with personalised number plates like BOB 1 and SCRU 2. I usually felt crap the next day and told myself I wouldn't go again, but somehow Dawn managed to persuade me.

I'd burnt the candle at both ends, driven myself into the ground and couldn't get rid of a cough. Ignoring a sharp stabbing pain in my right side, I carried on. A month or so later, sitting opposite Jane in her bed whilst Joe was downstairs making milky coffees for us, I bragged about the twenty-six-year-old. It was then that she had a serious word with me.

'I think you should stop this now, don't you?' Jane said, like she was talking to one of the kids.

'Stop what?' I frowned at her.

'All this party business. I know you're having fun. But I think you're overdoing it, and perhaps you should focus on Bee a bit more,' she said with pursed lips.

'Oh my god. Are you saying I'm neglecting her?'

'No. I'm not saying that. But listen to your chest. You sound like a chronic bronchitic on the chest ward.'

Pulling one of Joe's poppy-patterned pillows onto my lap, I stared out of the window, and so did she. I knew she was right, but I couldn't admit it.

It was all right for her, I thought. She had Joe to snuggle up to and give her comfort. She didn't feel the loneliness, the blame and guilt I felt. I'm not belittling her loss, but as she'd said to me on many occasions since, her life continued as before, but without her brother.

Bundling the three kids in the bath at teatime, I was struck by a sudden piercing pain in my left side. Dropping to my knees with the pain, I couldn't move, like I'd been stabbed by a bread knife. Joe picked me up. Jane put me to bed and immobilised my torso with pillows. Gave me co-codamol that she found in her bedside drawer.

The pain was as bad as my tubal surgery pain. I could only take shallow breaths; I was scared to move and had to sleep sitting up. Plus, my mood plummeted and I was full of self-loathing and regret. I felt like I'd let everyone down.

A couple of days later, Joe packed up my car and Jane reached across and strapped me in for my drive home.

'You'll listen to me now, won't you?' she said, squeezing my face and kissing me.

'I always do, don't I?' I said, trying not to cry again.

'Now concentrate. Don't drive over seventy. Call us when you get home,' Joe said through the window. I couldn't turn and wave like usual. Taking shallow breaths, I managed to drive the hour home. Bee helped lift our bags out of the car and got herself ready for bed.

The next day, my GP suspected pneumonia. Prescribed antibiotics and steroids and booked me an urgent chest X-ray.

Goosebumps made me shiver as I pressed my bare chest against the cold hard X-ray plate.

'Have you had an injury to your right side, Jane?' asked the radiographer.

'I don't think so,' I said, puzzled, as I held my side.

'I can see an old fracture on your right side, and three recent ones on your left. And both your lungs are congested. I suggest you call your GP tomorrow for the results.'

As I stood in the pale-blue hospital gown, the grey walls closed in on me. I had to sit down and absorb the news.

'But I don't understand,' I said to myself as I dressed, feeling like a ninety-year-old.

In a daze, I drove home. I couldn't understand why I was so ill. Pneumonia! Four fractured ribs! How had I ended up in such a state? It was obvious to those around me that I'd partied hard. Filled my lungs with tobacco. Blurred my brain cells with wine. Neglected my health. It was like I had a death wish. Maybe I did. It was only Bee who kept me going. I'd neglected her as well. That's a terrible thought that occurs to me now. I've since asked her about that time. She said she liked going to friends for sleepovers and spending time with both grandparents, her cousins and Auntie Janie's.

I was a perfect example of how poor mental health has a direct impact on your physical health. It doesn't end well.

Both Mum and Dad came to pick me up that day. Whilst Mum packed our clothes, I watched Dad out of my bedroom window chatting to the mums in the playground waiting for Bee to come out of school. I wanted to cry deeply, but I knew it would hurt. Sitting in the back of the car, Mum played I Spy with Bee. Staring out of the window, I barely spoke all the way home.

Mum had prepared Nanny's old bedroom. She'd put a fluffy pink hot water bottle in the bed, closed the curtains and placed four pillows like an armchair ready for me to slip straight into. When I woke, she brought warm milk and peanut butter sandwiches cut into triangles with no crusts, like she did when we were kids. She'd made the same for Bee, who looked tiny sat in Nanny's old chair to eat them. I was desperate to cuddle and kiss her, but the slightest wrong movements hurt me. Her face lit up when Dad peeped round the door and took her off for her bath. Despite regular pain killers, each time I coughed the pain stabbed deep into my lungs like a grabber crushing a car in the scrapyard.

Dad stepped up once again. He took Bee to and from school, helped with her homework, and read *The Little Girl in the Freezer* to her every night. In retrospect, Dad stepped up far beyond his Grandpa role; he became a surrogate father to Bee, and today she says that Grandpa is still the number one man in her life.

Pneumonia was confirmed by my GP the next day. He debated whether or not to admit to me to hospital. He was troubled by my fractured ribs. It was thought unusual for a forty-year-old to sustain fractured ribs from coughing alone. He wanted to do further investigations because of my history of skin cancer.

Back towards the end of the summer of 1989, when I was twenty-nine, Jane noticed a small, dark, irregular mole on my upper right arm as we lay by the lake. She was working as a health visitor at the time and had been to a half hour seminar about skin cancer.

'How long have you had that?' she said, inspecting and stroking it.

'No idea. I haven't seen it before. I'm covered in them,' I said, lifting up my skirt as I showed her my legs. 'A bloke at a nightclub played dot-to-dot on this leg once and made a giraffe,' I joked.

She made me to promise to make an appointment with my GP and ask to have it removed. The GP said it looked harmless and didn't think it needed removing. I insisted.

As he stitched my arm, he said, 'You can call for your results in ten days. I'm sure they will be fine.'.

He called me at home, six days later.

'Hello, Jane. It's Dr Barrett. Are you on your own?' he asked.

I was painting the landing at the time, so I laid my brush on the paint pot and said, 'Yes.'

'Well, you had better sit down,' he advised.

I knelt by the barley-white paint.

'I'm afraid the mole I removed was malignant. It is a malignant melanoma!'

All I heard was 'malignant'. And bang. I was dead.

'Are you okay, Jane?' he asked.

I don't know if I answered. He went on to say that I needed further investigations. He'd referred me to a plastic surgeon.

I ran downstairs to find my big *Black's Medical Dictionary*, and read:

'Malignant melanoma is a highly aggressive cancer and fatal form of skin cancer that tends to metastasize relatively early and aggressively, thereby spreading to other parts of the body. These cancers may be fatal if not found and treated early. They commonly affect people with red or blond hair, blue eyes with freckles or moles, and a history of sun burn.'

Through my tears, I read it again and again and again. It talked about me. I was that person.

Despite Mum telling me not to sunbathe as a teenager, I'd lay in the midday sun covered in coconut oil, like people did back then. On my first holiday to Torquay age fifteen, I wore a skimpy black bikini and lay on the beach all day. And when we went out on the boat, I wore vest tops. No sun cream. People only took sun cream with them on holiday back then. I'd gone through a spell of having sunbeds as well. All us nurses did. We'd compare our white bits when we got back to the wards.

There were times I'd exposed myself to so much sun that I could barely touch my skin. My shoulders were lobster red. In medical terms I'd given myself second-degree burns. I'd burnt down to the second layer of skin and caused pain, redness, swelling and blistering. My skin peeled off and I never went brown. I fashioned a shade of raw sienna.

For three hours I sat at the top of the stairs. *A fatal form of skin cancer. A fatal form of skin cancer. A fatal form of skin cancer*, I repeated in my head like a mantra. I was too young to die. I hadn't had a baby. *I wouldn't be able to have a baby now, would I?* I catastrophized.

And what about Simon? Thoughts flew round my head like a cricket ball had spun a million times and reduced everything to rubble.

My lower lip trembled and my Adam's apple swelled as Simon's key turned in the door.

'Hey, babe. You okay?' he shouted up the stairs.

Floating down the stairs, he met me at the bottom, pulled me by the waist and kissed my neck.

'What's up, babe? What's happened?'

I spewed my tail out like pouring paint too fast into a tray.

'I've got skin cancer. The fatal one. It's not good.'

He sat me down on the stairs and took my hands in his and said, 'Hey, hey. Calm down. Tell me again, slowly.'

When I finished, he let me go. Gripped his head with his hands and let out a primal scream.

'Fuck. Fuck, Fuck.'

He paced up and down the hall. I thought he would have put his fist through the wall, but we'd not long papered it.

I consoled him. Rubbed his back. Found myself saying, 'But it might be in the early stages. We may be overreacting.'

I felt his breath on my neck as we spooned in bed that night.

I went to see my parents on my own. I don't remember what I said. Mum nursed me on the settee, stroked the back on my hand. Dad was the closest to tears I had ever seen him. And from then on, my brother called me 'Lucky', because I never appeared to have any luck.

We went to see Brenda and Michael the next day. I sat on their kitchen table, swung my crossed legs as Simon told them. They looked solemn and gave us both a hug. Brenda said, 'But it's been caught early, hasn't it? I'm sure it won't be as bad as you think.'

That's what everyone said when I poured out my tale.

In the days leading up to my admission, I decorated the hallway. Scraped off wallpaper. Rubbed down the skirting. Emulsioned the walls. Didn't stop for lunch. Kept myself busy. I lost half a stone over four days. Two weeks later, I was an inpatient on the plastic surgery ward. Settled into another hospital bed, with a new plastic ID bracelet. My name above my bed. They took a wedge resection out of my arm. I was left with a scar like a Z and a dent in my arm.

The surgeon said it was caught in the early stages and I was seen in outpatients every three months to check it hadn't spread to my lymph glands. Over a five-year period, my visits reduced to yearly and the sun became my enemy. As soon as I felt its fire licking my skin, I covered up with cotton Indian tops and sarongs wrapped around my head and shoulders like a hijab. I was nicknamed Doris after Simon's grandma, who seldom left their beach hut as she had milk-white skin, like mine. Simon and Jane were brilliant. Reassuring. Gentle. Optimistic. They made me cover up. Brenda even bought me a wide-brimmed pink cotton hat that zipped into a bag and could be worn on a belt. It was hideous, but it made us all laugh.

I became obsessed with melanomas and trained other nurses to look for the signs. I was relieved when I reached the five-year mark. I hadn't expected to live past that. I felt inadequate, defective, sorry that Simon had to end up with someone with many imperfections.

Foolishly, however, I believed it was okay to have my face uncovered, so I freely faced the sun when I could until I noticed a small flaky spot on my nose, and then a few years later, on my ear. They turned out to be another form of skin cancer called BCC, basil cell carcinoma. They won't kill you, but if not treated they will eat your flesh away.

Because of my history, my GP fast-tracked me to Mount Vernon (the cancer hospital back then) for an MRI scan to eliminate secondary bone cancer. The words 'bone secondaries' repeated inside my mind like the ball in a game of ping pong.

Secondary cancer (metastases) is when a (primary) cancer that starts in one place in the body spreads elsewhere, like to the bones, liver, or brain, for example. I knew all about secondaries having nursed many people with cancer to their death. I kept thinking about the young mum I'd nursed on a female medical ward when I was diagnosed with skin cancer aged thirty. In the final stages of liver secondaries, I'd asked her where her primary was. She'd found a small mole on her leg that grew and became itchy. It was only when it started to bleed that she did something about it. Sadly, by then it had already metastasised into her liver. She died with her two young children and husband by her side.

As I muttered the words 'bone secondaries', sobbing in Mum's arms on their floral settee one afternoon after Dad had gone to collect Bee, Mum shushed my lips and said, 'I'm sure it won't come to that, dear. Try and think about something nice.'

But there was nothing nice in my life anymore, apart from Bee, of course. I wondered if this was how Simon had felt when he'd decided to take his own life. For the first time, I understood the desire to escape, to be free from pain.

Flicking through a tattered copy of *Gardeners' World*, Dad blended into the cold, slate waiting room in Mount Vernon as I waited to be called. Feeling chilly most of the time lately, I'd worn black leggings under my jeans, Mum's thermal vest and one of her plain crewneck jumpers that was easy to take off. I played with the wooden buttons on my old favourite bumpy brown, thick knitted cardigan. In a charity shop, I'd been attracted to the huge yellow and green sunflower on the back and hand-knitted sunflower faces sewn onto each pocket. It was more like a coat than a cardigan and also easy to remove in a hurry. Dad patted my knee and gave me a good luck wink when I was called into the scan room.

What I'd heard about the MRI machine was true. *They said it looked like a large polo, but it's more like one of those old people's toilet seats*, I thought as the radiographer gave me strict instructions not to move.

'We need you to stay still like a statue. It will be noisy, a bit like a washing machine. And there's an emergency button if you need it,' she reassured me.

In a thin pale-blue paper gown, I lay as still as a corpse as the radiographer slid me into the metal tube like a porter pushing the dead into the fridge in the mortuary. I'd turned off my hearing aids to stop the sound of the clunking machine. I tried to repeat a meditation I'd learnt to calm myself. In his sweet and mesmerising voice, Mooji Baba, The Spiritual Master, repeated:

*Pure. Awareness I Am. Pure. Awareness I Am. Om.'
Bone secondaries I've got. Bony secondaries I've got. Pure.
Awareness I Am…*

Drifting off, I pictured all my patients at my funeral wearing long white robes like monks, and Bee staring into my recently dug grave. I came to as they pulled me out, my limbs stiff. Sitting me up, they let me stretch and unravel.

'Does it look okay? Have I got secondaries?' I babbled.

The radiographer rested her hand on my shoulder, looked down into my lap and said, 'I can't tell you, my dear. We'll send the results to your GP. I'd just go and have a lovely Easter if I were you,' she said, leaving me with the impression that it was bad news!

What did she mean? Have a good Easter. *Is she saying it's going to be my last?* I thought as I continued to catastrophise about my nearing death.

'All done, Tozzy?' Dad said, linking my arm, gripping me tight, like I'd fall over if he let go. I had nothing to say. Absolutely nothing. Like someone had emptied the words from my brain.

I had some dark thoughts during that time and I believed it was my time to go. At least I would join Simon, I thought. I even thought about what would happen to Bee if I died. Would Jane have her, or Mum and Dad? I couldn't bare the thought of her losing me as well as Simon. I didn't let her out of my sight for a long time after that.

I thought my earlier grief had been lonely, but this felt desperate. I'd succumbed to the demon called depression. I didn't know it at the time, but I can see it clearly now. I had all the symptoms: the feeling of a hopeless outcome, loss of interest in anything, and increased fatigue, anxiety and uncontrollable emotions. I looked death in the face. It is only now looking back that I realise how ill I was. My body and soul were fucked. There was only room for negative thoughts. My usual positive, optimistic thoughts had migrated south.

A couple of weeks later my GP called and said that he was *reasonably* confident that I didn't have secondaries. To be certain, he fast-tracked me to an orthopaedic specialist. Mum came with me this time and squeezed my hand in her lap as we waited in outpatients.

The young Arab-looking doctor welcomed us with a warm smile and said, 'I have good news for you today. There is nothing wrong with your bones.'

I slumped forward. Let out a whimper. Dropped my head in my hands in relief.

'So why did she fracture her ribs then?' asked Mum, wiping her nose with one of Nanny's embroidered hankies.

'I believe that she coughed for so long without treatment that she weakened the bones. It's not unheard of in women. But don't worry. She'll make a full recovery. Just don't let her leave it so long before she sees her GP next time,' he said, raising his eyebrows at Mum as if to say, *Keep an eye on her*.

Biting her bottom lip, Mum reached across the desk and shook his hand. *Blimey*, I thought, *she too must have thought I was going to die*. I hadn't seen her so happy for a long time; she almost skipped out of his room, swinging her Margaret Thatcher handbag like it was empty.

'Let's go and treat you to something in Marlow, shall we? You can have anything you like. Your father will pay,' she said, squeezing my arm and holding my hand like she did when I was a child.

That night in Nanny's bed, I read Simon's letter again, and this time I heard, *I will never be able to change. I am only able to go a couple of months without things all feeling all too much. This won't be the case for you once I have gone. You will be able to grieve, but this will end. You will meet another man who will love you in a way that I haven't been able to.*

I heard his message for the first time. He was telling me to stop grieving. Telling me that he hadn't been able to love me like I deserved. Not because he didn't feel love for me, but because his self-love had gone. His mind had been ravished by bipolar and he had nothing left to give me, himself, or anyone else.

CHAPTER 44

Mum drove us straight to Marlow that afternoon, to Burgers, our favourite cafe, where we used to take Nanny for afternoon tea and chocolate éclairs. We'd sit in the corner by the window. Nanny liked that spot. To distract me and cheer me up, Mum encouraged me to tell her about the good times I'd had with Simon. So I told her about the time before Simon and I and Jane and Joe had children, and they had joined a water ski club.

Joe had bought a small speed boat that came with skis. On a picnic blanket printed with lemons, Jane and I lounged one Saturday afternoon whilst Joe prepared the boat for Simon and me to have a go at skiing. They'd been practising all week and could just about stay up in the water.

Struggling to get the tyre-like rubber wetsuit up his titanic thighs, Simon went puce in the face, and we all cracked up when he finally zipped it up as he could barely separate his thighs. Climbing on to the rocking boat, Jane and I squealed like playful kids for fear of falling in. The engine spluttered. Two-stroke engine petrol made us cough as Joe pulled the starter handle three times. Setting off, swirls of purple and blue oil trailed behind us like slug slime.

Treading water, Simon tucked his knees up to his chest as Joe hit the gas. Standing up, for all of three seconds, he came crashing down and bobbed in the water. Wiping tangled weed off his bald pate and water out of his eyes, six times he tried to get up, and like Norman Wisdom, the British comedy actor, he eventually stayed up long enough to get a third of the way round the lake. Jane and Joe still hadn't made it halfway around.

'Ginger. It's your turn now,' said Simon, wading like a deep sea diver out of the water.

'Oh no. I don't think so. What do you think, Jane? Shall I?'

Tucking into our cold beer, bread and oozing brie, we mused on the bank.

'Well, this is the deal,' Jane said. 'You'll get your hair wet. You won't like that. The water will go up your nose and in your mouth. You won't like that. You may get tangled in weed and you really won't like that. It's impossible to stand up. And when you do, you're not up for long, and it hurts like hell when you crash back down. Oh, and the boat pulls your arms out of your sockets. Apart from that, it's great when you're up!'

'Oh, for god's sake. You've put right me off,' I shrieked.

'Go on, babe. Take no notice of Jane. You'll be fine. If you don't like it, at least you can say you've tried,' said Simon, scooping the last of the brie onto his crust of French bread.

The beer had gone to my head, and it gave me the courage to do it.

Grappling to tug the wetsuit up over my thighs, my thumbnail split and my face turned cherry red.

'It had better be worth it. I'm not going through this again if it's not,' I shouted.

'Stop winging and get it over your fat arse in the water,' Simon said, chuckling.

Waddling like a penguin, in a onesie down the bank, I fished for the rope and belly-flopped in the lake as they cheered and clapped me from the back of the boat.

Like a sergeant major to his troop, Jane bellowed instructions.

'Tuck your knees under your chin. Point your skis straight in front and hang on tight. Don't let go, whatever you do.'

Simon followed on.

'And when you fall off, just stay where you are. We'll come back for you. I love you, babe,' he said, blowing kisses to me with both his hands.

Wobbling like a Weeble, and struggling to float in the foetal position, I gripped the bar with both hands.

'Just shout "HIT IT" when you're ready,' Joe yelled, hanging onto the stirring wheel.

Did he say hit it or shit it? I thought as they got further away.

Gluing my knees tight together and levelling my skis, I bobbed like a duck when the wash from the boat challenged my balance. Over the engine noise, I shrieked, 'HIT IT, HIT IT.'

With all my might I clung to the bar and dug my feet beneath my seat. In slow motion I rose like the Statue of Liberty with her flame reaching up to the gods. I was up. I was up. Oh my god. I screamed and screeched. I did it. I did it. I was water skiing. I was so pumped with adrenaline, I thought I could even attempt a jump. I beamed for so long that my cheeks ached.

Punching the air, Simon was gobsmacked. Jane jumped up and down with her thumbs up, and Joe pulled me skiing *all* the way round the lake. Feeling cocky, like Eddie the Eagle, I let go of one hand and lifted a leg in the air and landed splat, upside down in the weeds. I was breathless and like a dead seal, and they dragged me over the side of the boat and all patted me in disbelief.

We spent most weekends on the lake, and the following year we went to Poole Harbour, where I also mastered the sea waves until the boys took the boat out on their own on rough waters one day and came back with no windscreen. The boat was a right-off. As usual they'd gone too far.

Mum shook her head in amazement.

'You went water skiing? I didn't know you could do that. Wait till I tell your father, he won't believe it,' she said, blotting her lips and brushing crumbs off her tartan skirt.

265

CHAPTER 45

Seeing the sun peep between plump pearl clouds lifted my mood as I took a gentle walk to town to get Bee some books from the library, a week after my all-clear. *I'll have a coffee and pick up some flowers at the Tuesday market*, I thought, strolling down the hill past the local university. Students of all ages sprawled on the grass banks. I was surprised to see a couple of women of my age amongst the young students making the most of the spring sun. I felt envious of their laughter and youth.

As I passed the entrance, an idea popped into my head like a bath bomb being plopped into hot water. What if I gave up nursing? Go to uni? I'd always fancied myself as an arty student. Three years of fun, painting and drawing, meeting new people. No more smears or leg ulcers. Long uni holidays. The idea grew with every step. I'd have to choose something that would give me an income and support me and Bee.

As I walked a bit faster, my rucksack felt lighter on my back, and the spongy soles of my shoes bounced me up the concrete steps.

'Excuse me. Do you have this year's prospectus?' I asked a bored-looking middle-aged lady sat behind the desk.

With a long manicured nail, she pointed to a shelf in the corner.

'And when is the deadline for applications, please?' I enquired.

'Six weeks?' came the reply.

Like a child discovering the book corner at school for the first time, I picked up a handful of pamphlets and popped them in my rucksack, and before I knew it I was at the market, where my thoughts were broken by the words of the familiar curly blond fruit and veg bloke.

'Oi, oi, Ginge. Where have you been?' he called.

Dropping my head to one side to look in his direction, I felt my face flush pink as I gave him a wave, then headed straight to the Giddy Goat, my favourite coffee shop. I ordered a small cappuccino with extra froth and chocolate sprinkles, plus a warm pain au raisin. Scooping the froth with my teaspoon from around the edge of the heart shape floating on top, I settled in a spot by the window.

Covering the table with my pamphlets like spreading cards in a game of Patience, I noticed that there was a university in West London, only a forty-minute train ride away. The page stayed open on Multimedia Journalism BA (Hons) and I read:

'A journalism degree provides you with a range of core journalistic skills including researching, investigating, interviewing, reporting and writing, in addition to technical skills such as radio, video, photography and web design.'

There was an eruption in my skull, the type that was fuelled with possibilities. Hundreds of ideas flashed around my head like lightning in a black sky. It was an adventure calling me, making my pulse reckless, my breath brisk, and a rush shoot up the back of my neck.

It had my name all over it: investigating and interviewing, I'm good at that; I do it every day with my patients. Reporting and writing: I love writing and have had some of my poetry published. Radio, video, photography: I love photography and might even end up on the radio or TV. Imagine that! I wanted to jump up and tell everyone in the coffee shop what I'd discovered. Oh my god. There was hope. I could *actually* have a good time and enjoy myself again. *I must act quickly*, I thought. I squeezed the last raisin up from my plate between my thumb and finger, pressed the crumbs hard against the cool plate and sucked them into my mouth.

I whizzed to the library, picked Bee up a couple of Roald Dahl books and made my way back to the market. I treated myself to a small bunch of midnight-blue and letterbox-red anemones and then queued behind a couple of old ladies to buy some bananas and broccoli.

'Oi, oi, here she is again. Me favourite gal,' said the curly blond bloke, nudging his mate and winking at me at the same time.

'How can I help you then, young lady?' he said, grinning.

'I'll have four bananas and a small bunch of broccoli, please,' I said.

His arm touched my hand as he dropped them into my open rucksack and said, 'Where's little Roxy, then? She at school, eh?' he flirted.

He named her Roxy once as it was embroidered in silver thread on her black top some months ago. He'd called her Roxy ever since.

'Yeh, she's at school,' I called.

'Don't leave it so long next time, eh?' he responded.

'Okay,' I said as I walked away with a further spring in my step.

And by the time I went to collect Bee from school, I'd made up my mind. I was going to leave nursing and do a full-time degree. I'd found out about student loans, printed off the application form, and gathered all the relevant evidence, like exam results and past lecturers who would act as referees etc. I didn't know how I'd manage it. I just knew I would. Buzzing, I skipped across the road to join Rosalind and the other mums in the school playground. I felt like the Christmas lights had been turned on in London's Regent Street and I'd been lit up!

As I look back on my life, this was one of the most exciting things I've ever done. It was like I'd injected myself with courage. For the first time in my life I was doing something on my own. It was my idea. And deep inside me I knew I'd do it, partly to escape my grief and because I would be stimulated and energised again. It felt like when I left school at sixteen, I had no idea of what uni would look or feel like, but the anticipation itself was thrilling.

Working it all out in my head, I couldn't get to sleep that night. I decided to sell the house and buy something smaller around the corner. I'd already seen a house for sale that I liked, so I phoned the estate agent the next day and arranged a viewing with Bee after school. Predicting that Dad would go mad and try to talk me out of it, I decided not to tell him until I had a concrete plan. Over the weekend, I told Bee and she liked the idea. I'd talked to her a lot since Simon had died. I know she was only seven and I'm sure people would say that it was ridiculous or inappropriate, but when you are on your own, there isn't anyone else to share your thoughts with.

A year or so after Simon had died when she was standing on the edge of the bath as we cleaned our teeth, I broke down again and couldn't stop crying. She rubbed my back and said, 'Now, Mummy. I think you've cried enough now, don't you? It's time to be happy again.'

I scooped her up, sat her on my lap and let her wipe my tears away with some toilet paper.

'I'm sorry, darling. Sometimes the tears come and I just can't stop them,' I snuffled.

'But I don't like it when you cry, Mummy. It makes me sad.'

'I'm so sorry, my darling. I do try to not to let you see. But sometimes I just can't help it,' I said, sniffing.

It had worried me that Bee rarely cried, so more recently I looked it up on Google. It said: 'Children, more than adults, swing quickly between grieving and getting on with their normal lives. They can be upset one minute and asking to play a game or have some ice cream the next. It can be so quick that it's sometimes called "puddle jumping" – the puddle is their feelings of grief, and they are quickly in and out of the puddle.'

I had been relieved to read this, as it was Bee to a T. However, on this particular day as she wiped my tears away, her eyes looked like small glass marbles about to split.

'Please don't cry anymore, Mummy,' she repeated, staring up at me.

Crackles appeared around her smooth irises and bubbles of water leaked and strolled down her pink cheeks as she flopped her head into my chest clutching *my* wet tissue. There were many times during my grief when I'd felt she'd become like the parent and me the child. She appeared to have a wise spirit, even as a toddler.

Swinging hands, we skipped round the corner to view the new house. It was only at the end of our road, not even half a mile away. Our house had been valued for more than I had expected. I worked out that I would have enough to work part-time for three years with a little bit over. Brilliant; I had a plan. Time to tell Dad!

He'd come to do some paperwork and sort out my files. Sitting at the kitchen table before he went up to my office, he sat in Simon's chair, leaning against the radiator. I'd rehearsed what I was going to say and decided to tell him direct. Not ask his opinion, as he would challenge me. He *always* told me what to do, and *always* got the better of me.

I wasn't listening to a word he was saying as he made small talk about Mum taking Bee to see her friend whose child was the same age. My breath came fast as I drained the last drop of coffee to moisten my throat, then slapped my palms on the table. Stopped him in his tracks.

'Dad. I have something to tell you. I've made a decision about something you won't like. But I'm doing it anyway.'

Leaning back, he folded his arms across his chest and tucked his hands tight under his armpits. With downward eyebrows and straight lips, he said, 'I'm listening,' with a slightly amused smile.

Twiddling with my wedding ring under the table and looking down in my lap, I said, 'I've decided to give up nursing and go to uni to do a full-time degree in Journalism.'

He looked heavenward and asked, 'And how will you afford that then?'

Pulling myself upright, looking him directly in the eye like I'd rehearsed in the mirror just before he arrived, I replied, 'You don't have to worry as I've got it all worked out.'

'I bet you have,' he mocked. 'So tell me.'

'Well. I'm going to sell the house. I've already had it valued and seen a house up the road I like. That will leave me enough money to live on for three years. I'll carry on doing my part-time family planning job, and I could get some extra hours in the HIV Unit if I need to.' The words tumbled out like a confession.

Uncrossing his arms, he leant forward. Placed his palms upwards on the table.

Stay in adult mode. Don't buckle, whatever he says, I told myself as I too leant forward. Straightening my back, I met his eyes head-on. Not a position I would normally adopt, as usually I'd have slunk back down into naughty-child-about-to-be-told-off mode, but not today.

A long silence hung in the air until he replied, 'Well. You've certainly done your homework, haven't you. But I'm not happy about you selling the house. I think that would be madness.'

'I know, but I've worked it out,' I stated clearly.

'I dare say you have, but I can't let you do that, Tozzy,' he announced.

'But why?' I pleaded like a whining three-year-old being denied an ice cream.

271

Slipping under the table like a sulking child, I felt defeated and couldn't look at him anymore.

Reaching across the table with his strong, black-haired hands, he said, 'How about you stay here with Bee, which I think will be much more stable for you both, and I give you a loan to go to uni?'

'What do you mean?' I said, sitting bold upright, like the headmaster had just walked into the classroom.

'I will give you a small salary each month for you to live on. We can take it out of your inheritance.'

'Oh my god. Dad. Are you serious?'

'Do I joke about money matters?' he exclaimed.

Jumping up, I threw myself around the table and strangled his neck in a huge hug.

'That's amazing, Dad. Thank you so, so much,' I spluttered.

'I need to tell your mother and brother of course. You understand?' he questioned.

'Of course. Of course. Anything. Anything is fine.'

That was the most empowered I'd ever felt. Simon's death had given me a 'fuck it' attitude. I would say to myself, 'What's the worst thing that could happen? Could it be as bad as seeing my husband on a slab?' The answer was always 'No'! I've learnt that nothing you do is ever set in concrete. It can always change. You can *always* go back. But at least you've tried. If you never try, you will never know. *It's better to regret the things you have done, rather than regret the things you haven't.* This became my mantra.

I'd had some pretty duff years in my life: several ear operations; years of building the house; years of infertility, miscarriage and skin cancer; the final three years of Simon's illness, and then my grief that had weighed me down like a heavy military coat. I'd always lived a regimented kind of life where I wore the same uniform every day, worked within a strict nursing Code of Conduct and ran a strict appointment system where I saw patients

272

every fifteen minutes. And like most working people, I booked my twenty-five days' annual leave and marked it with a blue dot on the year planner in the office. I was about to be set free and be allowed to say goodbye to rules. As I found the courage and determination inside me, it was like I'd been given a year to live, and suddenly every day mattered.

CHAPTER 46

It was August 2000 and knowing I was going to be absorbed in study for the next three years I decluttered and decorated the lounge and dining room. Frank, one of my retired patients whose wife I looked after, offered his painting skills. Said he'd done a bit of painting and decorating since he retired. He brought Peggy weekly for a blood pressure check as it was dangerously high. They invited me for tea after Simon died, took me under their wing like grandparents.

'I'll bring my old mate, Cecil. Is that okay?' asked Frank as he opened the door for Peggy to leave one morning.

In preparation, I'd spent the previous week clearing and cleaning. Emptied the rooms, covered the sofas, dining room table and sideboard with dust sheets. I decided to rip off the old Designers Guild wallpaper, to paint everything white and freshen things up.

Once they'd finished, it was like someone had turned the lights on. Radiant and fresh, I only put back the things that I absolutely loved. It was minimal. I loved it. Simon would have loved it too. A vase of pale pink and white gerberas in the centre of our eight-seater pine table finished it off a treat. I'd painted Mum and Dad's vintage wooden chairs white and covered each seat in a two-tone velvet material, each one a different colour; I'd sourced the material in a market in Covent Garden.

'What about this hallway then? Do you want us to do that next?' said Frank, peering up the stairs as they left.

'I wouldn't mind,' I answered.

'We'll leave the paper on this time as it's good quality. It may need a couple of coats,' said Cecil with a twinkle in his eyes.

'Let me think about it and I'll let you know,' I called, waving them off like familiar friends.

They came back in August and spread Mermaid Turquoise paint throughout the hall and landing. Each time I opened the front door it was like walking into the Mediterranean Sea, where the water is clear and the horizon full of hope.

Arriving an hour before my first lecture, I felt a quickening in my pulse when I read *The London College of Music and Media* above the entrance. Being the oldest student at uni was a worry that swiftly left me as people older than myself rushed past me to grab a coffee on their way to lectures.

I'd chosen radio as my minor, and during the fourth week we went to the radio studios to look round. Feeling out of my depth amongst all the hundreds of dials, buttons and flashing lights, I panicked when I realised we were expected to wear headphones. How embarrassing would that be in front of my fellow students if my hearing aids whistled; plus, I didn't think my hearing aids would be compatible with wearing headphones. So I switched to photography.

One afternoon we were taken down the stairs into the bows of the basement of the university. Large metal industrial pipes lined the wide white corridors like arteries and veins. They reminded me of the passage that led to the mortuary in the hospital. It was cold, eerie and quiet. In the distance, a red bulb glowed indicating the entrance to the dark room where we were each issued with a bulky black Cannon A1 35 mm film camera that weighed a ton. My heart sank as I looked at the dials, knobs and numbers. I didn't have a clue where to begin or know how to put the film in, let alone how to make it work. The lecturer talked about shutter speeds, F stops and apertures. I only knew about the body's apertures, not camera ones!

Throwing my boots off at the front door when I arrived home that evening, I rushed upstairs holding my camera to find Dad bathing Bee. White foam wobbled on her head like candyfloss when she moved. He'd always been great at making bubbles when we were kids. He'd pour Matey in the bath and shake his hands, like waving at speed under water until our legs were covered with white mousse. As I leant down to kiss her hello, she spread the foam on my nose and chin. Drying his hands on Bee's Harry Potter towel, Dad then took the camera from me.

'Blimey, I've the exact same camera at home. Imagine that,' he said, inspecting it like a child thrilled with a new toy.

'But Dad, they talked about apertures, shutter speeds and F stops. They're talking another language to me. I don't know if I can do this.'

'Don't worry, Tozzy. I can teach you all that. You'll soon pick it up,' he said as he peered back at me through the lens.

Picking up an almost empty toilet roll, he demonstrated the apertures.

'Put most simply, the aperture is the opening in the lens. When you hit the shutter release button, a hole opens up that allows the light in,' he explained.

He made me look inside the lens so I could see it open and close at different speeds, known as F stops. He'd always been patient and calm as he explained things in a way that I could understand.

I couldn't wait to develop my film in the dark room where the only lights glowed red above each workstation. Everything was painted black: the walls, floor and ceiling. The only sound was from the radio that usually played chill-out music in the background.

Despite my first assignment coming out more grey than black and white, my tutor gave me a good mark for the subject matter and how I'd interpreted the brief. Technically I had to step up, but it was a good start. As the months went on, my images developed texture and contrast, and gradually popped off the paper like the classic black and white image of Audrey Hepburn or James Dean, for example.

I'd got through my first year, made new friends and finally began to feel like my old self again. I'd got into a nice routine, commuting on the train, stopping for a cappuccino and warm pan au raisin before my lectures. Bee appeared settled, and my focus was on getting good grades. For the first time in a few years, I felt content and I hadn't even thought about dating.

CHAPTER 47

One foggy February afternoon during my second year at uni in 2001, Bee begged me to go swimming.

'Please, Mummy, please,' she begged, looking up at me with her hands placed in prayer.

'Can't we go to the cinema instead?' I suggested.

'You haven't taken me swimming since Daddy died,' she pleaded further.

Plagued by guilt, I succumbed.

'Okay, but we're not staying all afternoon. Only for a couple of hours,' I said.

In the cold cubicle, I climbed into my faded one-piece navy costume and waddled like a mother duck into the lukewarm water. Windsor Leisure Pool was one of those with a wave machine and flumes. When it first opened we'd queued to be one of the first families to try it. State of the art at the time, with a pool side café and two Jacuzzis.

Bee couldn't wait to run off into the rapids. She'd go round and round. Start at one end of the snake-shaped channel and flow out at the other. With such a strong pull like the undercurrent in the sea, there was no going back, however much everyone tried; part of the fun was seeing if you could. Bee was a confident swimmer; she'd been taught by Simon from the age of two, and he'd encouraged her to swim underwater. He'd lift her above the waves and throw her in the water until she screamed and begged for more.

Crashing waves came every fifteen minutes or so; a siren blew to warn you to leave the deep end if you didn't want to be thrashed about. I'd timed it just right. The water had settled; it was safe swim. Breaststroke was my best and only style. Chin above the water. Random frogs-legs beneath, just like Mum. When she swam, she barely moved. I hoped I didn't look like that. I'd like to give the impression of someone sleek and athletic! Mum had worn a blue rubber swimming hat with floppy cut out flowers stuck to it. They fell off over time and left gaps. I didn't like getting my hair wet because it frizzed, made me look like Ken Dodd on acid. With no one else in the deep end, I managed a couple of widths – all of fifteen metres. Clinging to the edge, I watched Bee rush around the rapids. I pictured her now riding on Simon's back, clinging to his neck as he pretended to be the Lock Ness monster. They'd both be laughing as they ducked under, water pouring off their heads as they bobbed up.

Balancing on my elbows, my toes miles from the bottom, I sensed I was being watched. Squinting around the pool, I saw him. Reclining in the shallows, surrounded by splashing toddlers. Half laying, half sitting; his legs were crossed out in front of him. Wow. He was more handsome than George Clooney. Slicked back raven-black hair, a slim athletic body and a black diamond of chest hair that thinned towards his waist. He looked too good to be looking at me. So I double checked. No one behind me. No one either side. *It's me*, I thought as I clung to the ridged tiles to stop myself from sinking. I looked away. Looked back. Looked away again.

I decided to stare him out; in my best breaststroke, dipping my head like a moorhen to give the appearance of a sleek swimmer, I wafted towards his tempting glare. The corners of his mouth curled up into a smile that I could have warmed my hands on. I was that close that I saw laughter lines around his eyes that matched mine, and a dimple in his clean-shaven chin, like Simon's. Feeling the tiles under my feet, I realised that I'd gone too close, so I flipped like a display dolphin back to the deep end. I was trying to look cool; like a fish tempted by the bait, he'd lured me into his net. I saw naughtiness in his eyes that I liked. But not on a Sunday afternoon in a public pool, I thought as I caught my breath and clung to the edge to calm my breath.

Bee tugged at my costume and brought me back to earth. She then begged me to go up the shoot.

'Up the shoot?' I shrieked. 'I don't think so, darling.'

This guy would not fancy me if he saw how large my lardy bottom was out of the water – it would be game over. Bee persisted. I had a good hunt around and couldn't see him. Phew. It was safe to climb out.

Coldness wrapped around me like a wet towel as I tiptoed up the slippery steel steps to join others shivering at the top. Over the handrail, I searched for him amongst the semi-naked torsos below. Assuming he'd gone, I breathed out and psyched myself up to go down the fast flume known as the black hole. Usually, I loved rides like this. Once on holiday in Majorca we spent the day at a water park. I repeatedly went up and down a massive five-wide slide and wore a hole in my costume, exposing my backside to the world.

Secretly, I was disappointed that he'd gone. He was the hottest man I'd seen in months; plus, he looked like fun. As Bee ran on the spot to keep warm, I sensed being watched again. Glancing over my shoulder down the steps, I froze like an ice swan and gripped the handrail for support. Six steps below, he was rubbernecking right up my arse. Twisting my lower torso to face him so he wouldn't see how big my bum really was, I almost slipped off the steps. *Oh my god! Oh my god! He's so close*. And to prolong my agony, Bee insisted on going down first. Once she was out of sight, I swapped lanes to descend the slow one and worried that my ten bellies would bulge as I sat down. Like a stuffed penguin in a toy shop, I sat bolt upright all the way down. Acting as brakes, my toes clung and juddered on the sides of the slide as I spread my legs wide to slow myself down. Determined not get my hair wet, instead of plunging into the small deep pool at the end, I came to an abrupt and embarrassing halt. Caused a queue behind me as I prised myself off the edge. As my feet hit the bottom, I sprang up like a jack-in-the-box. *Not too much damage*, I thought as I glanced in the full-length mirror. A test for my waterproof blue-black mascara, and it had not let me down. And my hair was still in place.

I strolled like a pelican back into the main pool, where we came face-to-face and said hello.

Looking down at me through a curtain of wet black lashes, he said, 'I'm Ben.' Nice name, I thought as he reached to shake my cold hand. I giggled to myself. Shaking hands in a crowed swimming pool, and with only two pieces of material between us, felt surreal. I wanted to suggest we went into the Jacuzzi to get warm as we dripped and I shivered, but thought that sounded too forward.

'And your name is?' he asked.

'Ginger,' I said, pointing up at my frizzy hair.

Dodging numerous kids, we waded towards the deep end, settled at the edge of the pool, dangled our feet in the water and quickly exchanged biographies. He was nine days older than me, born on my due date; a carpenter, living on a narrow boat.

His voice softened as he told me he had five children.

'Five. Five. Are you serious? You don't believe in contraception then?' I teased.

'You're right. I don't,' he grinned, searching the pool for his kids. 'Over there, look. Those two dark-haired boys are mine. Eleven and seven.'

And there were two handsome, athletic mini versions of him bombing each other and making waves.

'And the others?' I enquired, tilting my head with a half grin.

He paused. Looked at his toes pointing up and down, and said, 'They're with their mothers.'

'Mothers! As in plural?' I questioned, shifting away from him. 'How many?'

'Don't worry, there's only two,' he said. 'Does that ring alarm bells?'

Mesmerised by his good looks, charm and wet hairy chest, in that moment, I didn't give a shit if he had ten children and five wives. He'd caught me. Hook, line and sinker!

He went on to explain that his second relationship had failed and that he and his wife were living separately. A glimmer of hope appeared in my optimistic brain; perhaps he was free after all. I told him about Finn, mentioned how I hated his shoes. I must have sounded shallow.

As he tilted his head sideways like a quizzical dog, a concern glowed in his eyes when I told him I was widowed with one child, and I pointed to Bee playing tag with a couple of girls the same age.

Interrupted by the siren, we jumped up as the waves began to roll.

'What's your number? I'll call you,' he said as we strolled towards the Jacuzzis, the pool almost empty.

'But you haven't got a pen.'

'I'll remember it. I'm good with numbers,' he said. I got him to repeat it.

Shivering and mottled mauve, Bee appeared. I pulled her close, rubbed her arms up and down. I turned around and he'd gone.

Did I dream that? I thought as I dried Bee's hair in a daze. Then once again I became aware of being watched. I turned around and there he was, leaning against the partition that separated the hair dryers. He winked and waved and strolled out of the swing doors. I went hot around my neck, clammy under my clothes. I dropped the hair dryer, ran out to look at his feet. I couldn't go out with another man who wore shoes like Dad's. I gasped as he slid out of sight. He wore black mud-scuffed wellington boots.

There was a brief message on the phone when we arrived home.

'I figured you'd be online. This is my email address…'

We started an online relationship. His emails were

descriptive, poetic and authentic. He wrote with sensitivity and talked sincerely about his failed relationships and love for his five children. He sounded like my dream man. He was into the moon, stars and the sea. Loved poetry, romance and hated sport. And, being a drummer, he was creative and loved music. He didn't mention that he was a fussy eater and didn't socialise!

It was like having an old-fashioned pen pal. I wrote in the evening. He'd respond by the morning. I couldn't wait to log on to see what he said. A week later he called from a phone box after his evening swim, where he swam forty lengths a day apart from Sundays. Sounding cheeky and mischievous, he made me laugh, although I felt slightly wary and a bit puzzled by him. He appeared sincere enough, but he was still living with his wife. He had explained how they were living separately on their boat, each in their own cabins. I had always said that I would never get involved with married men – ever – but he sounded separated enough for me to take a risk.

We arranged to meet at 10 a.m. by the park gates close to the river where I lived. I took ages deciding what to wear. It wasn't like a date. I couldn't dress up. I settled for a pair of faded jeans, a black polo neck and black corduroy coat with fur around the hood and cuffs. I topped up my lips with mango gloss as I climbed out of the car.

It was 9.55 and I was in position. I'd been trained by my parents to be punctual. Five past. Ten past. The drizzle became rain. My hair began to expand and I was forced to put up my hood. The bastard. He seemed so keen. *I'm walking at twenty past!* I thought to myself. Ten nineteen. *Last chance. That's it.* I turned to cross the road back to my car when he appeared in a black duffle coat with the hood up. And of course, his black welly boots.

I was struck by his calmness. He seemed to glide along the pavement next to me like a swan. And once in the coffee shop he was like a boy in a museum looking at and listening to the coffee machines. He genuinely hadn't been into a coffee shop for years and hadn't heard of a cappuccino or latte, and he didn't drink tea or coffee. He ordered a large glass of fresh orange juice.

He intrigued me. I couldn't judge him by his appearance. He wore black: black crew neck T-shirt and black jeans, and a black duffle coat and wellies. No watch. No mobile. No logos. Not even a key-ring. He smelt of Pears soap. His nails were short. He was clean-shaven. His chest hair was unruly. He was attentive, intuitive and at one with himself. He showed empathy and concern when I shared some of my tales and gazed at me intensely as if he already cared, and he appeared uncomplicated, calm and sincere. Too good to be true!

We talked about our weddings and he'd only been married once. He had two children by his first partner who'd left him for someone else and took the children with her. She'd reappeared when he'd met his second partner who became pregnant weeks into their relationship. Encouraged by her large Irish family, they married.

'Did you wear a suit?' I asked.

'Yes.' He grinned. 'It was the one and only time I've ever worn one. Plain black, small lapels,' he said, sniggering.

The next time you wear a suit is when you marry me, I thought as our stare lingered.

Sat on the loo whilst he paid the bill, I was puzzled by his genuine interest in me. He asked direct and open-ended questions, allowed me time to answer and then wanted to know more. His curiosity revealed an intensely inquisitive mind. I opened up to him like I would a counsellor, but not like Finn, who as I look back, went through the motions of wanting to know about me in the beginning, and was partly doing his job that came as second nature. But once he'd found out a few things, he was happy to talk about himself or talk trivia. Other men had referred to me as being a bit deep. I interpreted that negatively, as being intense. I tried to be less so, but it didn't come naturally. I wanted to know more and wasn't satisfied with superficial chit chat. That's what was refreshing about Ben: he too wanted to know more, but time ran out and three hours passed like three minutes.

Ben appeared different to any other man I'd met, apart from Simon, of course. He wasn't lively or animated like Simon, who you would know had entered the room because he would have commented on your appearance, done an impression, or made you laugh. Whereas you wouldn't notice Ben unless you brushed against him by mistake, and then he would leave an impression because he was enigmatic, mysterious and blindingly handsome. He'd flatter you with his eyes alone and come out with witty one-liners that would make you want more. I couldn't help but compare the two. What they had in common was that neither was mainstream and I'm attracted to these kind of eccentric, edgy men. But what comes with them is danger.

I've since learnt that true confidence is quieter and comes from an internal belief in your abilities, skill and value. Quietly confident people have accepted their strengths and weaknesses; they do not need to compare themselves to others to boost their self-esteem. This was Ben. Quietly self-assured.

Our elbows brushed as we crossed the road and walked back to the park. Taking my hand, he led me through the gates. When we stopped, he pulled me towards him, parted my fringe and popped a kiss on my forehead. Our lips coupled and we kissed like urchins gulping the air for breath. His lips were velvet soft and quick to respond. Our bodies swayed like the branches over our heads. I felt his warm breath linger over my mouth as we stood entangled. Reluctantly we said goodbye and I drifted in a daze back to my car.

To this day, I believe that Ben put a spell on me. Injected me with a cocktail of love drugs. Honestly. From that moment onwards, there was no room in my head for anything but him. I rushed to find the turquoise, satin, silver-mirrored journal that I'd been saving for something special. My need to capture my feelings was urgent. I'm holding that journal in my hand now. It bulges with our emails. Purple and turquoise words. I named it my Benzo book; his name when he was a professional drummer in an Indie rock band.

On the front page, in turquoise capitals letters, I wrote, *Awesome is an understatement.*

On my walk to school to collect the kids, I skipped and linked arms with Matt, who'd become a close friend.

'This could be it. I've met the one,' I chirped.

'But you've only met him twice!' he challenged.

'I know. But we've been writing every day for a week. And meeting him today confirmed how I feel. And... I think he feels the same...!'

'You're funny. You are,' he said, nudging my shoulder with his.

I know it sounds crazy. And it was crazy. I'd met a selection of guys, but none of them had suited me. None of them looked at me with genuine interest, like they wanted to know the true me. Me with battle scars. I didn't believe that someone could love me again because I wasn't properly healed, and I didn't think an incomplete woman who needed a bit of work to get her back to her former self would be an attractive proposition. I realise now that Ben saw past that. He saw my 'essence', as he liked to call it. Only now as a sixty-year-old woman can I see that he saw what Simon had seen – my vulnerability, my sense of fun, and readiness to say 'yes' to whatever came next.

That evening, he sent this email:

After we parted, your taste was on my lips and I smelt your scent all afternoon. I wanted to kiss you again. As I watched you drive off, you looked very quirky in a lovely sexy way. I felt like I had just met Pandora and had been left a gift. In my hands I held a small black box and the temptation to lift the lid was insatiable. The metaphor is real and so are the dangers, and yet I feel strangely reassured. I somehow know what to do. Amazing how a chance meeting can turn things upside down.

THE END

TWENTY-FIVE YEARS AFTER SIMON DIED

Ben and I felt like we'd met our missing halves. We wrote emails to each other day and night. We enjoyed six weeks of clandestine meetings until things came to a head, and Ben regrettably left his children to move in with me. Overnight, I went from a widow with one child to a step-mum with six children. His five children came most weekends. His two wives became best of friends, where they had previously despised each other. They made our lives difficult, to say the least. After a few years we moved away. Twenty-five years on, however, despite mountainous challenges, we have a good relationship with Ben's children who have produced six grandchildren so far! We live in the country with our Border Terrier called Twiggy, and our twenty-four chickens.

Bee, who has just turned thirty, left home to do her nurse training when she was twenty-one. But following her own mental health issues, she had to give up. She was diagnosed with Asperger's, diabetes, borderline personality disorder and depression. She has a strong biological family history of mental health. Currently, Bee is in the process of transitioning and prefers to be known as he/him. He lives with his partner and two hamsters in Birmingham, but due to his multiple health issues he is unable to work. Bee has regular Facebook contact with his birth mother and siblings, but to date has no plans to meet them face-to-face. His path hasn't been an easy one. And, after a few years under the mental health team, he is medicated and is still waiting for specialist talking therapy. So he, despite being under a mental health team, is one of those who has waited a few years for the correct treatment.

I returned to nursing a few years after my degree as I missed it, and I have worked in the field of mental health ever since. My most recent role was as an occupational health nurse working with depressed, traumatised and often suicidal police officers. It is my job to help them get them back to work and get them the help they need to make a full recovery and return to their duties.

Tragically and shockingly, a year ago, in the space of five weeks, Jane died following a three-year battle with cancer, Joe died four weeks later with a brain tumour, and my dad died a week later! So the most important people in my life had now joined Simon and Michael. My mum is managing well aged ninety-three. And Brenda is still going strong.

When I embarked upon the journey of writing this memoir, my feelings about Simon were all mixed up, like when you mix your colours with whites in the washing machine by mistake and everything comes out blighted and blue.

Through revisiting my life with Simon and some of the joyful moments we shared, I have truly made peace with the past and have fallen back in love with *my* Simon. The Simon whose essence was philanthropic, witty, quirky and reflective. I have been able to separate myself from the blame and shame that surrounded his illness and death. I now understand why he left us, and most of all, I forgive him.

I hope that this book will help you recognise the signs and symptoms of mental health, and bipolar in particular, and enable you to get help for your loved ones. And equally, if you become a 'survivor of bereavement by suicide', like me, I hope my story will reassure you and let you know that you are not alone in your journey, and that one day you too will recover.

Milton Keynes UK
Ingram Content Group UK Ltd.
UKHW010851120324
439019UK00002B/22

9 781916 981454